A GUIDE

TO THE

Middle English Metrical Romances

YALE STUDIES IN ENGLISH

ALBERT S. COOK, Editor

IX

A GUIDE

TO THE

Middle English Metrical Romances

DEALING WITH ENGLISH AND GERMANIC LEGENDS, AND WITH
THE CYCLES OF CHARLEMAGNE AND OF ARTHUR

BY

ANNA HUNT BILLINGS, Ph.D.

HASKELL HOUSE
Publishers of Scholarly Books
NEW YORK
1965

published by

HASKELL HOUSE
Publishers of Scholarly Books
30 East 10th Street • New York, N. Y. 10003

Library of Congress Catalog Card Number:

PRINTED IN UNITED STATES OF AMERICA

PREFACE.

THE plan of this book was suggested by the bibliography of the Middle English verse-romances in Körting's *Grundriss der Geschichte der englischen Literatur*. I have added to and expanded Körting's plan, with the purpose of giving some idea of the romance-stories, and a fairly full account of the results of scholarly investigation of the romances.

The whole field has not been covered, not quite one half of the romances named in the Introduction (pp. xii—xv) being treated in the main part of the book; but these represent far more than half of the most interesting romances. The romances that I have not considered are nearly all noticed by Körting (third ed. §§ 86—118, 122, 124—5). The first section of the book, 'English and Germanic Legends', is, I regret to say, not quite complete, the legendary nucleus of two romances, *Sir Gowther* and *Chevelere Assigne,* not having been recognized as of Germanic origin until after the first section had been printed. (See 'Additions and Corrections'.)

In the Introduction a general survey of the history and character of the English verse-romances has been attempted, for the benefit of those unfamiliar with the field under consideration. The survey is based, for the most part, upon the general reading done in connection with the main part of the work, not upon a close acquaintance with the romances themselves, my own reading of the romances,

a

made for the most part in 1897—98 and for the purpose
of summarizing the stories, having been necessarily a rapid
one. From my principal authorities for the history of the
English verse-romances, Ten Brink and Brandl, I have not
hesitated to quote freely.

I desire here to thank those who, in various ways,
have helped me in my work, and particularly to thank
Professor ALBERT S. COOK for encouragement in undertaking
and in continuing it.

December 30, 1900.

A. H. B.

Contents.

IV CONTENTS.

BOOKS AND JOURNALS

MOST FREQUENTLY REFERRED TO.

Angl. ... *Anglia.*

Ath. ... *Athenaeum.*

Arch. ... Herrig's *Archiv für das Studium der neueren Sprachen u. Lit.*

Brandl ... *Mittelenglische Literatur,* in Paul's *Grundriss,* Bd. II, Abt. 1, S. 609—718.

Child ... *The English and Scottish Popular Ballads,* ed. by Francis J. Child, Boston, New York, and London (L.), 1882—1898, 5 vols.

Child ... *English and Scottish Ballads,* Boston and N. Y., 1857—58.

DNB. ... *Dictionary of National Biography.*

Dunlop ... *History of Prose Fiction,* revised by Henry Wilson, L. and N. Y., 1888, 2 vols.

EETS. E. S. ... *Early English Text Society, Extra Series* (since 1867).

Ellis ... *Specimens of the English Metrical Romances,* revised by Halliwell, L., 1848.

E. St. ... *Englische Studien.*

Gautier ... *Les Épopées Françaises,* Paris, 1878—92, 4 vols.

Germ. N. R. ... *Germania, Neue Reihe.*

GGA. ... *Göttingische gelehrte Anzeigen.*

Gröber ... *Grundriss der rom. Philologie,* II. Bd., 1. Abt., 3. Lief., Strassburg, 1898 (*Altfranz. Lit.*).

Hartshorne ... *Ancient Metrical Tales,* L., 1829.

JB. ... *Jahresbericht über die Erscheinungen auf dem Gebiete der germ. Philologie,* Berlin, 1879—.

Julleville ... *Histoire de la langue et de la littérature française des origines à 1900;* ed. par Petit de Julleville, I, Paris, 1896.

Ker ... *Epic and Romance,* L. and N. Y., 1897.

Körting ... *Grundriss der Geschichte der engl. Literatur von ihren Anfängen bis zur Gegenwart,* Münster, 1891 (3d ed. 1899).

Ltbl. ... *Literaturblatt für germ. u. rom. Philologie.*

Lt. Cbl. ... *Literarisches Centralblatt.*

Ltzt. ... *Literaturzeitung.*

Mätzner, Spr. P. ... *Altengl. Sprachproben*, Bd. 1, Abt. 1, Berlin, 1867.
Mitteil. ... *Mitteilungen aus dem gesammten Gebiete der engl. Sprache
    u. Lit.* (Beiblatt zur *Anglia*).
Morris and Skeat, Specimens ... *Specimens of Early English*, Oxford,
    Part I, 2nd ed., 1887; Part II, 3d ed., 1884 (?).
Nutt ... *Studies on the Legend of the Holy Grail*, L., 1888.
Paris, G. ... *La Littérature française au Moyen Age*, Paris, 2nd ed.,
    1890.
    „   „   ... *Histoire poétique de Charlemagne*, Paris, 1865.
    „   „   ... *Histoire Littéraire de la France*, XXX, Paris, 1898.
Paris, P. ... *Les Romans de la Table Ronde mis en nouveau langage*,
    Paris, 1868—1877, 5 vols.
Paul u. Braune ... *Beiträge zur Geschichte der deutschen Sprache u. Lit.*
P. G. ... *Grundriss der germ. Philologie*, herausgegeben von H. Paul,
    Strassburg, 1891.
PF. MS. ... *Bishop Percy's Folio Manuscript: Ballads and Romances*,
    ed. Hales and Furnivall, L., 1867—1868, 3 vols.
QF. ... *Quellen und Forschungen.*
Reliques ... *Reliques of Ancient English Poetry* by Thomas Percy,
    1st ed., L., 1765.
Ritson, AEMR. ... *Ancient English Metrical Romances*, L., 1802, 3 vols.
Rhŷs ... *Op. cit.* on p. 85.
Rom. ... *Romania.*
Saintsbury, FLR ... *The Flourishing of Romance*, N. Y., 1897.
Schipper ... *Englische Metrik*, Bonn, 1881—89, 2 Bde.
Sommer ... *Le Morte Darthur* by Syr Thomas Malory, L., 1891, 3 vols
    (vol. III on the sources).
Ten Brink ... *History of English Literature*, translated by H. M.
    Kennedy, N. Y., 1889, 2 vols in 3.
Utterson ... *Select Pieces of Early Popular Poetry*, L., 1817, 2 vols.
Ward ... *Catalogue of Romances in the Department of Manuscripts in
    the British Museum*, I, L., 1883.
Weber ... *Metrical Romances*, Edinburgh, 1810, 2 vols.
Wilda ... *Über die örtliche Verbreitung der 12 zeiligen Schweifreim-
    strophe in England*, Breslau, 1888.
Wülker ... *Geschichte der englischen Literatur von den Anfängen bis
    zur Gegenwart*, Leipzig, 1896 (a popular account).
    „   ... *Altengl. Lesebuch*, Halle, 1874/79, 2 Teile.
ZsfdA. ... *Zeitschrift für deutsches Alterthum.*
ZsffSp. ... *Zeitschrift für franz. Sprache u. Lit.*
ZsfrPh. ... *Zeitschrift für rom. Philologie.*
ZML. ... *Old and Middle English Reader on the Basis of Zupitza's
    Alt- u. mittelengl. Übungsbuch*, by G. L. Mac Lean, L., and
    N. Y., 1893.

INTRODUCTION.

The French Verse-Romance.

THE mediaeval verse-romance was the child of chivalric France. It arose in the northern part of her territory, in the first part of the twelfth century, and flourished there until about the middle of the thirteenth. In the field of the secular epic, the verse-romances were preceded by the French national epos or *chansons de geste*,[1] which celebrated the early wars of mediaeval France—above all the wars of Charlemagne against the pagans, conceived as Saracens — and the wars of the feudal barons of the older period. By the twelfth century spontaneous epic production, which, it is held, had begun in popular songs of Merovingian and Carolingian times, had long ceased; the *chansons de geste* were now receiving at the hands of the jongleurs many additions, some of these doubtless under the influence of the romances or of the romantic spirit.

The verse-romances, as opposed to the national and popular *chansons,* were essentially court-epics. They were designed for reading in private audiences or in solitude, not for singing or recitation before large audiences, as were the *chansons.* They were frequently composed to please some noble person, who in more than one instance was a woman. Chrétien tells us that Marie, Countess of Champagne, daughter of the celebrated Eleanor of Poitou, gave

---

[1] For authorities on the *chansons* and the verse-romances, see *infra,* pp. 47, 85.

him both the *matière* and the *sens* of his *Conte de la Charrette* or *Lancelot*.[1] The verse-romances drew from many sources, classical and Oriental as well as European: Latin epic and myth, romances of the Græco-Latin decadence,[2] romances of Byzantine origin, religious legend, Celtic tales and songs, Norse and German myth, fairy and folklore, were all appropriated by the age of chivalry, and worked over into an expression of its life and ideals. Often, perhaps most frequently, the source of the French romance was only oral, the foreign material contributing as a rule only the nucleus, or the framework, or important elements, of the narrative.[3] The romances that treated their sources with the least freedom were those dealing with antiquity, but even in these romances the French poets made many additions. Many of the stories doubtless grew by successive oral and literary accretions, while later romancers borrowed from their predecessors or from a common store of stock situations. Several of the romances of adventure, however, were doubtless the product of their authors' invention.[4]

The distinctive features of the romances, chivalry, courtesy, and love,[5] find fullest and most complete expression in the romances of the Round Table, preeminently in those of Chrétien de Troyes.[5] The conception of love in the Arthurian romances was powerfully influenced by the Provençal love poetry.[6] These romances, whose more internal exposition was very different from that of the *chansons de geste,* 'are', says Paris, 'the veritable precursors of the modern novel'.[7]

---

[1] See also p. 43, n. 2 and p. 138, n. 1.

[2] On Alexander and on Troy.

[3] Of the romances based on Celtic legends, the *Tristan* seems to have retained most of the foreign material and spirit; see G. Paris, *Tristan et Isent* (*op. cit.* on p. 95).

[4] G. Paris, p. 105.

[5] See *Rom.* XII 534. For English prose translations and abridgments of Chrétien's romances, see Newell's *King Arthur and the Table Round,* Boston and New York, 1897, 2 vols.

[6] On *l'amour courtois,* see *Rom.* XII 534.

[7] *Hist. Litt.,* 16, 17.

At an early date the Charlemagne *chansons* and the romances, principally those of the Round Table, found favor beyond the borders of France, and the most famous of them, in poetical and in prose translations and adaptations, found their way into the rising European literatures. Anglo-Norman England had taken an active part in the development of the romantic material. The Normans brought with them into England the Charlemagne *chansons*; the Celtic legends, with which they soon displayed an acquaintance, they learned either in France from their Breton neighbors, or in England from the Welsh.[1] Many romantic elements must also have been brought into England by the Crusaders. In the twelfth century the development of romance received a most important impulse through the work of two writers on English soil, the *Historia Regum Britanniae* of Geoffrey of Monmouth, and the *lais* of Marie de France.[2] In this century and the succeeding one were also composed Anglo-Norman verse-romances based upon English or Anglo-Danish legends of a historical or semi-historical character.[3] With Norman-French the language of court and nobility, the French romances for many years supplied all demand, and even when their reproduction in English had begun, they were long preferred in courtly and aristocratic circles.

The Beginning of English Romance.

WE cannot say just when the romantic stories in favor among the Normans began to be written and sung among the English;[4] perhaps by the beginning of the thirteenth

---

[1] See Appendix A.

[2] On Marie, see Bédier, *op. cit.*, on p. 153.

[3] See Ten Brink, I 148—151.

[4] Romance had made a slight beginning in England before the Conquest: Ten Brink, I 114—115.

century, certainly not later than 1250.[1] Of extant romances,
however, only a few have been assigned to the thirteenth
century, but the first quarter of the fourteenth saw the
English verse-romance in full bloom.

The romances were circulated among the people by
the *disours, harpours, gestours,* or, as they were called in
pure English, 'seggers' and 'gleemen', who thus took an
important part in the intercourse fast uniting and blending
Norman and Englishman.[2] In promoting this intercourse
the gleemen could make use of some English material, for
English popular song had not been silenced under Norman
rule. Some of these songs, as we have already noticed,
had furnished the narrative ground work for Anglo-Norman
romances; while others, those of Horn and Havelok, developed under romantic influence, although the extant romances
are probably not adaptations of the French romances on the
same subjects.

The early verse-romances were composed for English
men and women of the higher class (though probably not
of the most courtly circles), who, although they had assimilated much of the superior civilization to which the Conquest
had opened wide the door of England, nevertheless did not
readily use the French tongue. The author of *Arthour and
Merlin,* writing not later than the first quarter of the fourteenth century, says that gentlemen use French, *Ac euerich
Inglische Inglische can, | Mani noble ich haue yseiȝe | þat
no Freynsche couþe seye.*[3] The circle of the minstrels'
audience grew wider from year to year, the romances finding
favor among the burghers and the common folk.

By far the greater number of the verse-romances are
based upon French originals. As a rule, the English versifier
follows his original with fidelity from incident to incident,
but in doing so he often speaks from his own English point

---

[1] On the date of *Bevis of Hampton,* cf. *infra,* p. 39, and Ten
Brink, I 193.

[2] Ten Brink I 225.

[3] vv. 23—26; cf. *Richard Coeur de Lion,* ed. Weber, II, vv. 22—32
(quoted by Ten Brink, I 242).

of view. He adapts his original to his audience by abridgment, by the more frequent use of direct discourse, by the
introduction of popular features, occasionally by the addition
of a passage of some length, and, less frequently, by the
use of another authority. Seeming changes may often be
due to differences between the source of the English translator and the extant French version or versions. The *seggers*
also, sometimes intentionally, sometimes owing to weakness
of memory or to misconception, often made changes in the
English text. 'In the mouth of the seggers, therefore', says
Ten Brink,[1] 'the form of these poems diverged ever more
from that of the original text. Industrious monks completed
their manuscripts from the text books of the minstrels ...'
We thus see 'how national and popular characteristics could
manifest themselves in such poetical imitations. Their
fortunes also involve a portion of English history, and in
them is uttered the English spirit, even though it seems to
"speak with tongues".'[2]

The metre of the majority of the early romances is
the verse of four accents.[3] In this verse alliteration frequently occurs, though not as a necessary part of the verse-
scheme. In several of the early romances appears a metrical
form, the twelve-line tail-rime stanza, which after 1350 was
to become 'a mark of the popular epic, while the more
aristocratic narrative retained the short couplet'.[4] In the
second half of the fourteenth century, the alliterative long
line was revived and used with considerable poetical power
in the southwest, whence its use spread northward.

---

[1] I 235.

[2] I 235—36.

[3] On its origin see Lewis, *The Foreign Sources of Modern English
Versification*, Halle, 1898, § 49.

[4] Brandl, p. 636. The tail-rime (*ryme couee*) was of Latin origin.
and used first in English in religious lyrics.

Periods.

The production of the verse-romances in the four periods of Middle-English literature will now be briefly outlined, following Brandl's *Mittelenglische Literatur*. The year 1350 may be considered as the dividing date between the earlier and the later verse-romances.

I. 1100—1250: The Transition Period.

The literature is prevailingly ecclesiastical, following Latin models. Only one romance, *King Horn*, from Kent, is assigned to this period.[1] Layamon's *Brut*, it should be remembered, was written about 1200.

II. 1250—1350: From Lewes to Crecy.

'Under the influence of Magna Charta, as well as of the succeeding struggles to make it practically effective, Englishmen won the ambition to vie with the Normans in poetry, as, in general, in the adornment of life. They transplanted the Norman poems bodily into English; the production was rich and manifold, although not yet original. Courtly material, models, and tendencies predominated, and even benefited ecclesiastical writers. The movement reached northern England.'[2]

Of the following romances all but *Havelok* and *Ywain and Gawain* are contained in the Auchinleck manuscript,[3] written 1330—40, and containing 'the flower of the contemporary poetry'.—*Romances:* Among the Saxons: *Lai le Freine, Sir Orfeo* (a *lai*), *Bevis of Hampton*.[1] In Kent: *Alexander, Arthur and Merlin, Richard Coeur de Lion, Seven Sages of Rome*.[4] Midland: (S. E.), (*Seven*

---

[1] Cf. Körting, § 87. The original English versions of *Bevis of Hampton, Floris and Blauncheflur*, and *Havelok* may belong to this period.

[2] Brandl, p. 609.   [3] See p. 15.

[4] Thomas Chestre's three romances, *Launfal, Libeaus Desconus*, and *Octavian*, though assigned by Brandl to the next period, belong in all probability to the second quarter of the 14th century; see *infra*, pp. 142—43, 151.

Sages),[1] *Sir Otuel, Guy of Warwick* (two versions), *Floris and Blauncheflur,*[2] *King of Tarsus;* (S. W.), *Sir Degaree;*[3] (N. W.), *Sir Tristrem;*[4] (N.) *Havelok,*[2] *Amis and Amiloun,*[4] *Horn Childe,* (*Bevis of Hampton*), (*Guy of Warwick*), *Roland and Vernagu.* North: (*Seven Sages*), (*Bevis of Hampton*), *Ywain and Gawain.*

III. 1350—1400: Prelude to the Reformation and Renaissance.

A period characterized by a wide expression of national self-consciousness, manifesting itself in (1) a democratic movement in political and social spheres; (2) the retirement of French in favor of English as the ordinary means of intercourse for high and low, and the use of English for the best artistic effort of cultivated writers; the origin of the Robin Hood ballads; the revival of alliterative poetry; the religious and the literary movement represented respectively by Wiclif and by Chaucer. 'If the feudal and ecclesiastical ideals of the late Middle Ages were best glorified by the French, Italians, and Germans, the democratic movement at the close of the Middle Ages won its most original expression among Englishmen.'[5]—In this period the minstrel romance enjoyed a wide popularity, being most cultivated in the provinces; at the same time it declined in quality.[6] *Romances:* More Southern England: *Arthur, Seege of Troy, Seege of Jerusalem,*[7] *Launfal,*[8] *Libeaus Desconus,*[8] *Octavian,*[8] *Sir Firumbras,* romantic tales by Gower and Chaucer.[9] S. W. Midland: *William of Palerne, Chevelere Assigne,*[10] *Joseph of Arimathie, Alexander, Destruction of*

---

[1] A new version. In the two periods following, I have, with one exception, not mentioned the new versions.

[2] See p. xii, n. 1.

[3] Ed. *PF. MS.* III 16; Utterson, I. (I give editions of romances not treated in this book and not named in Körting's index.)

[4] Close of the 13th century.

[5] Brandl, 609—610, 654.   [6] Cf. *infra,* pp. xx—xxii.

[7] Brandl, § 70.   [8] See p. xii, n. 4.

[9] See pp. xxi—xxiii.   [10] Ed. Gibbs, *EETS. ES.,* No. 6.

Jerusalem.[1]   N. W. England: *Sir Gawain and the Green Knight, Morte Arthure, Aunters of Arthur, The Avowing of Arthur, Sir Amadas.* The North: *Sir Perceval, Sir Degrevant,*[2] *Sege of Melayne, Duke Roland and Otuel, La Bone Florence of Rome,*[3] *Octavian, Sir Eglamour of Artois, Sir Isumbras.* N. Midland: *Ipomedon, Emare,*[4] *Athelston, The Erl of Toulouse,*[5] *Sir Gowther.*[5]

IV. The Fifteenth Century: Lancaster and York.

'THAT rude age of the Wars of Roses, which saw the first buds of humanism in England, but destroyed so many of them, and retarded the blossoming of all.'[6] 'Mediaeval customs and culture died a lingering death, and the light of a new era dawned slowly upon the world.'[7] Cultured and popular circles fell more widely apart than ever: the former cultivated the new court poetry (that of the school of Chaucer); the latter, the old courtly species. The literary movement was principally one of teaching and popularizing, a preparation for the Renaissance.[8]—Prose redactions of the French romances began in this period. The decline of the minstrel-romance continued. With this century the production of the verse-romances practically ceases. A number of short narrative poems, usually based on the romances and frequently in ballad style, belong to the sixteenth century or later.[9]— *Romances:* In the purer common speech, *i. e.* in the English of the school of Chaucer: Lydgate's *Troy-Book* and *Story of Thebes, Tancred and Sigismonda,*[10] *Generides, Partenay.* In an English 'more or less vulgar, but without a trace of Northern dialect': *Song of Roland, The Holy Grail, Merlin,*

---

[1] Körting, § 108.   [2] *Thornton Romances,* 1844.

[3] Ritson, III; Vietor, Marburg, 1893.

[4] Ed. Ritson, II.

[5] Or the beginning of the 15th century.

[6] Ten Brink II 322.   [7] Ibid., 310.

[8] Abridged from Brandl, p. 610.

[9] Cf. *infra,* pp. 31, 32, 189, 200 n., 208 n. 5. See Percy's *Reliques* and *PF. MS.*

[10] Brandl, § 108.

Parthenopeus of Blois, The Knight of Courtesy,[1] *Sir Tria-mour,*[2] *The Jeaste of Gawain,*[3] *The Marriage of Sir Gawain and Dame Ragnell,*[3] *The Green Knight,*[3] *The Squire of Low Degree, Sir Cleges.* North Midland or the North: *De-struction of Troy, Wars of Alexander, The Carle of Carlisle, The Turk and Gawain, Sir Torrent of Portugal, The Sow-done of Babylon, Le Morte Arthur.* Scotland: *Golagrus and Gawain, (Launfal), Tale of Rauf Coilyear, Lancelot of The Laik, Sir Eger, Grine, and Graysteel,*[4] *Roswell and Lillian.*[5]

Cycles and Types.

THE English verse-romances, while by no means re-producing all the French romances, yet represent a wide variety of legend-material. 'It was', says Ten Brink, speaking of the earlier romances, 'as if the full cornucopia of romantic poesy had been shaken out over the English people.'[6] In the very beginning of English romance, legends of English or Anglo-Danish origin were prominent. Arthurian legends, however, speedily gained the place of first favor, and romances based upon these legends are the most numerous. Nearly equal in number are those whose plot or nucleus came from the Orient or from antiquity. The French national epos is represented only by the Charlemagne legends and, with the exception of the *Chanson de Roland,* not by the most important of these. Other romances are based upon French romances of adventure, or upon those whose legend developed in France[7] around a historical or mythical nucleus.

---

[1] Ed. Ritson, III 193; Hazlitt, *Remains,* II 65.
[2] Ed. *PF. MS.,* II 78; Utterson, I.
[3] Bordering more upon the North.
[4] Ed. *PF. MS.,* I 341.
[5] Ed. Lengert, *E. St.* XVI 311, XVII 341.
[6] I 234.
[7] e. g. *Erl of Toulouse, Sir Gowther, Chevelere Assigne.*

Some of the later English romances, of comparatively little interest, have no known source, though important elements of the story are familiar. These romances may have been abridged from French sources, or they may have been strung together by some English minstrel. Of individual romances, *Bevis of Hampton, Guy of Warwick, Libeaus Desconus,* and *Launfal* enjoyed great popularity; *Sir Isumbras* was very popular in the North.

A glance at the types of romance represented in the earlier and in the later period may be of interest. These types may be distinguished in a general way, though they often blend or are combined. In the earliest romances the 'exile-and-return' motive,[1] always a favorite in mediaeval romance, is prominent. This motive outlines the narrative in *King Horn, Havelok, Bevis of Hampton,* and the first part of *Tristrem.*[2] Among the very early romances are two famous romances of love, *Floris and Blauncheflur* and *Sir Tristrem,* and one of devoted friendship, *Amis and Amiloun.*

Later, in the first years of the fourteenth century, when Englishman and Norman had become one under Edward I, 'the first truly English king', romances of a more heroic type began to appear, first in Kent and the S. E. Midland, and then in the North. Romances *à la King Horn* no longer suited the mood of the contemporary noble, says Brandl.[3] In the neighborhood of the victorious king, he won a self-consciouness which desired to hear the deeds of the greatest conquerors, extended heroic romances, where exile and love appear at the most as episodes. Such had formerly been accessible on English soil in the French language only, and possessed a pedagogic importance as a means of training for the youth fit for fighting, as a means of inspiration for the men. When King Robert Bruce in 1306 fled to an island, while in his boat he read, as Barbour reports, uninterruptedly from *Fierabras,* in order to maintain

---

[1] See p. 128, n. 2.

[2] Cf. *Sir Degaree, Sir Perceval, Libeaus Desconus;* see p. 131.

[3] p. 634.

his own courage and that of his companions. About 1300
these text-books of chivalry began to be translated into the
national speech, naturally with preservation of the short
couplet, and many introductory lines show that this was
proudly regarded as a patriotic act'. In the romance of
Richard Coeur de Lion we read:

> *Fele romanses men make newe,*
> *Of good knyghtes, strong and trewe,*
> *Off hey dedys men rede romance,*
> *Bothe in Engeland and in France.* [1]

The knights enumerated vv. 11—19, are: Roland, Oliver, and
'every doseper', Alexander, Charlemagne, Arthur, Gawain,
Turpin, Ogier the Dane, Hector, and Achilles. After 1350,
the new romances of the heroic type deal principally with
antiquity. With few exceptions they are heroic in theme
only, not in spirit. The spirit of the true hero-romance,
however, is that of the Scottish alliterative *Morte Arthure.*
Barbour's *Bruce,* the greatest of Middle English heroic poems,
is history in all essentials, yet history in itself romance,
and given a still further romantic coloring by popular
patriotic imagination.

Later, probably, than the early conqueror or hero-
romances appeared the first representative of the 'romance
of chivalric virtue', *Ywain and Gawain,* the only complete
English rendering of a romance by Chrétien de Troyes. [2]
The most highly chivalric of the French court-romances,
Lancelot, has no representative in English until the very
close of the fourteenth, or the beginning of the fifteenth,
century. Undoubtedly, however, the French versions were
well known in the higher spheres of society; Chaucer tells
us that Lancelot was held in great reverence by women. [3]

The favorite type of romance in the later period is the
romance of adventure and love, the element of adventure
being at first most prominent, that of love becoming increasingly so. The best representative of the romance of

---

[1] vv. 29—32.   [2] See Steinbach, *op. cit.* on p. 133.
[3] *Nonne Preestes Tale,* ll. 392—93.

adventure is probably Thomas Chestre's *Libeaus Desconus*, to which type his *Octavian* also belongs, while his version of the story of Launfal has two long adventurous additions. *Libeaus Desconus* represents a favorite sub-type of the romance of adventure: namely the story of a youth brought up in obscurity, but really of high birth, who goes forth into the world and by his knightly deeds wins for himself fame, position, and love. Another favorite sub-type is the story of the innocent persecuted wife; Chaucer's Constance is the most famous heroine of this type.[1] A combination of the two sub-types is made by the story of the knightly adventures of the heroine's son.

In Northwestern England, the romance of chivalric virtue finds a second representative[2] in the beautiful poem of *Sir Gawain and the Green Knight*. The influence of the Gawain-poet was strongly felt in northern England and in Scotland;[3] the theme of the chivalric test became a favorite, and, with or without this theme, Gawain, the most popular hero of Arthurian legend,[4] was celebrated in a number of short romances.

In a few romances—*The King of Tars, Joseph of Arimathie, The Holy Grail*—a religious motive is dominant, and the strong religious spirit of the Middle Ages is often manifested in other romances. The great religious romance on the quest of the Holy Grail has no representative in English verse, but Malory has told the story in poetical prose. Religious motives or features are prominent in the Charlemagne romances, in *Athelston* and in *Guy of Warwick*. In the latter, the religious motives resemble those in two legends of the lives of saints, *St. Eustachius* and *St. Alexius*.[5] Many of the mediaeval saints' legends are in reality only romances.[6] *Sir Gowther* is an interesting example of a

---

[1] Cf. *Florence of Rome, Emare, Sir Triamour*; see also G. Paris, § 27.

[2] Brandl (p. 654) sees a lineal descendant of this type in Spenser's *Fairy Queen*.

[3] See Brandl, pp. 663—65.

[4] Tennyson has been reproached for blackening his fame.

[5] See Brandl, § 40.   [6] G. Paris, § 50.

combination of two folk-tales worked over into a tale for religious instruction, and then still further transformed into a romance. The first part of the *Aunters of Arthur,* with a strong religious motive, is really not a romance at all. Frequently the English romance versifiers were clerics, who were not always averse to indulging in reflections against worldly minstrels.

General Character.

In mediaeval romantic poetry the English verse-romance has always been assigned a humble place. As an expression of the ideals of the feudal society in the days of chivalry, it is inferior to the verse-romance of both France and Germany. Even in its better representatives it has lost something of the chivalric, and has gained a more popular tone, a natural result of its origin among a simpler, ruder, more democratic people than the French, and in a period when the heyday of chivalry was past.

The English verse-romance is seen at its best in the poems of the earlier period,[1] particularly in those of the more southern counties, and, in the second half of the fourteenth century, in the alliterative romances of the West and of Scotland, where the romantic development was later than in the East. The rimed *Morte Arthur* is also worthy of special mention. The following characterization of these romances is partly quoted, partly condensed, from Ten Brink.

'The early English romance did not, as a whole, reach the level of its French model. Not only the honor of invention must be ascribed to the French (invention in composition, not in material), but also that of a more delicate execution and more harmonious presentation. The frequently abridged English versions are, as a rule, poorer, ruder, and of a less complete logical structure; and their excelling qualities, a more popular tone, a more vigorous painting

---

[1] The rimed *Alexander* (*Life of*) is probably the best.

b*

within narrower compass, do not make good these defects.[1]
But we are charmed by the joy they manifest in nature,
in the green forests, and in hunting, and we contemplate
not without satisfaction this rude primeval force that does
not exclude deep feeling, even if it often indulges in coarse-
ness.   Thus the English muse, if less delicate and dainty
than her French sister, was less artificial; if more passionate
was less lascivious; and in her enthusiasm for what is
grandly colossal, her joy in the actual, she showed, even
when repeating foreign romances, many of the features that
were to characterise her in the time of her full splendor.'[2]
The later alliterative romances show a certain reflection of
the stately splendor of the old English epos.   Two of these
romances, *Sir Gawain and the Green Knight* and the *Morte
Arthure,* reveal in their respective authors a highly poetical
disposition.   Of the Gawain-poet it may be said that few
mediaeval romance-poets can so justly lay claim to originality.   His romance is the work of a genuine poet and a
thinking artist, who, moreover, employed all his art in the
service of moral ideas.[3]

In the first half of the fourteenth century, the minstrel-
romance enjoyed what was, upon the whole, a noble popularity.   The romances of which we have been speaking expressed and stimulated a real, though often rude enthusiasm
for the conceptions and ideals of chivalry, especially on its
military side; but after 1350 the spirit of chivalrous society
experienced a change.   Outwardly the reign of Edward III
seemed the period of the greatest splendor of chivalry.   In
this period, too, the noble qualities of the heroes of romance
formed, nominally at least, an essential part of the ideal of
a gentleman and a warrior, and doubtless often found
embodiment in many a 'verray parfit gentil knight'.   But,

---

[1] They tell their story in a simple and naïve manner, with fresh-
ness of feeling, and not infrequently in warlike passages with considerable force and spirit; in such passages the English versifier is apt
to expand his original, while he condenses or omits passages of psycho-
logical analysis.

[2] I 253.   [3] I 336—48; II[2] 50—52.

though disguised by outward splendor and brilliancy, the passing of mediaeval chivalry had begun. The epoch is described by Ten Brink as 'a sort of Indian summer to the age of chivalry'. He says in part: 'The ideal which men strove to realize did not quite correspond to the spirit of the former age. On the whole, people had become more worldly and practical, and were generally anxious to protect the real interests of life from the unwarranted interference of romantic aspirations. The spirit of chivalry no longer formed a fundamental element, but only an ornament of life—an ornament, indeed, which was made much of, and which was looked upon with a sentiment partaking of enthusiasm. Devotion to chivalry was no longer the simple outflow of a dominant idea. The majority of people rejoiced merely in the splendor and in the festive, dignified existence that raised them above the common place and distinguished them from the vulgar crowd.'[1]

The changing spirit of the times is witnessed to by the character of the French poetry most favored in English court circles. In France, the time of conflict with the Middle Ages had long before been reached; a new spirit had awakened there of satire and of denial of the mediaeval view of life,[2] a spirit whose most notable literary expression was Jean de Meung's cynical continuation of Guillaume de Lorris' allegorical love poem, *le Roman de la Rose.* This romance, with the later French erotic poetry, produced under the influence of one or both parts of the *Roman,* and in which 'extravagant lady-worship was combined with occasional outbursts of sarcasm and cynicism', had now (1350—1400) begun to influence the sentiments of English chivalrous society. It was under the influence of this poetry that the earliest poems of the first English poet of great genius were produced.

The romances, though still read to some extent, were more and more neglected in higher society; at the same time they were widely circulated among the common people.

---

[1] II 34, 35.   [2] Ten Brink I 226.

Under these conditions, to quote Brandl,[1] 'the courtly, fashionable material forthwith sank to the masses and the streets'. The minstrel-romance grew poorer and ruder in content and in form: the tendency to abridgment and too often very empty abridgment to increased; portions of long romances were condensed into so-called ballads, and romance material was used in historical and political verse, or given a farcial turn, tendencies that became more marked in the fifteenth century.[2] In the *Tale of Sir Thopas*, Chaucer parodies the vulgarized romance of his day. He shows up its hollowness and incoherency, 'but still more in general the childish repetition of formal expressions, the passion for outward description, the wretched composition and tattered stanzas of the street-rhapsodies, into which the courtly romance style of two hundred years ago had by this time degenerated.'[3] The longer verse-romances of the later period, which were probably read rather than sung or recited,[4] were for the most part eminently uninspired.

In marvelous contrast to the body of English mediaeval romance produced after 1350 are the romantic poems of Chaucer. These poems, although they make use of old material, although they have their mediaeval features and tones, cannot be regarded as a late, brilliant flowering of mediaeval romance; they bear the impress of the Renaissance: 'Chaucer', says a recent writer, 'is the first modern epic poet.'[5]

With the romances of chivalry Chaucer seems to have been familiar, but to have entertained for them no very great respect.[6] He appreciated the picturesque features of

---

[1] p. 636; cf. Jusserand, *English Wayfaring Life in the Middle Ages*, transl. by Lucy T. Smith, Lond., 1889, p. 192.

[2] Brandl, §§ 77, 113, 114, 127, 128, 135.

[3] Brandl, p. 680.

[4] Cf. *Troilus and Criseyde*, V, l. 1797.

[5] 'Chaucer ist der erste moderne Epiker': Fischer (reviewing Ker's *Epic and Romance*) in *Anglia, Beiblatt*, X. 134.

[6] See Lounsbury, *Studies in Chaucer* (N. Y., 1892), II 302—5, III 330—32.

chivalry, and admired the nobler qualities of knighthood. His heroes of noble birth are usually represented as of the flower of chivalry: but he did not care to sing of arms, chivalric or heroic. In his two longest and most ambitious romantic narratives, the *Troilus and Criseyde* and the *Knight's Tale*, Chaucer expressly disclaims any intention of giving a full account of the deeds of war. The long and brilliant account of the tournament in the *Knight's Tale*, an event of central dramatic interest, is the only full presentation, in either romance, of a feat of arms. In this respect *The Knight's Tale* differs greatly from its source, the *Teseide* of Boccaccio. Such omissions on Chaucer's part were undoubtedly good art, but, on subjects that particularly interested him, he was not always so careful to avoid digressions. For the continuation of the unfinished *Squire's Tale* an elaborate chivalric program is outlined,[1] no part of which, however, is carried out. Was this due to lack of interest on Chaucer's part?—Some features of Chaucer's delineation of love, notably the figure of the despairing lover,[2] recall the romances; his attitude towards the chivalric ideal of love was, upon the whole, a critical one.

Chaucer's shorter romantic poems,[3] fittingly termed tales, have a very simple narrative basis, their amplification being seldom in the interest of additional incident, but in the interest of a deepened psychology. In the infancy of mediaeval romance, tales of even greater simplicity than those used by Chaucer had served, singly or combined, as a basis for the chivalric additions of the trouvères.

No renaissance of English romance followed Chaucer's work in this field; the romances of the fifteenth century were of the same old type. In several of them, however, Chaucer's influence has been pointed out; the increased number of romances treating of antiquity may have been due in part to the popularity of the *Troilus* and the *Knight's*

---

[1] vv. 651—662.

[2] *e. g.* Cf. Troilus with Chrétien's Lancelot.

[3] I have in mind the tales of the Man of Law, the Clerk, the Wife of Bath, and the Franklin.

Tale. These romances of the master certainly influenced Lydgate's *Troy-Book* and *Story of Thebes.*

Although the romances no longer held the place of honor, interest in them continued through the fifteenth century. This is shown by the numerous fifteenth century manuscripts of older romances, and by the number of French romances turned into English prose. When Caxton in 1477 had set up in Westminster the first printing press in England, among the earliest books issued from it were a number of romances, largely on classical themes, translated into English prose by the diligent Caxton himself, and another, *Le Morte Darthur,*[1] by "Syr Thomas Malory, Knight", the only English mediaeval romance that continued to be read down to modern times. Caxton's preface to this book shows the interest still maintained in Arthurian story, and the great renown of Arthur; it also shows that romances concerning 'the wordly acts of great conquerors and princes' were still regarded by many as veritable histories. As regards the historical truth of all that is written in the *Morte Darthur,* Caxton himself is rather skeptical, though he does not value the book the less. The fifteenth century saw a second edition of Malory's romance, and the sixteenth four more. The mediaeval romances, principally in prose but also in verse, were printed until the sixteenth century was well advanced,[2] until the Renaissance had come. After 1566, a new era was opened in the history of English fiction by the translations of Italian novels and tales that then poured into England.[3] Before the new interests thus aroused and so richly nourished by the drama in its ever widening scope, the old romances, with the exception of Arthurian story, soon lost any remnant of importance.

---

[1] Ed. Sommer; modernized text, Strachey, Lond. and N. Y., 1899, also, Gollancz in Temple Classics, 1899; Mead (see p. 208), Books 1, 2, 13, 17, 18, 21.

[2] See Ames-Herbert-Dibdin, *Typographical Antiquities,* Lond., 1749, 1785—90, 1812—19; Jusserand, *The English Novel in the Time of Shakespeare* (translation), N. Y., 1890, pp. 63—4.

[3] See Jusserand, *op. cit.,* pp. 68—86.

English and Germanic Legends.

I. King Horn.

1. Subject. The story of a prince, who, exiled from his native land by its conqueror, is brought up at a king's court, loved by the king's daughter, on this account is banished, returns in time to rescue the princess from another lover, and finally regains his heritage.

2. Specimen. Vv. 409—16:[1]

> heo makede faire chere
> and tok him bi þe swere.
> ofte heo him keste,
> so wel so hire leste.
>
> 'welcume Horn, heo sade,
> so fayr so Crist þe made!
> an euen and amoreȝe
> for þe ihc habbe soreȝe;
>
> haue ihc none reste,
> slepe me ne leste.
> leste me þis soreȝe,
> liue ihc noȝt to moreȝe.
>
> Horn, þu schalt wel swiþe
> mi longe soreȝe liþe,
> þu schalt wiþute striue
> have me to wiue:
> Horn, have of me rewþe,
> and pliȝt me þi trewþe!'

---

[1] Wissmann's numbering.

3. Story. Horn is the son of king Murry and queen
Godhild, of Suddene. Saracens invade the land, and Murry
falls in battle. Godhild takes refuge in a cave, while Horn
and his companions are set adrift in a ship upon the sea.
They land in Westernesse, whose king, Ailmar, takes them
into his service. Horn is loved by all, but most by the
king's daughter Rymenhild. She sends word to the steward
Athelbrus to bring Horn to her bower. Athelbrus, fearing
the king's displeasure, takes instead Athulf, Horn's comrade.
Rymenhild, unaware of the deception, embraces Athulf, and
tells him of her love. He whispers to her that he is not
Horn, whereupon she turns in wrath upon Athelbrus, who
promises to bring her Horn. When Horn comes, Rymenhild
receives him courteously, kisses him many times, and begs
him to plight her his truth. Horn replies that his lowly
birth and position make him an unsuitable mate for a king's
daughter. Rymenhild swoons from sorrow and Horn finally
promises to be her love when he is made a knight. When
this is brought about, Horn declares that, before he can
wed Rymenhild, he must prove himself a worthy knight.
On parting, Rymenhild gives him a ring that will protect
him in battle, if he will look on it and think of his love.
Horn rides forth, and, in the strength of his ring, kills one
hundred Saracens who have just landed; he returns to the
hall with the head of the leader upon his sword, and
presents the trophy to the king.

The next day, the king goes hunting, accompanied by
Fikenhild, a comrade of Horn's. Horn goes to the bower
of Rymenhild, whom he finds in tears over a dream of a
fish that broke her net. Fikenhild betrays the lovers to
the king, and accuses Horn of plotting against the king's life.

Ailmar, upon finding Horn with Rymenhild, banishes
him from the kingdom. Horn takes ship, and comes to Ireland, where he renders king Thurstan great service against
Saracen invaders. The king offers to make Horn his heir,
and to give him his daughter, but Horn remains true to
Rymenhild.

Seven years pass, and Rymenhild is to be forced to

wed king Modi of Reynis. Informed of this by a messenger from Rymenhild, Horn, with a company of knights, at once returns to Westernesse. In the disguise of a palmer, he gains admittance to the castle, and makes himself known to the bride; then, going out, he returns with his followers, attacks the castle, and kills all his enemies except Fikenhild, whom he pardons. The bridal of Horn and Rymenhild is celebrated, and Horn then starts at once for Suddene to win back his heritage there. In this he is successful; but, alarmed by a dream for the safety of Rymenhild, he hastens back to Westernesse, to find that he must again rescue her from another lover, the traitor Fikenhild. Disguised as a company of minstrels, Horn and a few knights gain admittance to Fikenhild's strong new castle, and kill him and his followers. Horn rewards his chief friends with crowns, and takes Rymenhild with him to Suddene, where she is made queen.

4. Origin. The legend of Horn is represented by an English song [1] and by a French romance, [2] both of the 13th century, by an English romance [3] of the 14th century, and by a number of Scottish ballads. In the 15th century, appeared *Pontus et Sidoine,* [4] a much amplified French prose version of *Horn and Rymenhild,* and, a few years later, an English and a German prose version of the French prose. To the 16th and 17th centuries belong the two parts of an Icelandic *Pontus-rímur,* and two Scandinavian ballads, [5] which were at least suggested by the romances of Horn.

The legend is undoubtedly of English origin. It is, perhaps, the oldest of those sagas of which Ten Brink [6] speaks as having their historical background 'formed by the invasion and settlement of the Danes, and the relations between England and Denmark growing out of them'. 'The

---

[1] *King Horn* (K. H.).

[2] *Horn et Rymenhild* (R. H.).

[3] *Horn Child et Maiden Rimnild* (H. C.).

[4] For the different versions of the *Pontus* - story, see ed. of the English version.

[5] Child I 193—4.   [6] I 150.

subject matter, taken as a whole,' he says,[1] 'points to a time when the Danish piracies were at their height.'

The localities of the poem cannot be identified.[2] Ward thinks that 'Suddene' and 'Westernesse' were probably only vague poetical designations. He finds, however, in Kemble's *Codex Diplomaticus*, several names of places in Southern England beginning with 'Horn', notably Hornesbeorh, a barrow in the isle[3] of Purbeck, Dorsetshire, near which the Danes had one of their strongholds in 876—77.

The genuine Germanic origin of the legend is shown in many features. Stimming[4] points out that all the names, even in the French romance, are thoroughly Germanic;[5] all expeditions, as in the *Beowulf*, are undertaken by sea; the residences of the kings are always near the sea; a coast guard watches the shore; in short, all the scenery is German, and, indeed, Low-German.

The nucleus of the story was, no doubt, the 'exile-and-return' motive, which enjoyed great favor in the romances of English origin.[6] This motive is, however, not peculiar to English legend. Wissmann[7] points out that almost all the leading features of *King Horn*, above all the flight to a strange land, the love of the king's daughter for the hero, the betrayal of this love, the banishment, service in a foreign land, return when danger threatens the loved one, disguise, recognition, and deliverance, appear in many mediaeval narratives[8] in the most varied combinations, and widely spread over the greater part of Northern and Middle Europe.

The origin of the extant poems now demands our attention. A comparison[9] of *K. H., R. H.,* and *H. C.* shows

---

[1] p. 231.

[2] For possible identifications, see Ward I 450—51.

[3] Cf. *K. H.* v. 1318.   [4] *E. St.* I 355—56.

[5] Ward, 454, says that some of the subordinate characters have names purely French.

[6] Cf. *Havelok* and *Beues of Hamtoun*. For historical influences shown in the legend, see Brandl § 22.

[7] *Angl.* IV 398.

[8] *Angl.* IV 352—398; Child I 192—201, and appendixes.

[9] *E. St.* XII 324—335.

that, while having the general plot in common, they differ widely in details. Both *K. H.* and *R. H.*, and *R. H.* and *H. C.*, as opposed to the third poem, possess a considerable number of common features, while *K. H.* and *H. C.* possess but one.[1]

In point of time, *K. H.* is undoubtedly the earliest, and *H. C.*, certainly in the extant version, the latest of the three poems. Upon the question of priority, Child[2] remarks: 'That the lay or geste of King Horn is a far more primitive poem than the French romance, and could not possibly be derived from it, will probably be plain to any one who will make even a hasty comparison of the two, and that the contrary opinion should have been held by such men as Warton and Tyrwhitt must have been the result of a general theory, and not of a particular examination.'[3] Wissmann,[4] comparing *K. H.* and *R. H.*, finds that every element necessary to the plot, every beautiful ancient feature of the French romance is also contained in the English poem, and that the latter has, besides, a number of old, truly poetical motives peculiar to itself. The French romance, with the exception of the popular 'tirade' form, is thoroughly courtly.[5]

Wissmann's[6] final conclusion in regard to the origin of the poems is that *K. H.* must have been the ultimate source of the other two, though it cannot have formed the direct source of *H. C.*; both *R. H.* and *H. C.* may have had special sources, which, in turn, must derive from *K. H.* In opposition to the view of Wissmann, Stimming[7] thinks that *K. H.* cannot be regarded as either the direct or indirect source

---

[1] The play upon the name of Horn, and this is introduced in a different connection. Cf. *K. H.* vv. 205—210, *H. C.* vv. 385—86.

[2] p. 192.

[3] For the views of earlier scholars upon this point, see *QF.* XVI 65.

[4] *Untersuch.* 113.

[5] For illustrations of the above points, see *Untersuch.* 114—20, and *E. St.* I 356—60.

[6] *Angl.* IV 344. [7] *E. St.* I 352—56.

of the later poems, which show too many changes and additions to admit of such a possibility; a mediaeval poet would not have departed so far from his original. Both *H. C.* and the ballads give popular versions of the legend, and the most probable view of the origin of the Horn poems is that all drew independently and directly, or nearly so, from a popular legend composed of numerous songs,[1] differing considerably from one another, which arose in different places as the popular saga spread gradually over England. Of the different versions, the one earliest fixed lies before us in *K. H.* Another completed form was probably known to the French poet, or he may have drawn from single songs. That such songs, treating of one or another episode of the Horn legend, existed at the time of the composition of the romance, is shown from the passage in *R. H.* (v. 2783) where Lemburc asks her brother to sing to her the song narrating the love history of Horn and Rymenhild.[2]

In the opinion of Caro,[3] *R. H.* may have had several sources, one of which was *K. H.* This view is supported by the features common to the two. *H. C.*, he thinks, can hardly have been drawn directly from the saga. Investigation of the style[4] shows that motives and whole sentences have been borrowed from other poems; it would also be the first time that the source of a romance in twelve-line stanzas is to be sought directly in popular legend. Caro, however, asserts[5] that *H. C.*, though the latest poem, contains the most popular version of the legend. Wissmann,[6] on the other hand, maintains that the seemingly ancient features contained in *H. C.*, such as the sword 'Bitter-fer' (v. 403), and the magic well (vv. 577—88), either do not

---

[1] W. also speaks of the probable existence of earlier songs; see under 5, p. 8.

[2] S.'s view of the origin of the Horn poems is preferred to that of W. by both Child (I 195) and Zupitza (*Anz. f. d. Alt.* IV 150).

[3] *E. St.* XII 333; cf. p. 328, C. ff.

[4] pp. 347—50.

[5] *E. St.* XVI 306; see also, Wolf, *Ueber die Lais*, Anm. 61, p. 217.

[6] *Angl.* IV 343—44.

fit into the connection or are superfluous additions. It can be shown, he thinks, that the poet borrowed motives from other poems and worked them over only superficially. Other diverging features, W. thinks, are neither ancient nor organically developed as the legend spread. In points where *H. C.* agrees with *K. H.* against *R. H.*, the latter gives the more ancient version.[1]

Some incidents of *H. C.* seem to W. to be historical reminiscences, taken perhaps from older songs, but not belonging to the genuine Horn legend. For example, the story of Horn's father,—the two battles following one after another, the feast from which he is called to his last fight, remind us of the history of the Saxon Harold. Another incident of the legend in *H. C.*, pointing to a later origin is mentioned by Ward,[2] namely, that the exiled children do not arrive in Houlac's kingdom in a boat, but are brought by land. Brandl[3] remarks that certain features in the plot of *H. C.* remind us of *Sir Tristrem* (which is alluded to in *H. C.* v. 311) and that single expressions resemble expressions in *Sir Tristrem* and in *Amis and Amiloun*.

The eight ballads, or rather versions of a ballad, on *Hind Horn,* printed by Child, are all of Scottish origin. They begin, almost immediately, with the love of Horn for the king's daughter. In one or two points,[4] the ballads resemble the version of *H. C.* as opposed to that of *R. H.* or *H. C.*

Wissmann,[5] who did not know all the ballads, thinks that they have come from *H. C.*; Stimming[6] considers them the remains of separate songs, drawn, like *H. C.*, from a northern form of the legend. Child,[7] also, thinks that there

---

[1] pp. 344—352.

[2] I 461, see also p. 460.   [3] § 52.

[4] Viz.: the discoloration of the ring, and the elopement of the bride in versions C, G, and H. (In *H. C.* the elopement is prepared for, but not carried out, see vv. 1027—32). The last stanza of A, B, and C agrees with vv. 1111—12 of *H. C.*; see Child I 192—93.

[5] *Untersuch.* 121—24.

[6] *E. St.* I 355, 361.   [7] p. 193.

is no necessary filiation between the ballads and *H. C.*, and that, were filiation to be accepted, there would still be the question of priority; for the oral traditions represented by the ballads, are not younger, necessarily, than what was committed to writing centuries ago.

The relation of the three MSS. of *King Horn* perhaps demands a few words, as it is unusually complicated. Wissmann [1] finds that the readings of two MSS. frequently correspond as against that of the third, and each one seems, in places, to have alone preserved the original. W. concludes that the MSS. are all independent of one another, and that no two form a group or MS. class. C is the most trustworthy; its changes seem unintentional. O stands pretty near to C in worth, while H deserves less confidence; it seems to be the work of a redactor who tried to remove difficulties in the subject-matter, and to give the poem a smoother, more artistic form.

The only explanation of the relation of the MSS., lies, W. thinks, in the view that the song of King Horn was handed down orally from one singer to another, and that no one followed the original version closely. Zupitza,[2] as opposed to W., maintains that MSS. O and H must have had at least a common oral source, in order to account for the readings in which both agree in opposition to the genuine readings of C. Brandl,[3] however, thinks that the result reached by W. as to the relation of the MSS. is probably incontrovertible.

5. Metre. 1548[4] verses in short riming couplets. In King Horn we have the chief representative of the so-called 'national rime verse', i. e. the short riming couplet developed from the alliterative long line, as distinguished from the short couplet imitated from Latin or French models. According to Wissmann,[5] the greater number of

---

[1] *Untersuch.* 4—7; *QF.* XLV ii—xiii.
[2] *Anz. f. d. Alt.* IX 184—88.   [3] *Litbl.* 1883 (4) 133.
[4] Wissmann's text.   [5] *Untersuch.* 48.

verses have four stresses (four stresses, if the ending is masculine, three stresses, if feminine, in which latter case W.
supposes a fourth [secondary] stress to rest on the feminine
ending). Schipper, whose principles of word-stress in ME.
verse are opposed in some respects to those of W.,[1] says[2]
that 3-stressed verses occur much more frequently than do
4-stressed, a not inconsiderable number (e. g. vv. 93/4,
263/4) having three stresses and masculine endings. Luick[3]
gives the two main types of couplets occurring in *K. H.*
as represented by, (a) vv. 5/6, 3-stressed, with feminine
endings; (b) vv. 9/10, 4-stressed, with masculine endings.
A less number of 4-stressed verses with feminine endings
occur (vv. 817/18).

The national riming verse of *K. H.* was doubtless
influenced in its development by the short riming couplet
known through foreign models, and already imitated in
English verse.[4] Schipper[5] points out this influence in the
decided and, on the whole, successful striving for equality
in the feet. Brandl[6] sees it in the free use of both masculine and feminine rimes; Wissmann[7] suggests it when he
alludes to the less frequent use of alliteration and the
fuller development of rime, as compared with *Layamon.*

Many of the verses are alliterative, though not strictly
so. A trace of the alliterative long line is seen in the
frequent occurrence of alliteration between the lines of a
couplet. A considerable number of the alliterative expressions in the poem are also found in *Layamon.*[8]
Schipper[9] considers these as formal expressions[10] that
were common poetical property. From the remains of
alliteration in the poem, W.[11] concludes that *K. H.* was
probably preceded by alliterative songs of like content.

---

[1] For a brief statement of the main point of controversy, see
The Nation, No. 902 (Oct. 12, 1882), quoted in *Angl.* V, *Anz.* 110.
[2] I 162, 182.   [3] *P. G.* II 1 p. 1005.
[4] Schipper I 108, 162—63.   [5] p. 188; see also p. 162.
[6] *Litbl.* 1883 (4) 134.   [7] *Untersuch.* 58.
[8] *Untersuch.* 59.   [9] p. 189.   [10] *e. g.* vv. 154, 387, 542.
[11] *Untersuch.* 58. Cf. Kölbing's *Sir Tristrem,* p. LII.

Better evidence of this, Schipper thinks, is found in the occasional verses (*e. g.* vv. 121, 212, 289, 1253, 1375/6) having only the two stresses of the old half line.

W.[1] sees in the poem traces of an originally strophic structure: here and there the same rime occurs four times (*e. g.* vv. 127—30, 1121—24); frequently two couplets form a whole, as in short speeches, comments, etc.; sometimes strophes of six lines occur.

In the poem, vv. 2—3, listeners are promised a song. W.[2] thinks that the narrative portions, which are treated with less care, were given in more of a recitative; the couplets that make the transitions to the conversation may have been almost spoken, while the direct monologue and dialogue, to which the greater space is given, and which have, almost without exception, a strongly strophic structure, were really sung. Schipper[3] thinks that the delivery was a recital with musical accompaniment but that there could hardly have been singing in the true sense of the term.

6. Dialect. Southeastern[4] or Midland.[5]

Wissmann finds that the vowel-system of the poem has no definitely marked character, but, in general, is that of the S. E., differing, however, from that of Kent in many points. Other scholars[6] assign the poem to the Midland. Brandl,[7] after criticising W.'s vowel-phonology in some respects, declares the poem to be pure Midland, and adds, 'Of all the characteristics of the Kentish dialect, not one is authenticated in the rimes.'

7. Date. Before the middle of the 13th century. Wissmann[8] thinks that since the rimes in *K. H.* are in-

---

[1] *Untersuch.* 62, 63, and *QF.* XLV p. xix—xxii. Cf. Schipper, 191, Luick, *op. cit.* p. 1005, § 17.

[2] *QF.* XLV p. xxii.   [3] p. 191.

[4] Wissmann, *Untersuch.* 33.

[5] Lumby's ed. pp. v—vi; Morris, *Early Eng. Allit. Poems,* pp. xviii—xxxvi; Brandl § 22, and in *Litbl.* 1883 (4) 132—5.

[6] See n. 5.   [7] *Litbl., op. cit.* 135.

[8] *Untersuch.* 58.

extricably united with its style and tone, and since, therefore, the verse represents the final stage in the gradual change of the alliterative long line into the short riming couplet, the poem cannot be earlier than the second quarter of the 13th century: but that it need not be proportionally earlier than *Layamon* B, which represents an earlier stage of the change; for *Layamon* arose in a monastery, where, naturally, the old tradition was maintained longer, and untouched by foreign influences.

8. Author. Unknown.

The author of the French romance, who is spoken of in the poem (v. 3) as 'mestre Thomas', was probably an Anglo-Norman.[1] He is not however to be identified with Thomas the author of *Tristan*.[2]

9. Bibliography.

Manuscripts: C. Cambr. Univ. Gg. 4, 27, 2, probably not later than the middle of the 13th cent.;[3] described in Lumby's ed. pp. v—vi.

O. Oxford, Bodl. Laud 108, *ca.* 1300.[4]

H. Brit. Mus. Harl. 2253, 2nd decade of the 14th cent.[5]

Editions: C. Michel, in his ed. of the French romance. Lumby, *EETS.* No. 14, 1866. See *E. St.* III 270, for a few emendations.

Mätzner, *Spr. P.* I, 1, 209.

Wissmann, a critical text, *QF.* XLV, Strassburg, 1881; for a general introduction, see *King Horn, Untersuchungen zur ME. Sprach- und Litteraturgeschichte, QF.* XVI. Revs.: *E. St.* I 151—162 (Stimming), IV 99, V 408—9, VI 150—53, 153—57; *Ltzt.* 1882 (11) 14—15; *Lt. Cbl.* 1883 (2) 61; *Ltbl.* 1883 (4) 132—35 (Brandl); Zupitza in *Anz. f. d. Alt.* IV 149—53; and IX 181—92.

Morris, *Specimens* I 237.

---

[1] G. Paris, § 68; Michel, p. xlix.

[2] Michel, pp. li, lii and *Rom.* XV 575 ff.

[3] *QF.* XVI 3.   [4] Horstmann in *Arch.* 1872, p. 39.

[5] Horstmann, *op. cit.*

H. Ritson, *AEMR.* 91; see *QF.* XLV pp. i, ii for a collation of Ritson's text with the MS.

O. Horstmann, *Arch.* 1872, p. 39. For a collation of the texts of Wissmann, Horstmann, and Ritson with the MSS., see *Anz. f. d. Alt.* IX 182—83.

The OF. romance, *Horn et Rimenhild*, by F. Michel, P., 1845.

By Brede and Stengel in *Ausgaben und Abhandlungen* VIII, Marburg, 1885 (diplomatic print).

The Ballads: Four are printed by Michel, *op. cit.,* pp. 393—409, eight by Child, I 195 ff. *Refs.: QF.* XVI 121 ff. *E. St.* I 355, 360—63; XII 335—36.

The Prose Version: King Ponthus and the Fair Sidone, Publications of the Mod. Lang. Assoc. of America XII, No. 1; see *Rom.* XXVI 468; *Mitteil.,* 1897, p. 197.

General References: Ten Brink, I 149—150, 227—232, II² 10; Brandl, § 22; Ward, 447—67; *Hist. Litt.,* XXII 551—68 (Analysis of OF. poem); Child, I 187—208.

Monographs: Wissmann, *Studien zu King Horn, Anglia* IV 342—400; Mettlich, *Bemerkungen zu dem agn. Lied vom wackern Ritter Horn,* Münster 1890, prgr., see *E. St.* XVI 306—8.

On the metre see Wissmann, *opp. cit.* and *Zur ME. Wortbetonung, Anglia* V 466—500; Schipper Ab. 3, Cap. 9,— *Anglia* V, *Anz.* 88—111, (see p. 88 n. 1 for other refs., also *JB.* 1882, No. 1003)—in *P. G.* II 1 pp. 1038—40; Luick, *P. G* II 1 pp. 1005—7.

II. Horn Childe and Maiden Rimnild.

1. Subject. See *King Horn,* 1.

2. Specimen. Vv. 985—996 (st. 84):

> Forþ sche went, þat maiden fre,
> & feched drink, þat men miȝt se,

> To þat beggere:
> "For Hornnes loue y pray þe,
> Go nouȝt, ar þis drunken be,
>   ȝif ever he was þe dere!"
> Þe maiden bi him stille stode,
> To here of Horn, hir þouȝt it gode,
>   He lay hir hert ful nere;
> Of þe coppe he drank þe wine,
> Þe ring of gold he keste þerinne;
>   "Bitokening, lo, it here!

3. Story. See *K. H.*, 3. [The following are the principal points in which the story of *Horn Childe* differs from that of *King Horn* as told above.

Hatheolf, the father of Horn, rules north of the Humber. Foes from Denmark come against him, who are all slain; then three kings come from Ireland, who defeat and kill Hatheolf in a great battle. An earl of Northumberland seizes Hatheolf's dominion. Horn and his comrades are taken by Arlaund far into the south of England, where Houlac rules. When Hatherof, and, afterwards, when Horn, visits Rimnild in her chamber, she does not so openly and warmly express her love as in *K. H.* She bestows upon each knightly gifts, and when she learns that her first visitor is not Horn, she is not angry. After Horn has been made a knight, he is the victor in a tournament, and the king gives him leave to choose from among the maidens in the king's bower; he chooses no one but Rimnild. When the accusation is made against the lovers, the king beats Rimnild until the blood comes, and then shuts himself into his chamber until his wrath against Horn has cooled; the next day, he threatens to have Horn drawn and hung if he is found in the country. In parting, Rimnild gives Horn a ring. When the stone turns pale, she tells him, then the thought of his love changes; when the stone waxes red, she belongs to another. Horn tells Rimnild that when she sees his shadow in a certain well she may know that he is about to wed. Horn rides into Wales, where he enters the service of king Elidan. He is sent to Ireland, and there helps Finlac, Elidan's son, to defeat his enemies. Atula, the daughter of Finlac, falls deeply in love with Horn, and tells him of her love. He gives an evasive answer. Upon looking at his ring, he sees that it has changed its hue. Horn enters the castle of Houlac disguised as a beggar. When Rimnild recognizes her lover she swoons, and is led to her room; she sends word to Horn that she will steal away to him towards night. After the feast, there is a tournament in which Horn unhorses the bridegroom, king Moioun, but will not kill him. Moioun goes away, and Horn is married to Rimnild. Horn assembles forces to win back his father's land in Northumberland . . .]

4. Origin. See *K. H.*, 4.

5. Metre.[1] 1136 verses, written in the twelve-line tail-rime stanza, with the rime-order *aab aab ccb ddb*.[2] A considerable number of stanzas (31, 37, 56, 69, 74, 76, 78, 80, 83, 88) show a rime-order diverging from the type. Stanzas 52, 67 and 96 are incomplete. Assonance and alliteration are very frequent.

6. Dialect. The North Midland is the region to which Brandl[3] assigns the romance. Caro[4] assigns it to the Southern part of North England, near the boundaries of the East Midland, for he finds that the poem contains some specifically Northern characteristics, as opposed to the common Northern and East Midland peculiarities. The Southern characteristics found in the poem he attributes to the scribe.

7. Date.[6] Probably the first quarter of the 14th century. Since the author knew *Sir Tristrem*, which Kölbing places in the last decade of the 13th century, and since the romance is found in the Auchinleck MS., it cannot have been written before 1290, nor after 1325.

8. Author. Unknown.
The author of the French romance is spoken of in the poem (v. 3) as 'mestre Thomas', and this led Sir Walter

---

[1] Caro's ed. 343—47.
[2] Class I of Kölbing's scheme, *Amis and Amiloun*, p. XIV.
[3] § 52.   [4] Ed. 341—43.   [6] Caro, 350.

Scott,[1] who held *H. C.* to be the older poem, to conjecture that the author of *H. C.* might be Thomas of Erceldoune. This conjecture is, however, unfounded.

9. Bibliography.

Manuscripts: Auchinleck, Advocates Libr., Edin., first quarter of the 14th century.[2] The end of *H. C.*, and at least one leaf after v. 783, are missing. For a description of the Auchinleck MS., see *E. St.* VII 178—191.

Editions: Ritson, *AEMR.* III 282—320.

Michel, 341—89 (*op. cit.* under I 9).

Caro, *E. St.* XII 323—366. See *Angl.* XIV 309 (emendations).

General References: Brandl, § 52; Ten Brink, I 248—50; see under I.

III. Havelok The Dane.

1. Subject. The story of an exiled Danish prince, who is brought up in a menial position, marries the heiress to the English throne, herself deprived of her rights, and finally becomes king of Denmark and England.

2. Specimen. Vv. 945—958.
Havelok while in the service of the earl's cook:

>   Of alle men was he mest meke,
>   Lauhwinde ay, and bliþe of speke;
>   Euere he was glad and bliþe,
>   His sorwe he couþe ful wel miþe.
>   It ne was non so litel knaue
>   For to leyken ne forto plawe
>   Þat he ne wolde with him pleye:
>   Þe children that yeden in þe weie
>   Of him he deden al her wille,
>   And with him leykeden here fille.

---

[1] *Sir Tristrem*, Edin. 1819, pp. LIX—LXI.
[2] Kölbing, in *Arthour and Merlin*, p. LX.

Him loueden alle, stille and bolde,
Knictes, children, yunge and holde;
Alle him loueden, þat him sowen,
Boþen heyemen and lowe.

3. Story. King Athelwold of England upon his death bed commits his only child Goldborough to the guardianship of the Earl of Cornwall, who swears to protect her, and to give her in marriage to the best, strongest, and fairest man that lives. In Denmark, little Havelok and his two sisters, upon the death of king Birkabeyn, their father, have been commited to the care of Earl Godard. Godard breaks his oath, murders the little girls, and gives Havelok to a fisherman, telling him to drown the child in the sea. But that night, in his cottage, Grim the fisherman sees a bright flame issuing from the mouth of the sleeping Havelok, and, upon examination, finds on the boy's shoulder a 'king's mark', which causes him to believe that Havelok will one day be king of Denmark. With Havelok and his own family, Grim escapes to England. He lands at the mouth of the Humber, and there founds Grimsby.

Grown a strong youth, Havelok enters the service of the cook of Earl Godrich of Cornwall, where he becomes famous for his good nature and for his strength both at work and in the popular games. The earl hears of Havelok, and resolves to marry him to the princess Goldborough, thus degrading her, and, at the same time, keeping his promise to her father. Against the wishes of both Havelok and Goldborough, the marriage is celebrated, and Havelok takes his wife to Grimsby.

At night, as Goldborough lies sorrowing because she is wedded unsuitably, she sees around her a bright light, which comes from the mouth of Havelok, then perceives on his shoulder a cross of gold, and hears the voice of an angel saying: 'Goldborough, cease to sorrow. Havelok is a king's son. He shall be king of England and Denmark, and you shall be queen'. Then Goldborough is glad, and kisses Havelok, who awakes.

At Goldborough's urgent request, they sail the next day for Denmark. There Havelok wins the friendship of a powerful earl, Ubbe, who soon discovers, by means of the breath of flame, the royal lineage of the young stranger, and wins for him the support of the leading men of Denmark. Havelok is acknowledged king, and Godard, by the sentence of the people, is flayed, drawn, and hung.

After four years, Havelok returns to England, conquers Godrich, and is crowned in London.

4. Origin. The legend of Havelok undoubtedly sprang up on English soil during the period of the Danish invasions.[1] Evidence pointing to the local origin of the legend, probably in Lincolnshire, is found in the definite geographical references of the poem, and in the name, local traditions,[2] and ancient seal,[3] of the city of Grimsby.

From the number of chronicles,[4] for the most part Anglo-Norman and of the 14th century, in which Havelok is mentioned or his story told, it seems clear that he was once regarded as an historical character. In the two French metrical versions[5] of the story, and in the version found in the prose chronicle of the *Brut*,[6] the events are referred to the times of Arthur or a little later. This fact, together with the resemblance seen by him between the story of *Havelok* and Layamon's account of events in the reign of Æthelbert of Kent, has led Skeat[7] to the conclusion, that 'the tradition concerning Havelok arose from facts connected with the history of Northumbria and Lindesey in the sixth century'. But the English version does not place the story in the times of Arthur, and this allusion in the French versions is doubtless a mere interpolation, made, under the influence of the Arthur legends,[8] by the OF. poem, now lost, from which the versions just referred to have descended.[9]

---

[1] See *General Refs.* § 9, and Wohlfeil, 13.
[2] See Skeat, § 18.
[3] See Skeat, § 19, and title page.
[4] See Skeat, pp. iv—xix.   [5] See **9**, p. 23.
[6] See Skeat, § 12.   [7] § 18.   [8] Wohlfeil, 14.
[9] See p. 21, n. 5.

The historical source of the name and fame, and perhaps of the story, of Havelok, has in all probability been
more correctly traced[1] to the life of Olaf Sitricson, a Danish
prince, who, about the middle of the tenth century, reigned
for a few years in Northumbria. This Olaf is known in
the sagas by the same surname or nickname, *Cuaran*[2] (*i. e.*
of the sandal) which Havelok, in the French versions, also
receives; and in certain Welsh chronicles,[3] Olaf and his
kinsman Olaf Godfreyson, appear as *Abloyc* and *Abloec,* and
in the *Anglo-Saxon Chronicle* as *Anlaf*; once, under the
date of 949, as *Anlaf Cwiran.* Now, according to Storm,
the Norse *Ōlafr,* originally *Anleifr,* corresponds with the
OE. *Anlāf,* the Irish *Amlaib* (pronounced *Awlay*), and the
Welsh *Abloc,* from which come the Anglo-Norman *Aveloc,*
later, *Havelok*; in the old Grimsby seal the name is *Habloc.*

That the name Havelok became associated with an
historical Olaf is shown from the fact that, in the *Metrical
Chronicle of England,*[4] written probably in the reign of
Edward II, Olaf Tryggvason, king of Norway from 995 to
1000, is called 'Haueloc'; and in the ballad of *Guy and
Colebrande,*[5] Olaf Cuaran appears as 'Auelocke'.

The main facts in the life of Olaf are, briefly, as follows.[6]
His father Sitric, who was of the famous race of the Hy
Ivar, ruled in Northumbria for a few years, and married,
as his second wife, the sister of king Æthelstan. Upon
the death of Sitric in 927, Æthelstan at once annexed
Northumbria, driving out Olaf. Probably a few years later,
Olaf married a daughter of Constantine II of Scotland, and
in 937 we find him the leader of the great confederacy of
Scots, Danes, and Britons against Æthelstan. The famous
battle of Brunanburh, so nobly sung in the *Anglo-Saxon
Chronicle,* witnessed his disastrous defeat. After the death

---

[1] By Storm, *E. St.* III 533—35. See, also, Ward, I 429—37.
[2] See *Rev. Celt.* III 189, n.; quoted by Ward, 430, n.
[3] See Storm, 534; Ward, 429—32.
[4] Ritson, II 270 v. 797.
[5] *P. F. MS.* II 528.
[6] See *Dict. Nat. Biog.* XLII 82.

of Æthelstan in 940, the Northumbrians recalled Olaf to
his father's kingdom, which he extended southward to
Watling Street. In 944, he was driven from the country
by king Eadmund. In 949, he regained his kingdom in
Northumbria, only to be finally expelled in 952. He then
went through a long career as king of Dublin, dying, at
an advanced age, in 981.

One rather striking correspondence between the historical
facts and the Havelok legend, as told in the French
metrical versions, lies in the fact that the persons corresponding to Athelwold and Godrich in the English story
(Adelbrict and Edelsi in Gaimar, Ekenbright and Alsi in
the *Lai*), are both kings and brothers-in-law; and in Gaimar,
Adelbrict is a Dane, Edelsi, a Briton.

In the history of Olaf, Storm finds 'elements enough to
account for the romantic epos of Aveloc'. On the other
hand, it has been suggested [1] that the names of historical
characters may merely have been grafted upon the nucleus
of an entirely unrelated legend, as was often the case in
popular ballads. A position in regard to the origin of the
legend, between the two preceding, is suggested by Ward
when he says, [2] 'The connection between the two heroes,
which the editors [3] of "Havelok" have regarded as a mere
mistake, existed really (we believe) at the very foundation
of the Havelok-Cuaran legend, and helped to give the
romance its present form.' And again, [4] 'The camp-stories
told and the lays sung about Anlaf Cuaran, one of which
is preserved by Malmesbury (in his *Gesta Regum* [5] and also
in his *Gesta Pontificum*) must have influenced the development of many romances that were current before his time.'
Previously existing elements of mythology and folk lore,
or elements common to romance, are found in such features
as the marvellous flame-breath, [6] the Valkyria-like rôle
played by Argentille [6] (Goldborough), the dead men tied up

---

[1] *JB.*, 1891, xvi, 443.   [2] p. 430.
[3] See Skeat, p. xviii, n. 1, xix, n. 2.   [4] p. 435.
[5] i 143.   [6] Ward, 428, 429.

to stakes in the ranks of battle[1] (French versions), the points of likeness[2] between the story of Havelok and that of Hamlet[2] (Amlethus), as told by Saxo Grammaticus, and between the story of Havelok and the account in the Icelandic saga of the youth of Olaf Tryggvason.[3] The greater fame of this Olaf, who is said to have married Olaf Cuaran's sister Gyda, and who, as we have already seen, has been called Havelok, perhaps gave an added impulse to the development of the legend.

One of the strongest motives underlying the development of the Havelok legend may well have been political or national,[4] namely, the desire of the Danes to prove their right to sovereignty in England. This desire would naturally have been at its strongest in the reign of Canute, until which time, Ten Brink[5] thinks, the legend was probably not completed; for, 'at the end of the tale, Denmark and England are at peace, and a Danish king rules over England'. Even after the legend had received a complete poetic form, new elements, embodying features of contemporary history, may have been added by later redactors. Thus several features peculiar to the English version have been

---

[1] pp. 428, 434.

[2] p. 435. See Grundtvig, *North. Myth.*, 1832. p. 366; K. Köster, *Sagnet om Havelok Danske*, Copen., 1868. Here, perhaps, should be given the report in the *Athenaeum*, 1896, no. 3603, p. 681, of the paper of Mr. Gollancz, read before the Philological Society. 'His Hamlet researches had led him to the conviction that the Icelandic *amlothi*, a fool, and the Aberdeen *ablich*, a fool, *ablach*, a carcass, worthless person, were the same. The early mythical stories of Havelok and Hamlet became merged, and their names too. Havelok was the Scandinavian Anlaf Cuaran, of whose name there were twenty different forms, one "Aleifr", in Welsh "Abloyc", in Irish "Amlaidhe" and "Amlaibh", and in Giraldus Cambrensis, "Amalacus". „Amlaidhe" was "Amlothi" or "Hamlet". The English form occurs in the *Wars of Alexander*, where Darius' courtiers show him as an "Amlaghe", an ape, dwarf; and Porus, in his letter says, "thou Alexander, thou ape, thou Amlaghe out of Greece"'.

[3] pp. 436—37. For the Olaf-sage, see *Heimskringla*, transl. Laing, 1889. II 71—246.

[4] Wohlfeil, 17.   [5] p. 234.

adduced by Hales[1] as pointing to so late a period as the reign of Edward I.

Was the legend first poetically treated by Danish, Welsh or English minstrels? Storm and Ward, chiefly upon etymological grounds, claim this honor for the Welsh. Besides the Welsh origin of the name Havelok, two names of women, Orwain and Argentille (in the French versions), are derived by Ward[2] from a similar source. As evidence of a Welsh origin, Storm attaches importance to the expression in the *Lai* (v. 21), 'Q'un lai en firent li Breton', 'Whereof the Britons made a lay'. This may, however, be merely a conventional expression, as Breton lays had become very popular and were imitated by the Norman poets;[3] or the term 'li Breton' may refer simply to the inhabitants of Britain. It is the opinion of Ward[4] that the theme was treated at one time by Welsh minstrels, that the Anglo-Danes then took up the theme, and connected Havelok's foster-father with the founder of Grimsby.

The relations of the extant poetical versions and the prose version in the OF. chronicle of the *Brut* have been investigated by Kupferschmidt,[5] with the following results. These versions, as a comparison of their incidents show, all go back to a common OE. original. The French versions, however, do not draw directly from this common source, but each comes, independently, from the same intermediate OF. poem. Of the two French metrical versions, that of Gaimar, dating from about 1150, is the earlier;[6] while the *Lai d'Avelok*, judging from phonological evidence afforded by the rimes, does not go further back than the 13th century.[7] The extant English version has developed independently

---

[1] *Athenaeum*, 1889, I 244. [2] pp. 432, 433.

[3] Cf. G. Paris in *Rom.* IX 30, VII 2.

[4] p. 429. [5] *Rom. Stud.* IV 423—30.

[6] Madden, p. vii, and Skeat, p. ix, consider Gaimar's version as an abridgment of the *Lai*, which Skeat, § 4, assigns to the middle of the 12th century.

[7] An opinion already expressed by the Abbé de la Rue, and based principally upon linguistic grounds. *Essais historiques sur les Bardes*, 116—19. Caen, 1834.

near the two French poems. Both Brandl[1] and Wülker[2] seem to think that the author of the English poem was at least acquainted with a French rendering.

5. Metre. 3001 verses, whose general metrical scheme,[3] to which, however, there are not a few exceptions, is that of 4-stressed[4] iambic verses, rimed in couplets. In contrast to *King Horn, Havelok* shows the short couplet imitated from foreign models.[5]

The verses are grouped in divisions of very unequal length. Instead of the couplets, we sometimes find 'tirades' of four, six, and, once, (vv. 87—105) of nineteen verses. The rimes are, upon the whole, correct. Alliteration occurs but rarely.

The poem, according to Ten Brink,[6] was probably not designed for singing, but for non-musical delivery by a *segger*, who, in more than one place, addresses his audience on his own behalf.

6. Dialect. That of the North of East Anglia.[7] Hupe thinks that the evidence of verb inflection and of rime makes against Lincolnshire as the home of the poet; he is inclined to accept Norfolk. Upon grounds of phonology, rime, and conjugation, he decides that the home of the scribe was further to the W., perhaps in the S.W. part of the diocese of Lincoln, and therefore near Oxford.

7. Date. In its present form, about the end of the 13th century. It was used by Rauf de Boun,[8] who wrote in 1310, and must, therefore, have been composed before that date. Madden and Skeat place it about 1280, a date generally accepted by later scholars (Storm, Wohlfeil, Hupe). Brandl gives the date as about 1300, and 1296 or, possibly, 1300 is assigned by Hales.[9] The date of the MS. cannot,

---

[1] § 52.   [2] p. 98.   [3] For full details, see Wittenbrink.

[4] Cf. Wittenbrink, 22, § 6, and Skeat, p. xliv, n. 1.

[5] Schipper I 269—70.   [6] p. 232.

[7] Hupe, 193, so Wittenbrink, 38.

[8] Skeat § 7.   [9] See p. 21, n. 1.

according to Skeat,[1] be later than the end of the 13th century, but Hupe,[2] on paleographical grounds, would refer the MS. to about 1380.

8. Author. Unknown.

From the Latin words and expressions scattered through the poem, Wittenbrink[3] judges that the author was a monk or cleric.

9. Bibliography.

Manuscripts: Laud 108, Bodl. Libr., Oxford; desc. by Skeat, § 26; by Wittenbrink, 3—5, and § 3.

Editions: Madden, for the Roxburghe Club, L. 1828. Skeat, *EETS. ES.* No. 4, 1868. Collation by Hupe, *Angl.* XIII 194. Emendations by: Zupitza, *Angl.* I 468, VII 145, — *ZsfdA.* XIX 124; Stratmann, *E. St.* I 423, V 377; Hupe, *Angl.* XIII 197—200; Wittenbrink, § 2; Kölbing, *E. St.* XVI 299 ff., XIX 146 ff.; Holthausen, *Angl.* XV 499—504, XVII 442.

Selections, in *ZML.*, 85 (vv. 1—183); Morris' *Specimens,* I 237 (vv. 339—748); Wülker, *AE. LB.* I 81 (vv. 2052—2265); see *E. St.* XVII 297 for emendations.

Editions of the French Versions. *Lai d'Havelok,* Madden, *op. cit.,* 105—146; F. Michel, P. 1883; Th. Wright, in his ed. of Gaimar for the Caxton Society, L. 1850, App. pp. 3—34. Gaimar's version in his *Estorie des Engles*: Madden, 147—180; *Monumenta Historica Britannica* I 764 ff.; Th. Wright, *op. cit.,* 2—27; Hardy and Martin, L. 1888, I.

General References: Ten Brink, I 149—50, 232—234; Brandl, § 52; Wülker, 81, 97 f., 105; *Hist. Litt.* XVIII 731 —38; Morley's *Eng. Writers,* III 267—76 (abstract); Ward, I 423—446. *Dict. Nat. Biog.,* XLII 82.

Monographs: Kupferschmidt, (on Gaimar's Version and its relation to the *Lai*), *Rom. Stud.* IV 411—30; see *Rom.* IX 480. — Wittenbrink, *Zur Kritik und Rhythmik des alt-engl. Lais von H. dem Dänen,* Burgsteinfurt, 1891, prg; revs., *E. St.* XVI 299—304, *Mitteil.,* 1891 (8) 244. — Ludorff,

---

[1] p. xxxv. [2] p. 192. [3] p. 5.

Ueber die Sprache des altengl. Lay H. þe Dane, Münster, 1873, diss. (see Wohlfeil, 8, 9). Hohmann, *Ueber Sprache und Styl des altengl. Lai H. the Dane,* Marburg, 1886, diss.; Wohlfeil, *The Lay of H. the Dane. Ein Beitrag zur ME. Sprach- und Litteraturgeschichte,* Leipzig, 1890, diss.; Hupe, *H.-Studien, Anglia* XIII 786 ff.

IV. Guy of Warwick.

1. Subject. The deeds of an English knight, undertaken to win the favor of his lady; his later life as a pilgrim, in order to win the favor of Heaven.

2. Specimens.[1] a) From version A, vv. 1151—4. Felice's terms:

> Ac mi loue no schaltow haue
> For noþing þatow may craue,
> Er þou perles holden be
> & best doand in þis cuntre,

b) From version α, st. 270. After the departure of the Danes:

> Bliþe were þe Inglis men ichon:
> Erls, barouns, & king Aþelston
>   Þai toke sir Gij þat tide,
> & ladde him to Winchester toun
> Wiþ wel fair processioun
>   Ouer al bi ich a side.
> For ioie belles þai gun ring,
> 'Te deum laudamus' þai gun sing,
>   & play, & michel pride.
> Sir Gij vnarmed him, & was ful bliþe:
> His sclauain he axed also swiþe:
>   No lenger he nold abide.

---

[1] From Zupitza's ed. of the Auchinleck MS.

3. Story.[1] Guy, son of Syward of Wallingford, steward
of the Earl of Warwick, becomes enamored of the earl's
daughter, Felice la Belle. Felice at first scornfully rejects
the love of her father's cup-bearer, but later, touched by
his devotion and despair, promises to accept his love when
he shall have become a famous knight. Knighted by the
earl, Guy crosses the sea, and, victor in many tournaments,
wins wide renown. Returning to England after a year, he
is received with honor by king Æthelstan; but Felice,
fearing that marriage may win him from love of arms,
refuses to listen to his suit until, as a knight, he has no
peer. So Guy goes forth again. Victorious alike in knightly
contests and in war, he becomes the first knight in Christen-
dom. His greatest achievement is the deliverance of the
emperor of Constantinople from the Saracens, his reward
being the offer of the emperor's daughter in marriage, with
half the kingdom. At the very altar, Guy recollects Felice
and swoons. The marriage is deferred, and circumstances
soon give him a good pretext for leaving Constantinople.
Returning through Germany, he devotes himself for some
time to the rescue of two lovers, Sir Tirri and the fair
Oisel, from their difficulties, then crosses to England. Hearing
that a dragon is ravaging Northumbria, Guy hastens thither,
and, after a terrible fight, kills the beast. Returning home,
he finds that his father is dead. At Warwick, he is received
with great honor, and his marriage with Felice is celebrated
with prolonged festivities.

After a month of happiness, Guy, standing alone one
night in a turret, looking upon the heavens thick beset
with stars, thinks sorrowfully of the war and woe that he
has wrought: all has been done for the love of Felice;
nothing for the love of 'Jesus omnipotent', who gave him
all his honor. He vows to expiate his sins, as a pilgrim,
and, in spite of the anguish of his wife, leaves Warwick
that night, bidding her give their expected son to Sir
Haraud of Ardern, his former master and companion-in-arms,

---

[1] MS. A.

to educate. In parting, Felice gives Guy a ring. For many years, through many lands, the pilgrim 'with glad chere' pursues his way. Once in the East, in behalf of Christian prisoners, he lays aside his pilgrim's garb to fight the Saracen giant Amorant, and in Germany, he again rights the affairs of the much oppressed Sir Tirri. Finally, an old man, he returns to England. England has been invaded by the Danes under Anlaf, and Æthelstan, directed by an angel, begs the pilgrim to fight for England against Anlaf's champion, the African giant Colbrand. After a desperate fight near Winchester, Guy kills the giant, and then, after visiting Warwick, and unrecognized partaking of his wife's bounty, he retires to a hermitage in the forest. Finally, warned by an angel of his approaching end, he sends to Felice her ring, and lives to look upon her once; she survives him but a fortnight, and is buried by his side.

Reinbrun, Gij, sone of Warwike.

Guy's son, Reinbroun, when seven years old, is stolen by foreign merchants, who present the child to king Argus of Africa. Heraud, going in search of Reinbroun, is wrecked upon the African coast, and imprisoned in a Saracen city. The lord of this city, Amiral Parsan, hearing that his prisoner was once a famous knight, asks Heraud to fight for him against king Argus, who, by the aid of a valiant knight, has almost conquered the Amiral. This young knight and Heraud meet in battle. During their desperate encounter, Heraud repeatedly adjures the knight to reveal his name; Reinbroun, for it is he, finally complies, and the combatants embrace.

On their way back to England, they stop for the night at the castle of Amis of the Montayne, an old friend of Guy's. Amis, as they learn from his sorrowing lady, has been driven from his country because he had been a friend to Guy. Now he has disappeared; his wife thinks he has been captured by a fairy knight. Reinbroun rides out to seek Amis, and finds him in an enchanted palace. The lord of this palace he overcomes, thus freeing Amis and three hundred other knights.

In Burgundy, Reinbroun has an encounter with a formidable young knight, who proves to be Heraud's son Haslak, he having set forth in search of his father. All three proceed to England. Having been honored by Æthelstan in London, they go to Warwick, where Reinbroun receives the homage of his men.

4. Origin. The earliest known version of the story of *Guy of Warwick* is the Anglo-Norman romance of the 12th century,[1] of which the different versions of the English romance are translations. Neither chronicle nor legend, previous to the romance, makes any mention of the hero or his achievements; additional details by the chroniclers of the 14th century, such as the identification of the scene of combat between Guy and the giant,[2] have not been shown to belong to the original legend. The work of the Anglo-Norman poet, however, was, in all probability, based upon Old English traditions of the 10th and 11th centuries.

Guy's crowning achievement, his defeat of the Danish champion in behalf of Æthelstan, seems to point to Brunanburh as the inspiration of the legend, but there is no known historical source for the part played by Guy. Ellis,[3] seeing some resemblance between the name of Guy and that of Egils[4]—a Northern viking who, according to the Danish 'Egils saga' of the 11th or 12th century, with his brother Thorolf, aided Æthelstan at Brunanburh—conjectures that Egils, 'becoming the hero of one of the many odes composed on the occasion of that much celebrated battle, may have been transformed by some Norman monk into the pious and amorous Guy of Warwick.' Upon this point, Tanner,[5] in substance, remarks, that it is not improbable that Æthelstan was aided at Brunanburh by one or more sea-faring

---

[1] Ten Brink I 246; *DNB* XXIII; G. Paris, p. 250, gives the first third of the 13th century.

[2] See *DNB*, and Ward, 480—81.   [3] p. 188.

[4] The two names cannot be identified etymologically.

[5] p. 45.

adventureres, and that the memory of aid received led gradually to the transformation of the foreign into a national hero.

It will be observed, however, that the scene of the combat with Colbrand is laid at Winchester, where the spot was identified by local tradition in the 14th century. Now, though the site of Brunanburh is not positively known, it certainly was not at or near Winchester; moreover Winchester, though not approached by the Danes in the reign of Æthelstan, in the reign of Æthelred, in 993, was threatened by Olaf Tryggvason, who, as we have already seen, has been confounded with Olaf Cuaran.[1] The confusion as to the name may have led to the identification of the danger to Winchester with the battle of Brunanburh and king Æthelstan, the scene, however, being kept at Winchester.[2]

Several of the names in the romance are known to English history, though not to that of the tenth century. The name Guy is possibly a Norman reproduction of the OE. Wīgod, or of wīg, war.[3] 'Wīg,' says Ward,[4] 'was a common name down to the Conquest: it would naturally be pronounced Gwi by many of the Normans.' An historical Wīgod of Wallingford was cupbearer to Edward the Confessor, and in favor with the Conqueror. 'There is at least nothing absurd,' remarks Ward,[5] 'in the conjecture that Guy might stand for some mythical ancestor of Wīgod of Wallingford.' When, in the 14th century, Guy had become famous, and was treated by the chroniclers as an historical character, Rous, the chaplain and genealogist of the Beauchamps, the Norman Earls of Warwick, claimed to trace their descent from Guy through Wīgod of Wallingford.[6]

Guy's father, in the French romance, is called Siward or Seguard, and his master is Harald or Heraud d'Arderne. Now Thurkill, the last Anglo-Saxon lord of Warwick and,

---

[1] See III, § 4.   [2] This is the view of Ward, pp. 472—3.

[3] Price, in Warton's *Hist. of Engl. Poetry*, 1840, § 5, I 171 n.

[4] p. 474.   Cf. *Onomasticon Anglo-Saxonicum*, Cambridge, 1897, pp. 486—92.

[5] p. 474.   [6] See Ward, 475—76.

according to Rous, a descendent of Wīgod and the father
of Margaret, the first Norman countess of Warwick, had a
son Siward, who founded the family of Arden.[1] Furthermore, Siward of Arden had, according to documents quoted
by Dugdale,[2] a daughter of the unusual name of 'Filicia'.
We also learn through Dugdale of a certain Leticia, spoken
of by one of her descendants as daughter of Siward de
Arden and a mistress of Henry I. As Leticia was not
daughter, but granddaughter to Siward, Ward thinks that
the name in the above connection is a mistake for Felicia,
and he is, upon the whole, strongly inclined to connect the
Felice of the romance with the granddaughter of Thurkill
of Warwick. 'We need hardly add,' he remarks,[3] 'that if
she was really one of the acknowledged mistresses of Henry I,
the probability of her being addressed by a Norman poet
would be decidedly increased.'

The mass of detail in the romance is no doubt
pure fiction, either the invention of the poet, or drawn by
him from the common 'romance fund'.[4]

Of the conclusion of the story, Ward[5] says that it 'is
imagined more in the spirit of the twelfth century than of
any earlier period. The conclusion, however, is in excellent
dramatic keeping with the rest of the hero's home adventures;
and it is not at all improbable that the story of the Winchester champion obtained its ascetic character by being
treated in a Saxon cloister.'

The French romance was done into English several
times. According to Zupitza,[6] we possess the whole, or
considerable fragments, of at least four different ME. versions.
The poem of *Guy and Colebrande,* which tells the story of
Guy's fight with the Danish champion and of his life and
death at the hermitage, is probably a very old version.
Kölbing[7] thinks that it undoubtedly goes back to a source

---

[1] See Ward, 476.   [2] See Ward, 477—78.   [3] p. 478.
[4] See Brandl, § 37; and *Germ. N. R.* XXII 191—94.   [5] p. 479.
[6] Ed. of 1875—76, pp. v—viii; cf. refs. under 9, *MSS.*, pp. 30—1.
[7] *Germ. N. R.* XXII 193.

nearly related to that which lay before the poet of the Auchinleck version.

The treatment of Guy by the chroniclers[1] and the traditional development of his history at Warwick,[2] it hardly falls within our province to report.

5. Metre. Version A[3] of the Auchinleck MS. has 7306 verses; version α[3] has 299 twelve-line stanzas. All the versions mentioned by Zupitza[4] are in short couplets, except, in the Auchinleck MS., (1) the second version (α) and (2) the sequel to the romance,—*Reinbrun, Gy sone of Warwike,* both in the twelve-line tail-rime stanza. α is divided by Wilda into two parts, according to the rime order: stanzas 1—46 belonging to class I, the remaining stanzas, and those of *Reinbrun,* to class III.

6. Dialect. The versions noticed by Brandl are assigned by him as follows: A,[5] to a region between S. and W. Midland, perhaps even to S. Warwickshire; α,[5] to a region a little further north,—Wilda[6] thinks that this version arose in the S. E. Midland, in a region bordering upon Essex— c[7] and P[8] to the N. Midland; *Reinbrun,* Wilda[9] assigns to the E. Midland, more to the S. than to the N., and N. W. from the home of *Guy of W.*

7. Date. The earliest English translation was probably made during the first quarter of the 14th century, the period to which the oldest extant MS. belongs.

8. Author. Unknown. Some parts of the poem suggest the hand of a monk.[10]

9. Bibliography.

Manuscripts: A.[11] Auchinleck, Advocates' Libr., Edin., first quarter of the 14th cent. (Kölbing, *Arthour and Merlin,* p. ix); desc. in *E. St.* VII 178 ff.

---

[1] See Tanner, pp. 20—38. [2] *DNB.* [3] See under 9, *MSS.*
[4] Ed. of c, pp. v—viii. [5] Br. § 37. [6] pp. 46—55.
[7] Br. § 80. [8] Br. § 52. [9] pp. 56—61.
[10] See the conjectures of Ellis and of Ward, pp. 27, 29.
[11] Lettering of Zupitza in *Szgsb.*

In this MS., the romance is composed of two versions, the second (α) beginning after Guy's fight with the dragon (after v. 7306 of Z's ed.)

C. Cajus 107, Cambr., beginning of the 15th cent.

c. Ff. 2, 38, Univ. Libr. Cambr., 15th cent.

S. Sloane 1044, Brit. Mus. (fragment of 216 vv.), 14th cent.; desc. *Szgsb.* 623.

P. Addit. 14408, Brit. Mus. (fragment of 11400 vv.), 14th cent.; desc. in *Szgsb.* 635—36.

On the MSS. and the relation of the versions, see Zupitza, in his ed. of 1875, pp. v—viii, and in *Szgsb. der phil.-hist. Classe d. kais. Akad. d. Wiss.* LXXIV 623—68; cf. Kölbing in *Germ.* XXI 354—59, 365—67, and in *E. St.* II 248.

Old prints, and editions: d. By Copeland (a copy in the Brit. Mus.), about the middle of the 16th cent.; it is a modernization of P; the first twenty leaves are wanting.

P. Privately printed by Sir Thomas Phillips (Middle Hill, 1838); reprinted by Turnbull in his ed. of A, p. xxviii ff.

For notices of other prints, prose versions, &c., see Z.'s ed. of c; p. vii; *DNB.*, XXIII p. 388; *Mod. Lang. Notes,* 1896, pp. 406—408; *Ang.* II 193.

a. Turnbull, for the Abbotsford Club, 1840.

c. Zupitza, *EETS. E. S.,* Nos. 25, 26, 1875—76; text criticism by Kölbing, *E. St.* XIII 136.

a and c. Zupitza, *EETS. E. S.,* Nos. 42. 49. 59, 1883—91 (texts only); noticed in *Angl.* XI 324.

S. Printed in *Szgsb.* 624 ff.

The French text has never been entirely edited. Herbing has edited the beginning of the romance from the Wolfen-büttel MS. in the *Programm der grossen Stadtschule zu Wismar,* 1872.

Short Poems and 16th *and* 17th *century Versions.* See Ward 494—501.

1. *Guy and Colebrande,* in *P. F. MS.* II 527; for date, see *Germ. N. R.* XXII 193.

2. *Guy and Phillis,* in *P. F. MS.* II 201, 608; Ritson's *Ancient Songs and Ballads,* 1829, II 193.

3. Lydgate's *Guy*. About 74 8-line stanzas on Guy's fight with the giant, and his life and death at the hermitage. In *Szgsb.* 649—65; *P. F. MS.* II 520 (Harl. MS. last 78 vv.); *ZML.* pp. 114—15 (sts. 59—64).

4. A version of the whole romance by John Lane, 1621. About 17450 ll.; not printed. See *Szgsb.* 645—46. The prose introduction is printed in *P. F. MS.* II 521—25.

5. *The famous historie of Guy, Earl of Warwick* by Samuel Rowlands, a poem in 12 cantos, published before 1630. A portion of this poem is found in

6. *Guye: And Amarant*, printed in *P. F. MS.* II 136, and in the *Reliques* (1847) III 152.

General References: Ten Brink, I 150, 182, 246—48; Brandl, § 37, 53, 80; Wülker, 98, 105; Ward, 471 ff.; *Dict. of Nat. Biog.* XXIII; Ellis, pp. 188—238; *Hist. Litt.* XXII 841—51; *PF. MS.* II 509—20.

Monographs: A. Tanner, *Die Sage von Guy von Warwick, Untersuchung über ihr Alter und ihre Geschichte*, Heilbronn, 1877, diss.; rev. by Zupitza, *Angl.* II 192—99; by Kölbing, *E. St.* II 246—48.—Wilda pp. 46—61.

V. Athelston.

1. Subject. King Æthelstan and his three friends: how one falsely accuses another to the king.

2. Specimen. Vv. 1—12:

> Lord, þat is off myʒtys most,
> Fadyr and sone and holy gost,
>   Bryng vs out off synne
> And lene vs grace so for to wyrke
> (To loue boþe god and holy kyrke),
>   Þat we may heuene wynne.
> Lystnes, lordyngys, þat ben hende,
> Off falsnesse, hou it wil ende,

A man, þat ledes hym þer-in.
Off foure weddyd breþeryn I wole ȝow tel,
Þat wilen yn Yngelond gon dwel,
    Þat sybbe were nouȝt off kynne.

3. Story. Four messengers, one of whom is Athelston, cousin to the king of England, meet by a cross in a forest. For love of this meeting, they swear to be 'wedded brethren' for ever. When Athelston becomes king, he makes one 'brother' Earl of Dover; another, Earl of Stane, giving him his sister Edyff in marriage; the third, a clerk, he endows with the bishopric of Canterbury.

The king greatly loves the Earl and Countess of Stane and their two fair sons. The Earl of Dover, becoming jealous, after first exacting from the king an oath not to reveal his informant, accuses Stane and his wife of plotting against Athelston's life and throne. Under the pretext of knighting the sons, Athelston summons Stane and his family to London. Upon their arrival, they are at once cast into prison. The queen, persisting in her intercession for the prisoners, is silenced by Athelston with a blow that kills her unborn child. The queen now sends for the archbishop of Canterbury. The next day Athelston goes to church and prays that the truth may be revealed concerning the prisoners. Looking up he sees the archbishop, who intercedes for them. The king becomes very angry, and tells the archbishop to lay down the insignia of his office and leave the kingdom. The archbishop, after excommunicating the king and placing England under a ban, rides away, but is soon recalled by the now submissive king.

The archbishop proceeds to subject the accused to the ordeal of fire, by requiring them to walk barefoot over nine red-hot plowshares. This they do without receiving the least injury. The countess after having passed the ordeal, gives birth to a son, who becomes 'Saint Edemound'. The king and the archbishop christen the child, and the king names him his heir.[1] Athelston is constrained by the arch-

---

[1] The successor of Æthelston was his brother Eadmund.

bishop to reveal the name of the accuser, and Earl Wymound is summoned to London. As he solemnly denies before his peers ever having made the accusation, he is subjected to the ordeal. He falls upon the third plowshare. Questioned as to why he made a false accusation, he replies, 'Because the king loved him too much, and me too little.' He is drawn by five horses and then hung. Jesus grant that no traitor ever have a better ending!

4. Origin. No original for this romance is known, and, so far as the editor is aware, no story concerning Æthelstan like the one narrated here has been pointed out elsewhere. The poet, however, refers to authorities both oral and written;[1] and, from the expression frequently repeated, 'In romaunce as we rede', Zupitza[2] concludes that there was without doubt a French source.

No historical basis for the romance can be shown. There are, however, certain stories told of Æthelstan's reign, in which a general resemblance to features of our romance will be readily perceived. Thus William of Malmesbury[3] quotes Æthelstan as telling, in a charter to the abbey of Malmesbury, how a certain Ælfred, being accused of conspiracy against the king, went to Rome to defend himself by oath before pope John. But the very instant he had sworn at the altar of St. Peter, he fell down, and died three days later at the English college. Again William of Malmesbury, this time drawing from old ballads, tells how Æthelstan's cup-bearer accused Eadwine, the king's brother, of being connected with the conspiracy of Ælfred. Although Eadwine took an oath before the king, declaring his innocence, the king caused him, with his armor-bearer, to be set adrift in an old boat.[4] Eadwine, in despair, leaped into the sea, and was drowned. Æthelstan repented that he

---

[1] See ed. II, n. to v. 19.   [2] Ed. III 325.

[3] Under dates 924—933.

[4] For the statement of different chronicles on this point, see *DNB* II 217. The *A. S. Chronicle* merely mentions that Eadwine was drowned in 933.

had slain his brother, and did penance for seven years. The cup-bearer, one time when presenting wine to the king, slipped, and, as he bore himself up with the other foot, exclaimed, 'So brother helpeth brother'. This reminded Æthelstan of the share the cup-bearer had had in his brother's death, and he ordered him to be put to death. The correspondence between the stories just noticed and leading features of our romance are, in the opinion of Zupitza,[1] only accidental, and belong to generally popular motives. Certain details, while in some respects agreeing with history, in others, diverge from it.[2]

5. Metre.[3] 811 verses. The MS. is not divided into stanzas, but the metrical scheme for the greater part of the poem is that of the twelve-line tail-rime stanza, of which there are 59 (class III). The incompleteness of the 16 remaining stanzas is due, in the opinion of the editor to a defective text. Alliteration is plentifully used.

6. Dialect. North Midland. Wilda[4] calls the dialect purely Northern. Zupitza,[5] however, thinks it 'more advisable' to consider it N. Midland, upon the grounds that no specifically Northern words occur, and that the poet has probably used *i* rather frequently before the perfect passive participle. Brandl,[6] who also assigns the romance to the N. Midland, remarks that perhaps the entrance of London speech forms had already begun to obliterate the boundaries of the dialects.

7. Date. About 1350. Zupitza[7] agrees with Kölbing[8] in assigning the MS. to the second half of the 14th century. The vocabulary shows almost no ancient feature.

8. Author. Unknown.

9. Bibliography.

Manuscripts: 175, Caius Coll., Cambr.; desc. in *E. St.* XIV 321—22.

---

[1] Ed. III 325.   [2] See ed. III 325.   [3] Ed. III 326—30.
[4] p. 64.   [5] Ed. III 337.   [6] § 80.   [7] Ed. III 337.
[8] *Sir Beues* p. vii.

Editions: Hartshorne, *Ancient Metrical Tales*, L. 1829.
Th. Wright, *Reliquae Antiquae*, L. 1895, II 85.

Zupitza, *E. St.* XIII 331—414 (I, text,—II, notes), XIV
321—44 (III, introduction, and index to the notes).

General References: Brandl § 80; Zupitza, *E. St.* XIV
325 (a few lines on the general character of the romance).

VI. Sir Beues of Hamtoun.

1. Subject. The wrongs, adventures, wondrous feats,
and successes of an English knight, principally in the East.

2. Specimen. a) Vv. 313—18. Beves to his mother:

'Ac o þing, moder, i schel þe swere:
3if ich euer armes bere
     And be of elde,
Al þat haþ me fader islawe,
And ibrou3t of is lif dawe,
     Ich schel hem 3ilden!'

b) Vv. 771—82. Beves goes to fight the boar:

Þo Beues in to þe wode cam,
His scheld aboute is nekke a nam
And tide his hors to an hei þorn
And blew a blast wiþ is horn;
Þre motes a blew al arowe,
Þat þe bor him scholde knowe.
Þo he com to þe bor is den,
A se3 þer bones of dede men,
Þe bor hadde slawe in þe wode,
Ieten here flesch & dronke her blode.
'Aris!' queþ Beues, 'corsede gast,
And 3em me bataile wel in hast!'

3. Story. Beves, son of Guy, Earl of Southampton,
when fifteen, is sold into slavery by his mother, who has

married the emperor of Almaine, the murderer, at her instigation, of her aged husband. Beves is presented to the Armenian king, who offers him his daughter Josian if he will renounce Christianity, which he refuses to do. By his valor, Beves wins Josian's heart. At first he rejects her proffered love; but, when weeping she comes to the door of his room, promising to become a Christian, he relents, and they kiss in token of betrothal. The king, misinformed concerning this interview, determines to rid himself of Beves, whom he dispatches with a sealed letter to Brademond, king of Damascus, a rejected suitor of Josian's. Brademond casts Beves into a dungeon, where he must defend himself with a stick against dragons. After seven years, he escapes. Josian is forced by her father to marry Yvor, king of Mombraunt. But by a charm she preserves her virginity.

Beves, learning of Josian's marriage, goes as a palmer to Mombraunt, where he hears her complaining of her lover's falseness. Entering the castle, he is recognized by Josian, who begs him to take her away, telling him she is still a virgin. The lovers escape, and, after encountering many perils, reach Cologne, where Beves' uncle is bishop. Here Josian is baptized. After killing a terrible dragon, Beves goes to England to assist his foster father, Saber, against the emperor.

During his absence, Josian is forced to marry Earl Miles. Upon the wedding night, she strangles him with her girdle, and for this is condemned to be burned. She is rescued by Beves, and sails with him to the Isle of Wight. Beves and Saber defeat the emperor, who is put to a horrible death; Beves' mother falls from the castle, and breaks her neck. Beves and Josian are now married.

Incurring king Edgar's displeasure, Beves sets out for Armenia. On the way, Josian gives birth to twin sons, 'Gii' and 'Miles', and, soon after, is carried off by king Yvor's men. Beves commits the babes to the care of a forester and a fisherman. Entering a large town, Beves tilts so brilliantly in a tournament that a princess wishes to marry him; upon learning that he has a wife, she proposes that he shall be her lord in a pure manner, and if, before the end of seven years, Josian is found, she herself will marry Terri, Saber's son. Beves consents.

Meantime, Saber, guided by a dream, rescues Josian, who, assuming a palmer's dress, travels with him and is finally reunited to her husband and children. Yvor, coming against Beves with a large army, is defeated and killed. The victor receives his kingdom.

Beves, with a considerable force, accompanies Saber into England to restore to Saber's son his estates, of which king Edgar has deprived him. Beves and his sons have a terrible encounter with the citizens of London, but come off victorious, and Miles is promised the hand of the king's daughter. Beves and Josian return to the East, and finally die in each other's arms.

4. Origin. The story of Beuve or Bovon de Hanstone is widely spread in the Mediaeval literature of Europe.[1] In France, the story was treated at least thrice in verse and once in prose. From France, it wandered to Italy, where six different versions are now known. Besides the English romance, there exist Scandinavian, Netherlandic, Celtic and Slavonic versions.

Did the romance first take shape in England or in France? Kölbing, in his Introduction,[2] says, 'The story no doubt originated in France'. But Ten Brink speaks of the romance as an Anglo-Norman poem of the 12 th century, combining 'widely dispersed materials of song and story, naturally including some English ones'. Some of the most striking episodes, such as the fights with the dreaded boar, with the dragons in the dungeon, and, later, with a dragon[3] near Cologne, recall to him traditions of Germanic folk-lore embodied in *Beowulf* and in the *Niebelungen*. G. Paris also speaks of the romance as 'Anglo-Norman',[4] and as having

---

[1] Kölbing's ed. p. xxxiv—v.   [2] Ed. p. xxxvi.

[3] This last episode is an addition of the English poet's. See Kölbing p. xxxvii.

[4] *Rom.* XXIII 487.

a 'Germanic origin'.[1] Upon this point, Wülker,[2] after remarking that the story recalls that of Hamlet,[3] says, 'Since adultery is the chief motive, we may perhaps conjecture a Celtic source for the original groundwork, and, indeed, we still possess a Celtic redaction of the material.'

The English version is something more than a mere translation. It treats several of the important episodes[4] in a more detailed and interesting way than does the French,[5] and shows, besides, three large additions, the two most important of these being the fight with the dragon near Cologne (A. vv. 2597—2910), and the resistance of Beves and his sons against the inhabitants of London (A. vv. 4287—4538).

The existing MSS. represent only copies or reproductions, considerably changed, of the original English version in the beginning of the thirteenth century. In order to account for the readings of the existing MSS. and of the oldest print, Kölbing[6] assumes the existence of six other English texts. He also finds that A, although by far the oldest MS., does not stand particularly near the original text; and that, in many cases, a paper MS. of the 15th century, and even the old print, preserve better the original wording.

5. Metre.[7] 4620[8] verses, in two different metres. The first 474 verses are written in the six-line tail-rime stanza, with the rime order, for the stanzas beginning at vv. 61, 73, 301, *aab aab*; for the remaining stanzas, *aab ccb*: the *a* and *c* lines have four stresses, the *b* lines but two. Kölbing remarks[9] that it is more than probable that Chaucer borrowed from *Sir Beues* the metre for most of his *Sir Thopas*. From l. 475, the short couplet is used.

---

[1] § 27.   [2] p. 98.

[3] In the *Hist. Litt.* XVIII 748, the legend is compared to that of Orestes.

[4] See Kölbing's ed. p. xxxvi.

[5] The English poem is not derived directly from either of the two known French MSS. G. Paris, in *Rom.* XXIII 487.

[6] p. xxxviii ff.   [7] Kölbing's ed. pp. x—xiii.

[8] K.'s text, 350 lines are supplied from MS. S.   [9] Ed. p. x.

Other ME. romances in which the metre is changed in the middle of the text are:[1] *Guy of Warwick* (MS. A., though here two versions are supposed), *Rouland and Vernagu, Sir Firumbras,* and *Richard Coer de Lion* (MS. A.)

6. Dialect.[2] That of the South of England (MS. A). Since A shows but few of the phonological characteristics[3] of the eastern and western counties of Southern England, it must have been composed on their borders, perhaps in the neighbourhood of Southhampton, where the fabulous hero of the poem is said to have born.

7. Date. The earliest extant version (MS. A) belongs to the first quarter of the 14th century; but Kölbing[4] assigns the first English translation to the beginning of the 13th century.

8. Author. Unknown.

9. Bibliography.
Manuscripts:[5] A. Auchinleck, Advocates Libr., Edin.; see II, 9, *MS.*

E. No. 175, Caius Coll. Cambr., 2nd half of the 14th century.

S. MS. of the Duke of Sutherland, *ca.* end of the 14th century.

N. XIII, B 29, Royal Libr., Naples, 15th century.

C. Ff. 2, 38, Univ. Libr., Cambr., 15th century.

M. No. 8009, Chetham Libr., Manchester, 15th century.

Editions: (For the old printed texts, see Hazlitt's *Hand-Book,* L. 1867.) A. Turnbull, for the Maitland Club, Edin., 1838; collated with the MS., in *E. St.* II 317 ff., and in Kölbing's ed. pp. ix—x.

A (with the variants), Kölbing, *EETS. E. S.* 46, 48, 60, 1885, 1886, 1894; revs. *Angl.* XI 325, *E. St.* XIX 261—68, *Rom.* XXIII 486 (G. Paris); *E. St.* XXIV 463—4.

---

[1] See Kölbing's ed. p. xi.   [2] Kölbing pp. xiii—xxi.
[3] Cf. *E. St.* XIX 262.   [4] p. xxxviii.
[5] For refs. on the MSS., see Kölbing pp. vii—viii.

The OF. poem has not as yet been published.

General References: Ten Brink, I 150, 182, 246; Brandl, § 30, 53; Wülker, 98; Ellis, 239—281; *Hist. Litt.* XVIII 748 ff.

Monographs: Schmirgel, *Stil und Sprache des ME. Epos Sir B. of H.*, Breslau, 1886, diss.; reprinted in English in Kölbing's ed.— *Die Allitteration in Sir B. of H.* (Auchinleck MS.), *E. St.* XIX 441—53.

VII. William of Palerne.

1. Subject. The love-story and strange adventures of William, Prince of Palermo, and Melior, daughter of the Emperor of Rome, a werwolf playing the part of good angel to the hero.

2. Specimen. Vv. 161—69:

þus passed is þe first pas · of þis pris tale,
& ȝe þat louen & lyken · to listen a-ni more,
Alle wiȝth on hol hert · to þe heiȝ king of heuene
preieth a pater noster · priuely þis time
for þe hende erl of herford · sir humfray de bowne,
þe king edwardes newe · at glouseter þat ligges.
For he of frensche þis fayre tale · first dede translate,
In ese of englysch men · in englysch speche;
& god graunt hem his blis · þat godly so prayen!

3. Story. [1][William, the little son of the king of Apulia, is in great danger. As heir to the crown, enemies are plotting against his life. But a werwolf, who is really Alphonse, prince of Spain, transformed by his stepmother, carries William away from Palermo to a forest near Rome.] Here the child is adopted by a cowherd, and is finally taken by the emperor of Rome, and made page to the

---

[1] From the French text; the opening lines of the English text are missing.

emperor's daughter Melior. William grows up a model knight, and Melior falls desperately in love with him. Her friend and confidant Alexandrine, knowing something of charms, causes William, by means of a dream, to fall even more desperately in love with Melior. At last, Alexandrine brings them together, and they confess their love. But the emperor has determined to wed Melior to the prince of Greece. On learning of this, William nearly dies of grief; but Melior promises to be true to him. By Alexandrine's aid, they escape from Rome, sewed up in the skins of white bears, and hide in a den, where the werwolf brings them food. Great is the commotion in Rome, when the bride is missing at the wedding. The disguise of the lovers becoming known, they are pursued, and find themselves in the greatest peril. Dressed up as a hart and hind, and guided by the werwolf, after many adventures, they reach Palermo. The king is dead, and Palermo is now besieged by the king of Spain, who wishes to force queen Felice to give her daughter Florence in marriage to his son. Through a strange dream, the queen is led to see her deliverer in the disguised knight. William espouses her cause, defeats the Spaniards, and takes prisoner the king and his son. The werwolf appears at court, and does obeisance to the king of Spain, who then suspects that the wolf may be his eldest son. William imperatively demands that Queen Braunden shall disenchant the werwolf. This is done, and William is overjoyed to receive his faithful friend as the noble Alphonse. Queen Felice now learns from Alphonse that William is her son. William is married to Melior, Alphonse to Florence, and his half-brother to Alexandrine. Alphonse soon becomes king of Spain. William rules wisely in Apulia, and, in course of time, becomes emperor of Rome. He then rewards the cowherd with a castle and a 'tidy' earldom.

4. Origin. The romance, as we learn from the poet [1] himself, is a translation from the French. In the original,

---

[1] Vv. 165—8 (see under **2**), vv. 5529—33.

the Old French *Guillaume de Palerne*,[1] which belongs to the
second half of the twelfth century, and is, therefore, about
two hundred years older than the English poem, we read
that the countess Yolent [2] caused the poem to be translated ' de Latin en Roumanes '. This claim of a Latin
origin, as well as the designation of William as Prince of
Palermo, seems to point to Sicily or Southern Italy as the
original home of the romance. The nucleus of the story
was, probably, the primitive tradition of the werwolf,[3]
which may have been brought by the Normans into Sicily,
and there combined with features of Byzantine origin. The
legend of the werwolf, as known to the Normans, may have
been of Scandinavian origin, or, since the tradition is found
among the Celts also, the werwolf story in *Guillaume de
Palerne* may have been taken from some Breton tale or
lai.[4] The leading features of the poem, the tender and
sentimental love intrigue between William and Melior, and
the strange adventures in which it involves them, show the
influence of Greek romance.[5]

As nothing is known of the Latin original, we cannot
determine how much of the romance was due to the invention or arrangement of the trouvère. G. Paris [6] classes
Guillaume de Palerne among the romances that passed into
the French from the Greek through oral transmission.
Michelant [7] thinks that the theme of the poem was only a

---

[1] Vv. 9655—59.

[2] Yolande, daughter of Baldwin IV, Count of Hainault. She
became Countess of Soissons, and, afterwards, of St. Paul. She seems
to have been one of those ' grandes dames ' who inspired the trouvères,
and suggested to them subjects of composition.

[3] See Hertz, *Der Werwolf* (a classic on the subject); Baring-
Gould, *Book of Werwolves*; Grimm, *Deutsche Mythologie*; Kirby
F. Smith, *An Historical Study of the Werwolf in Literature, Publi-
cations of the Mod. Lang. Assoc. of America*, IX 1—42.

[4] See G. Paris, § 67. *Bisclaveret*, a lai of Marie de France, is
based upon this tradition; see Warncke, *Die Lais der Marie de France*,
Halle 1867. See also Skeat, pp. xxvii—xxix.

[5] See Ten Brink, I 335. G. Paris, § 51, 52.

[6] § 51.   [7] p. iii.

fragment from some Italian chronicle, like that of the romance of Cligès.

After a detailed comparison of the English with the French poem, Kaluza concludes[1] that the translator shows a much greater independence than is usual in English romance poetry. In both the amplifications and the abbreviations of the English poem, the adaptation to a different people and a different society is clearly seen. Madden says that the romance is translated with surprising closeness from the same text as the French prose version of Durand. Kaluza, who did not have access to this prose version, thinks that, although the MS. original, if extant, might show the source of many apparent elaborations of detail in the English romance, yet, from the very nature of these elaborations (or additions), his results would not be changed.

5. Metre.   5540 alliterative long lines. Every half line has, as a rule, two primary and two secondary stresses. Next to *Joseph of Arimathie,* this is the earliest of those poems of the fourteenth century that represent the revival[2] of the old alliterative verse. The alliteration is, as a whole, consistently carried out, though not so regularly and completely as in some of the later poems[3] of the same class.

6. Author.   In v. 5521, the poet speaks of himself as 'William'. From vv. 165—8[4] and 5529—33, we learn that he was commissioned to translate the poem from the French by Sir Humphrey de Bohun.[5] It is not unlikely, therefore, that 'William' was one of the earl's ministrels.[6] Ten Brink[7] sees the personality of the poet reflected in his poem.

---

[1] *E. St.* IV 272.   [2] See Ten Brink, I 329—32.

[3] Viz. the *Alexander* fragments, A and B, *Sir Gawayn, Cleanness, Patience,* and, especially, the poems of Langland.

[4] Quoted under 2.   [5] See Skeat, pp. ix—xiii.

[6] See vv. 5070—73, 5454—58. The mention of gifts to ministrels, made in these verses, is not in the original.

[7] I 335; cf. Kaluza, *op. cit.,* pp. 272—74.

7. Date. Probably about 1350. In 1349, Sir Humphrey de Bohun returned from a journey into France, perhaps bringing with him the French romance, which he may have then given to William to translate. Sir Humphrey died in 1361.

8. Dialect. The West Midland; according to Schüdde-kopf, the S. W. Midland, probably Shropshire. Kaluza [1] maintains that the dialect of the poet cannot be shown from the text in its present form, which, on account of various kinds of defects, and especially on account of the gaps shown, cannot be the original. As there are no rimes, that aid in determining the original dialect cannot be used. The MS. shows a mixture of Northern, Southern, and Midland speech forms. The alliterative metre used points to a home in the West Midland.

9. Bibliography.

Manuscripts: [2] Cambridge, King's College, 13. For a few emendations by Stratmann, see *E. St.* IV 99.

Editions: Madden for the Roxburghe Club, L. 1832.
Skeat, *EETS. E. S.* No. 1, L. 1867; (remarks on the text, Kaluza, *E. St.* IV 280—87).

Selections: Morris, *Specimens,* II 138 (vv. 1—138); Wülker, *AE. LB.,* II 76 (vv. 170—550); Hartshorne, *Anc. Metr. Tales,* p. 256 ff. (vv. 3—633, text worthless).

A prose fragment, printed, probably, by Wynkyn de Worde, corresponding to vv. 5047—5228 of the English poem, and evidently based upon it, or upon a prose translation of it. Facsimile in Bodl. Libr., Oxford. See *Acad.,* No. 1088, p. 223.

The OF. poem ed. by Michelant, *Société des anciens textes frçs.,* P. 1876. There is a prose translation of the OF. poem, supposedly by Pierre Durand, 16th century, three editions, see Skeat, pp. xvi—xvii.

---

[1] *E. St.* X, 293 ff.
[2] Bryant (the discoverer of the MS.), *Observations,* L. 1781, pp. 14—23.

General References: Ten Brink, I 329—332; Brandl, § 73; G. Paris, § 51, 52, 67; Julleville, pp. 254—340; *Hist. Litt.* XXII 829—41 (an analysis of the OF. romance).

Monographs: Kaluza, *E. St.* IV 197—287 (on the relation of the poem, as a translation, to its OF. source).—Asclöf, *An Essay on the Romance of William and the Werwolf* (on the grammar and etymology, not valuable).—Schüdde-kopf, *Sprache und Dialekt* etc., Erlangen 1886: rev. by Kaluza in *E. St.* X 291—5; by Hausknecht, *Ltzt.* 1886, (9), 1755.—Pitschel, *Zur Syntax des ME. Gedichtes, W. of P.*, Marburg 1890.

The Charlemagne Legends.

General References. See Gautier's *Bibl. des chansons de geste* (1897), and the bibliographies in G. Paris; Gröber, II 1. 3, pp. 447, 461—2, 538; Julleville, 168—170. G. Paris in: *Litt. Franç.*, §§ 15, 18—32; *Hist. Poét.*; *Rom.* XIII 598 ff. (a long review of Rajna's *Le Origini dell' epopea francese*); *Rom.* XI 149 ff., (on *The English Charlemagne Romances*). Gautier, especially Vol. III, and in Julleville, Ch. II. Gröber, *op. cit.* In English, Ten Brink, I 122, 124—5; Saintsbury, *FlR.*, Ch. II; Ker, Chs. I (IV), and IV.

VIII. The Sowdone of Babylone.

1. Subject. (1) The destruction of Rome by the Saracens. (2) As in *Sir Firumbras*.

2. Specimen. Vv. 695—702:

> Now speke we of Sir Gӯe
> That toward Rome hied with his Oost.
> Whan he approched there-to so nyʒe,
> That he myght se the cooste,
> Alle on a flame þat Cite was,
> That thre myle al abowte,
> Ther durst no man, þat ther was,
> Come nyʒe the Cite for grete dowte.

3. Story. Laban, Soudan of Babylon, in order to avenge the plundering of one of his ships by the Romans, sails with his army from Agremore in Spain to attack Rome.

He is accompanied by his son Firumbras and his daughter
Floripas.

The Saracens land near Rome, and devastate the sur-
rounding country. The Pope calls his council, in which
Duke Savaris advises fight before asking aid from Charlemagne. The next day, Savaris attack the Saracens, who
lose two-thirds of the force engaged. Lukafer of Baldas
captures ten thousand Christian maidens, who are all slain
in order that the seed of Christianity may be destroyed.
Lukafer asks the Soudan for Floripas as his wife, and promises to bring Charlemagne and his peers as prisoners to the
Soudan. Floripas says that when he does this, she will be
his darling. Lukafer makes an unsuccessful assault upon
Rome. The next day, when Savaris comes out to battle,
Lukafer, by displaying a banner like that of Savaris, gains
admittance to Rome, killing all in the main tower. Savaris,
with his force almost totally destroyed, finds the city gate
shut against him, and is killed.

The Pope's council dispatches messengers to Charlemagne.
Laban assaults the city by water, but unsuccessfully. The
Pope summons all his people to St. Peter's, and proposes
a sally against the enemy; the next morning he leads
twenty thousand men against the Saracens. In the battle
that follows, he is unhorsed by Firumbras, who thinks
his opponent is a sovereign; upon seeing the Pope's tonsure,
Firumbras tells him to go home and 'keep his choir'. Guy
of Burgundy is ordered by Charlemagne to march to the
relief of Rome. Through the treason of the guard of the
principal gate, the Saracens gain possession of the city. All
the streets and lanes are soon covered with dead men.
Firumbras takes from St. Peter's the holy relics, the cross,
the crown and the nails. The city is burned, and the
Saracens, rejoicing, retire to Spain.

Guy of Burgundy approaches Rome only to find the
city in flames. Charlemagne swears by God and St. Denis
to be revenged. He takes ship with his army for Spain.
Near Agremore, a battle occurs between the Saracens under
Firumbras and the Christians. Well fight the twelve peers.

Charlemagne takes an active part. The Saracens withdraw with great loss. Charlemagne thanks God, Saint Denis, and Lady Mary of Paris; he praises the elder knights for having won the victory, and exhorts the younger ones to take example by them. Laban again sends Firumbras with thirty thousand men against the Christians.

[For the remainder of the story, see *Sir Firumbras*; cf. ed. of *S. of B.*, pp. xxvii—xxix.]

4. Origin. The narrative of the *Sowdone* consists of two parts, each of which is a free and greatly condensed reproduction of an OF. original. The first part, to about l. 938, corresponds, in this general way, to the *Destruction de Rome*; the second part, to the romance of *Fierabras*. From the resemblances in expression and in proper names, Hausknecht[1] concludes that the *Destruction* was, most probably, the original of the first part of the *Sowdone*; the original of the second part[2] cannot be identified with any of the extant versions of the *Fierabras*, though the differences between the *Sowdone* and the *Fierabras* as edited by Kroeber and Servois are not significant. There can be no doubt but that the original of the second part was a version similar to the Hanover MS.[3]

The historical kernel[4] of the narrative in the *Destruction* was, in all probability, the expedition against the Lombards, who were menacing the Papacy in 773. The popular imagination, inflamed by the spirit of the Crusades, substituted the Saracens for the Lombards.

The greater part of the story told in the *Destruction* is found in general outline, though differing in important details, in the riming chronicle of Phillippe Mousket[5] (about 1243). After the destruction of Rome, however, while the *Destruction* transfers the scene of action to Spain, the

---

[1] Ed., pp. xxii—xxvii.

[2] See pp. xxvii—xxxiii and xlix—lii.

[3] So G. Paris, as quoted by Herrtage in his ed. of *Fierabras*, p. xiv, n. 1.

[4] Gautier, III 52, II.   [5] Vv. 4664—4716.

4

ancient poem analyzed by Mousket treats of the reconquest
of Rome by the army of Charlemagne, the most important
episode of this part of the narrative being a combat between
Oliver and Fierabras. Gaston Paris has pointed out [1] that
the romance of *Fierabras*, in its rather abrupt opening and
numerous obscure allusions, presupposes an earlier poem, like
that known through Mousket (which Paris designates as
Balan), and that *Fierabras* is an amplified and considerably
altered version of an episode of the second part of the old
poem. Does the *Destruction* represent the first part of this
poem? Gröber [2] maintains the affirmative, though he does
not consider the *Destruction* identical with this first part,
but as representing a later redaction. He also holds that
the *Destruction* and the first part of the present *Fierabras*
romance had, in their original form, the same author. Hausknecht,[3] however, points out that, while some of the allusions
in the *Fierabras* are not explained by the account in the
Destruction, they are explained by the summary of Mousket,
and that there is even an instance of the *Destruction* being
in contradiction to the *Fierabras*. He therefore concludes
that the account of Mousket is based on the old *Balan*
poem, and that the *Destruction* was composed as a kind
of introduction [4] to the *Fierabras*, though not by the same
author, in order to clear up allusions to preceding events
noticed in that poem — 'whereby it happened that some
allusions remained unexplained.' [5] The so-called 'episode' [6]
of six hundred lines at the beginning of the Provençal
Fierabras, he concludes was also composed as an explanatory
account, whereas Gröber [7] considers it an amplification of
the account at the close of the *Destruction*.

---

[1] *Hist. Poét.*, 251—52.

[2] *Verhandl.*, 205 ff., and *Zs. f. rom. Phil.* IV 160.

[3] p. xiv.   [4] Cf. *Rom.* XVII 22, n.

[5] G. Paris (*Rom.* XI 149) thinks that the author of the *Destruction*
may have known an old poem more or less well.

[6] The attack of the Saracens on Charlemagne's advance guard
commanded by Oliver.

[7] *Zs. f. rom. Phil.* IV 169.

5. Metre.[1] 3274 generally 4-stressed verses, composed in the 4-line ballad measure[2] (rime-order, *ab ab*). Instances of variously rimed eight-line stanzas, however, occur.

6. Dialect.[3] East Midland. The phonological and inflectional peculiarities of the *Sowdone* agree throughout with those of other East Midland works. The grammatical inflections show that the language of the poem agrees closely with that of Chaucer. The final *e* is, in the opinion of Hausknecht, very frequently, though not always, silent. Schleich thinks that it is probably silent.

7. Date.[4] The beginning of the 15th century. From the resemblance of the language to that of Chaucer, and from certain passages indicating a knowledge of some of the later parts of the *Canterbury Tales*, (*The Prologue* and *The Knight's Tale*), the author must have been at least a contemporary and a late contemporary, of Chaucer. But since, contrary to the usage of Chaucer, the final *e* seems often to have been silent, Hausknecht concludes that the author lived some time later, probably at the beginning of the 15th century.

8. Author. Unknown.

8. Bibliography.
Manuscripts: The only MS., which formerly belonged to Sir Thomas Phillips, is now in the possession of the Rev. J. E. A. Fenwick, Thurlestane House, Cheltenham.

Editions: In the publications of the Roxburghe Club, L. 1854.

Hausknecht, *EETS. E. S.* No. 38, 1881; revs., Schleich, *Angl.* V, *Anz.* 69—73.

The OF. originals: (1) *Destruction de Rome,* in *Rom.* II 1—48. (2) See *Sir Firumbras.*

---

[1] See Hausknecht, pp. xl—xlv; cf. Schleich.
[2] Brandl, § 125.
[3] Hausknecht, pp. xxxiv—xl; cf. Schleich, 71—72.
[4] Hausknecht, pp. xlv—xlvii.

General References: Hist. Poét., 251—2; Gautier, III 366—80; Brandl, § 125; Ellis, 379—404 (analyzed under the title of *Sir Ferumbras*). See further under IX 9.

Monographs: Gröber, *Verhandlungen der 28sten Versammlung deutscher Schulmänner in Leipzig,* Leipsic 1873; rev. by Bartsch in Ebert's *JB.* XI 219. — Hausknecht, *Ueber Sprache und Quellen des ME. Heldengedichts S. of B.,* Berlin, 1879, diss.; rev. in *,Litbl.* 1880 (3) 100; *Arch.* LXIII 460; *Rom.* VIII 479; *Zs. f. rom. Phil.* IV 163 (Gröber). — See also IX 9.

IX. Sir Firumbras.[1]

1. Subject. The reconquest by Charlemagne in Spain of the relics carried away from Rome by the Saracens; including the heroic episode of the combat between Oliver and Firumbras, and the romantic episodes connected with the imprisonment of the twelve peers.

2. Specimen. (1) Vv. 672—7. The combat between Oliver and Firumbras:

þey foȝten to-gadres þanne ȝerne ꞉ þys wytherwyns wilde &
⟶ wroþe,
& smyte strokes smerte & sterne ꞉ in haberkes & helmes boþe.
Wiþ þe strokes þat þis frekes slente ꞉ flyngande to-gader in fiȝte,
Hur helmes & haberions þay to-rente ꞉ þat arst wer fair & briȝte,
& hure scheldes stronge & grete ꞉ þey were al to-hewe;
Vnder hure boþen fete ꞉ þan miȝte me þe peces schewe.

(2) Vv. 5059—66. The relics save the Christians from the assaulting Saracens:

þᵉ tour þay hauede y-take þo Nadde duk Naymes y-lope hem to,
As hit ful þorw grace,

---

[1] i. e. Fier-en-bras = Fier-à-bras; see ed., pp. xvii—xviii.

With þe releques þat he þo bar Riȝt to wyndowes þer þay war,
& schewede hem on hur face.
þorw þᵉ vertue of þat syȝt þe Sarsyns þanne gunne waxe affriȝt,
þat abide þay ne durste,
Bote fullen a-doun of þe walle, and so heȝe þay fullen alle,
þat hure bodies al to-burste.

3. Story. [1][While the army of Charlemagne is advancing against the Saracens, the van, commanded by Oliver, is suddenly attacked, and only saved from destruction by the arrival of Charlemagne and his old knights.] That evening Charlemagne declares that the old knights bore themselves better in fight than the young barons. The next day, a huge Saracen, Firumbras, king of Alexandria, appears before the army, and boastfully challenges one or more of Charlemagne's peers. No knight offers himself for the combat. Charlemagne begs his nephew Roland to undertake the fight; but Roland, angered at Charlemagne's boast of the preceding evening, promptly refuses. A mortal quarrel is only averted by the intercession of Ogier. Oliver, hearing the news, rises from his bed, staunches his bleeding wounds, and begs that the king will grant him the battle against the Saracen. Charlemagne reluctantly assents. Firumbras, though scorning to fight with a knight of low rank, such as Oliver declares himself to be, is finally forced into combat. The fight is long and terrible. After a while, Oliver confesses his name, and Firumbras is 'gladdere' than he was, because he has his peer. At last, Firumbras is terribly wounded. He begs for mercy, and promises to become a Christian. While Oliver is bearing Firumbras to the French camp, a party of Saracens breaks from ambush. Oliver and four of the knights that have come to his aid are captured, and carried off to Aigremont. Firumbras is found by the French; he is baptized, and his wounds cared for. Roland and the six remaining 'douzeperes',

---

[1] According to the French text; the opening lines of the English text are missing.

having been sent to demand the release of their fellows
and the return of the relics, are also held prisoners. Balan
determines to put them all to a cruel death. Florippe takes
charge of Roland and his fellows for a while, and conducts
them to her chamber, where they find Oliver and the four
other knights, whose rescue from a dungeon by Florippe
the poet has already described. Florippe has loved Guy
of Burgundy since witnessing his valor at the siege of
Rome. She promises to help the knights, if Guy will become betrothed to her. To this Guy finally agrees.
Florippe, now 'comforted', delivers to the knights the sacred
relics, which they reverently worship. Advised by Florippe,
the knights attack the Saracens, most of whom are slain.
Balan escapes from the castle. He assembles a great army,
and besieges Florippe's tower. After various thrilling experiences, such as the theft of Florippe's magic girdle (which
is a protection against famine), sallies for food, the capture
of Guy of Burgundy and his rescue at the foot of the
gallows, Richard of Normandy is dispatched as a messenger
to Charlemagne, and reaches the French camp just as
Charlemagne in despair is starting for France. The king
at once marches to the rescue of his peers. After some
terrible fighting, the Saracens are defeated, and Balan is
made prisoner. In spite of the entreaties of Firumbras, he
refuses baptism and is beheaded. After her father's death,
which she has unfeelingly urged, [1][Florippe is baptized and
married to Guy. Charlemagne divides Spain between Firumbras and Guy. The relics are delivered to Charlemagne;
their genuineness is proved by their remaining for some
time suspended in the air. Charlemagne returns to France,
and in Paris distributes the relics, instituting in their
honor the fair of 'Lendit'.[2] Within three years occurs the
betrayal of Roland by Ganelon].

4. Origin. The original of *Sir Firumbras* is the OF.
Fierabras, which arose in the second half of the 12th cen-

---

[1] According to the French text.   [2] See p. 61, n. 2.

tury, was early translated or imitated in nearly all the
languages of Europe,[1] and has been reproduced even down
to the present day. Of all the Charlemagne romances it
obtained the highest degree of popularity.

The present English romance, Hausknecht concludes,[2]
is a pretty close translation of some unidentified French
version, which perhaps belonged, or at least was nearly
related, to the type *y*,[3] the original of the OF. poetical
versions; it shows but few significant variations from the
known versions of this type.

A version of the romance was known to the Scotch
poet Barbour.[4] From the outline given by him, Hausknecht[5]
concludes that this version was not identical with any of
those extant.

As has been already stated in the discussion of the
origin of the *Sowdone, Fierabras,* as we now possess it, is
the amplification and development of an episode in an
earlier poem, now lost. The ancient legend of the taking
of Rome by the Saracens has here been welded into another, the legend of the relics of the Passion.[6] The origin
of *Fierabras* has been discussed in a most interesting
monograph by Bédier,[7] the substance of whose final summary,
together with a few points from the body of the monograph, now follows.

Fierabras is divided essentially into two parts, one,
ancient, going back to a source which is the poem known

---

[1] For the different foreign versions, see the editions (*EETS*) of
Sir Firumbras, pp. v—x, and of the *Sowdone of Babylone*, pp. v—ix.
Cf. *Hist. Poét.*, 97, 143, 155, 214, 251; Gautier, II 307—9; and the
French ed. of *Fierabras*, pp. xiv—xvii.

[2] *Sowdone of Babylone*, pp. xxi—xxii.

[3] For the stemma of *Fierabras*, see Gröber, in *Handschriftl.
Gestalt.*, 27. Cf. Gröber, in *Zs. f. rom. Phil.* IV 170; G. Paris, in *Rev.
Crit.*, 1869, 2, p. 125; *Rom.* XXIV 55.

[4] See *The Bruce*, ed. Skeat, 1870, Bk. III 435 ff.

[5] *Angl.* VII 160.

[6] See G. Paris, in *Rom.* IX 32—35.

[7] *Rom.* XVII 22—51.

to Mousket, the other, of later invention, which has many
sources, the contemporary 'chansons de geste.' These two
different parts have been associated by the occasion that
gave birth to *Fierabras,* the fair of l'Endit, whose original
pretext was the worship of the relics enshrined in the
abbey of St. Denis.   A poet, a 'jongleur' undoubtedly,
wished to recount the history of the relics of the Passion,
but he could not create it out of whole cloth. It was necessary to rest upon an already accredited legend, and the
poem known to Mousket has furnished him with just this
aid. This poem, towards 1170, was already old and beginning to fall into oblivion. It contained some fine parts,
celebrated fragments, which could be revived.   He kept
what he could of it, the long episode of the combat between Oliver and Fierabras, in which the old poem really
lives again (the scene has been transferred from Italy to
Spain), and has welded to it a whole series of epic
episodes, borrowed, with a thousand and one commonplaces,
from the contemporary 'chansons de geste'.

5. Metre. 5852 lines.   In vv. 1—3411 the septenar,
with internal rime, is used; from v. 3411, the six-line tail-
rime stanza, with the rime-order *aab aab,* each couplet
being written in one long line.   There in nothing in the
French version that corresponds with this change in metre.
Though not alliterative, the romance yet contains a large
amount of alliteration.

6. Dialect.[1] Southern, probably Devonshire, but not
pure. Carstens,[2] agreeing essentially with the editor, concludes that the romance is written in a S. W. West Saxon
dialect, influenced by a dialect spoken in S. Yorkshire near
the boundary of the Midland. The Northern influence is,
however, denied by both Wülker and Sarrazin. Some of
the evidence adduced by Carstens in favor of a Northern,
points rather, in the view of Sarrazin, to a S. E. (Kentish),

---

[1] Ed. pp. xviii—xxvii.   [2] p. 40.

influence; the mixture of dialects can best be explained by
supposing that the author, a native of Kent or a territory
bordering directly upon it, settled in Devonshire. Upon
the conclusion of the editor,[1] not questioned by Carstens,
that the poet and the scribe are one, Wülker thinks that
a thorough investigation of the rimes would cast doubt.

7. Date. The second half or last quarter of the 14th
century. Since the final *e* is usually sounded,[2] the romance
cannot have been written after 1400. From the date (1377)
of the document forming the inner parchment cover of the
MS., Black concludes that the romance was composed shortly
after 1377, or early in the reign of Richard II.

8. Author. From evidence furnished by documents
forming the parchment covers of the MS., Black concludes
that the author was a clergyman living in the diocese and,
probably, in the city of Exeter.

9. Bibliography. *Manuscripts:* Ashmole 33, Bodl.
Libr., Oxford; desc. by Black, Catalogue of the Ashmolean
MSS., col. 14; see also ed., pp. xv—xvi and Carstens, 3, 4.

Editions: Herrtage, *EETS. E. S.* No. 34, 1879. Revs.:
by Reichel, with textual criticism, *E. St.* XVIII 270—82; by
Stratmann, with remarks on the text, *Litbl.* 1880 (10) 374.

Selections: ZML. III (vv. 1104—59).

The OF. poem. *Fierabras*, ed. by Kroeber and Servois,
in *Anciens Poëtes de la France*, P., 1860.

The Provençal poem: *Der Roman von Ferabras pro-
venzalisch*, edited by Bekker, Berlin, 1829.

General References: Hist. Poét., 251—53, 155; Gautier,
III 381—97; Brandl, p. 659. On the popularity of the romance, see p. 55, n. 1., and Brandl, § 70.

Monographs: Gröber, *Die Handschriftlichen Gestaltungen
der chanson de geste Fierabras*, Leipsic, 1869; rev. by G.
Paris, *Rev. Crit.* 1869, 2, p. 121 ff.; cf. *Rom.* XXIV 1—55.

---

[1] pp. xv—xvi.   [2] Carstens, 4.

Angl. VII 160 (on the version known to Barbour). — Bédier, *La Composition de Fierabras, Rom.* XVII 22—51. — Carstens, *Zur Dialectbestimmung des ME. Sir Firumbras,* 1884, diss.: rev. by Einenkel, *Angl.* II, *Anz.,* p. 4; Sarrazin, *Litbl.* 1884 (10) 387; Wülker, *Lit. Cbl.,* 1885, (12) 390. — Reichel, C., *Die ME. Romanze Sir Firumbras und ihr Verhältnis zum altfranz. und provenz. Fierabras,* Breslau, 1892, diss.

X. Roland and Vernagu.

1. Subject. The journey of Charlemagne to Constantinople, and his campaign in Spain against the Saracens, concluding with the single combat between Roland and Vernagu.

2. Specimen. Vv. 797—808:

> Þo rouland kneld adoun,
> & maked an orisoun
>   To god in heuen liȝt,
> & seyd, 'lord, vnder stond
> Y no fiȝt for no lond,
>   Bot for to saue þi riȝt.
> Sende me now miȝt & grace,
> Here in þis ich place,
>   To sle þat foule wiȝt.'
> An angel com ful sone,
> & seyd 'herd is þi bone,
>   Arise, rouland, & fiȝt'.

3. Story. One hundred and three winters after God died upon the tree, Constantius, emperor at Constantinople, bidden by an angel, asks the aid of Charlemagne, then ruler over nearly all Europe, including France, Denmark, and England, against the Saracen Ebrahim, king of Spain, who has exiled the Patriarch of Jerusalem. Charlemagne proceeds with a large army to Constantinople, where he is received with honor by Constantius, and offered costly gifts. Refusing these, he begs for some relics of the Passion, whose sweet odor cures three hundred sick people. He receives the crown of thorns, a part of the cross, 'God's clothing', 'our Lady's smock', the rod of Aaron, the spear, and one of the nails. The genuineness of the relics is attested by a heavenly light.

After returning to Gascony, Charlemagne sees in the sky one night a line of stars pointing toward Galicia, and the voice of St. James thrice bids him win Galicia, where the apostle's body lies. Charlemagne and his host advance into Spain, and, by miraculous aid, regain the cities. Upon his prayer for help, the walls of Pampeluna and Lucerne fall to the ground.

One day, a black giant forty feet high comes as a champion from the Sultan of Babylon. Four renowned knights in turn, and then ten together, are carried off under the giant's arm. Then Roland takes the field, and the giant, in a two days' combat, finds him no mean adversary. At length, Vernagu the giant, weary of stone-throwing, requests time for a nap. Roland grants this, and when his slumbers become too audible, kindly places a stone under his head. When Vernagu awakes, a theological dialogue ensues, in which Roland explains the possibility of the Trinity, the Incarnation, the Resurrection, and the Ascension. Vernagu, at first incredulous, finally says he understands it all, and now they will fight to see whose religion is the better. Roland, hard pressed, prays for victory, since he fights to save the right. An angel appearing, says, 'Thy prayer is heard'. He now fights with a free heart, and after a terrible struggle, gives the death-wound to the giant, who in vain calls upon Mahomet and Jupiter for help. Roland cuts off his head, and presents it to Charlemagne. There is a thanksgiving procession, with cross, and banner, and merry song. The report of all comes to a stern Saracen, Otuel.

4. Origin. The closing verses of *Roland and Vernagu*[1]
suggest that it is only a part of a longer narrative. In its
present form, the poem represents the first and second parts
of a cyclic poem in six-line stanzas, called by G. Paris[2]
Charlemagne and Roland, which was intended as a kind
of *résumé* of the wars of Charlemagne against the Saracens.
Its divisions are as follows: (1) the journey of Charlemagne
to the Holy Land, according to the Latin legend; (2) the
beginning of the war with Spain, including the Vernagu
episode, according to the chronicle of Turpin;[3] (3) *Otuel,*[4]
in a version inferior to that of the Auchinleck MS.; (4) the
end of the narrative of Turpin.[5] The third and fourth parts
of our cyclic poem are known only through Ellis'[6] description
of a MS., now lost, once in the possession of W. Fillingham.

The legend underlying the first part of *RV* (vv. 1—140)
has its historical basis,[7] doubtless, in the friendly relations
of Charlemagne with Eastern powers, and in his devotion
to the Church. From the time of Einhard, Charlemagne
was supposed to have desired to visit Constantinople. The
legend early made its appearance both in the popular poetic
and in the monastic literature,[8] and, from the 12th century
to the Renaissance, was almost universally accepted as
historic fact. Gautier enumerates about thirty narratives
of which it is the object.[9]

The source, directly or indirectly, of the account in
RV is a Latin poem of the 11th century, known as the
Descriptio,[10] the earliest of the extant poems based upon
the legend. The *Karlamagnùs Saga* (Norse prose, 13th cent.)

---

[1] To be designated as *RV*.   [2] *Hist. Poét.*, 156.
[3] Chs. II—XVI, XX.   [4] See XII.   [5] Chs. XXI—IX.
[6] pp. 357, 373—79. Ellis analyzes part 4 only.
[7] See Einhard's *Vita Caroli Magni,* chs. XVI, XXVII, and *Annales
Einhardi* under date 800.
[8] The earliest extant version is found in the chronicle of Benedict,
a monk of St. Andrew's, who wrote in the second half of the tenth
century.
[9] III, 283 ff.
[10] *Descriptio, qualiter Carolus Magnus clavum et coronum Domini*...

gives the *résumé* of a still more ancient poem, which, in the opinion of G. Paris (*Rom.* IX. 33) and of Morf (p. 211), the author of the *Descriptio* must have used. *RV* follows the general outline of the *Descriptio*. In the latter poem, however, the foes of the Patriarch are merely the heathen, not the Saracens of Spain. The author of the *Descriptio* states, with no details, that Charlemagne, after reaching Constantinople, conquered Syria and took Jerusalem.[1] The *Descriptio* recounts more miracles than does *RV*, and closes by telling that the relics were deposited in Aix-la-Chapelle, and later, under Charles the Bald, were removed to the abbey of St. Denis, where their veneration became the occasion for the fair of l'Endit.[2]

In the *Descriptio*, the original legend has doubtless undergone some change. Morf,[3] in his study of the *Pèlerinage de Charlemagne*,[4] concludes that the old lost song from which the *Descriptio* must have drawn was of an essentially warlike nature, and spoke of a journey to Constantinople only, where Charlemagne received the relics for delivering the Greeks from their Saracen foes. To this original tradition was joined later, as an introduction, and, if we may judge by the abstract in the *Saga*, in a form little developed, the tradition of a pilgrimage to Jerusalem. In the *Descriptio,* the popular poem is modified in the service of monasticism. The number of relics is larger, there is added the detailed recital of miracles, and but five lines are given to the combats of Charlemagne against the infidels.

Morf thinks that the original author of the *Descriptio* was a French monk of Aix, who, in the 11th century, made use of a popular poem in order to defend the authenticity of the relics at Aix against the rival claims of the abbey

---

[1] In *RV.*, after v. 88, the scribe may have omitted a stanza to this effect. Wächter, p. 15.

[2] See IX, 4. The word 'endit' corresponds to the Mediæval Latin, 'indictum', an official announcement, especially of a festival. *Rom.* IX 31, n. 4.

[3] p. 213.

[4] End of the 11th century, Gröber, p. 465.

of St. Denis. Then a monk of St. Denis audaciously took possession of the poem, making an addition that was all in favor of the genuineness of the relics of St. Denis. St. Denis seems to have won the victory, for it became greatly venerated as the shrine where the relics in question were preserved. In their honor the *Pèlerinage de Charlemagne* and the *Fierabras* are thought to have also been composed.[1]

The source of the second and fourth part of our cyclic poem, the chronicle of the pseudo-Turpin,[2] is also the production of the monks. The English narratives correspond[3] in general with the Latin. In *RV* the verbal correspondence is often pretty exact, but much is omitted, and there are some additions.

The considerable number of these divergences, together with the fact that some of them agree with other versions of the legend, and that other narratives,[4] earlier than our poem, unite Charlemagne's journey to Jerusalem and Constantinople with his campaign in Spain, leads Wächter to conclude[5] that the English poet did not draw directly from two separate sources, but from some work in which the two narratives were already united. That this source was a French, not a Latin narrative, seems probable from the French form given to many of the proper names. It is true that the poet refers (vv. 328, 429) to his source as Latin, and (vv. 1, 481) to its author as an eye-witness of what he tells; but these references may have been in the French source, or the English writer himself may have known the Latin chronicle.

5. Metre. 880 verses, in the twelve-line tail-rime stanza (class III). Eight verses, probably no more, are missing at the beginning.

6. Dialect. The NE. Midland, with a Southern scribe.[6]

---

[1] See IX 4.   [2] See G. Paris, § 34.
[3] See Wächter, 16—29.   [4] Wächter, p. 30.
[5] p. 30.   [6] Wächter, 33—34.

7. Date. Not later than the first quarter of the 14th century, since found in the Auchinleck MS.

8. Author. Unknown.

9. Bibliography. *Manuscripts:* Auchinleck; see II, 9.

Editions: Nicholson, for the Abbotsford Club, Edin., 1836. Herrtage, *EETS. E. S.* No. 39, 1882, p. 35; cf. Wächter, 36—42 (notes on the text).

General References: Hist. Poét., p. 156; Ten Brink, I 245—6; Brandl, § 52, 53; Ellis, pp. 346—357, 373—9. On the underlying legends, see Gautier, III 283—308; G. Paris, in *Hist. Poét.* pp. 53—59, 337—44, and in *Rom.* IX 29—35 (on the *Pelerinage*); H. Morf, in *Rom.* XIII 208—232.

Monographs: Wächter, *Untersuchungen über die beiden ME. Gedichte R. und V., und Otuel. I. R. und V.,* Berlin, 1885, diss.

XI. The Sege of Melayne.

1. Subject. The siege of Milan, which the Saracens have taken, by the army of Charlemagne, led and inspired by Archbishop Turpin.

2. Specimen. Vv. 913—924. Turpin arms himself:

> The Bischoppe þaw keste of his abytte
> And aftir armours he askede tytte,
> For egernesse he loughe.
> A kirtill and a corsett fyne,
> Þer ouer he keste an actow syne,
> And it to hym he droughe:
> An hawbarke with a gesserante,
> His gloues werew gude and auenaunte;
> And als blythe als birde one boughe
> He tuke his helme and sythew his brande,
> Appow a stede a spere in hande
> Was grete and gud ynoghe.

3. Story. The Sultan Arabas has harried Lombardy, and sacked Rome and Milan. Charlemagne, in a dream, is bidden by an angel to assist Alantyne, the lord of Milan. Turpin encourages him to do this. Upon the suggestion of the traitor Ganelon, Roland, with a considerable force, is sent on in advance. Arrived before Milan, the French challenge the Sultan to battle, which results disastrously to them. Alantyne and Richard of Normandy are killed; Roland, Oliver, Gawter, and Guy of Burgundy are captured.

They are led before the Sultan, whom Roland urges to believe in the Trinity. Arabas scornfully orders a cross to be burned before them, but the fire will not consume it. Fire bursts from the cross, blinding the Saracens. Guy kills Arabas, and, after throwing the Saracen lords into the fire, the prisoners escape. Horses are miraculously provided for their journey to Paris.

Turpin, overpowered with grief at the fate of the French army, reproaches the Virgin for deserting them. He proclaims a crusade against the Sultan, and one hundred thousand of the clergy assemble. Advised by Ganelon, Charlemagne refuses to accompany Turpin. The archbishop excommunicates Charlemagne, taunting him with cowardice. Turpin threatens to shut Charlemagne up in Paris and to besiege and burn the city, against which he leads his army. Upon the advice of Naymes, Charlemagne finally yields, and leads a large army into Lombardy.

Turpin offers a mass for the French that have been slain, and bread and wine are sent down from heaven. In the battle against the Saracens, Turpin leads the van; his clergy win the day. Turpin vows that he will neither eat nor drink until Milan is taken. Severely wounded in an assault upon the city, he refuses all attention. An army, supposedly of Saracens, coming into sight, he prepares to charge them singly, but soon discovers them to be friendly Bretons under their Duke Lionel. Sixty thousand Saracens come up, but are cut to pieces by the Bretons. Charlemagne makes Lionel Duke of Burgundy, and gives him his daughter. Turpin, sorely wounded, and having

now fasted for three days, can scarcely speak, yet still refuses all attention. All mourn greatly for the bishop, and prepare again to assault Milan . . . .
[Poem unfinished.]

4. Origin.[1] Although no original is known, the *S. of M.*[2] is undoubtedly a translation from the French. The original seems to have been composed as an introduction[3] to *Otinel*, for it is only in *Otinel* that we find a Garcy reigning in Lombardy, as here. Thus the *S. of M.* resembles the *Destruction de Rome*, which was intended for an introduction to the *Fierabras*; though the author of the *Destruction* may have known more or less well some old poem, while the *S. of M.* seems drawn from the imagination. Since *Otinel* had a great success in England, we may suppose that the author of the *Siège de Milan* was an Anglo-Norman, who wrote, probably, at the end of the 12th century.

5. Metre. This unfinished poem contains 1602 verses in the twelve-line tail-rime stanza (class III). Alliteration[4] occurs frequently, but by no means regularly; it serves merely as an ornament, especially in formal expressions.

6. Dialect.[5] Northern, and tolerably pure, as witness the large number of ON. words, and many words and expressions prevailingly or exclusively Northern. There are but two marked departures from the Northern dialect (the present participle *discomforthynge* 240, and the perfect participle *wepe* 89).

Herrtage[6] thinks that the scribe was Southern; Dannenberg[7] sees no essential difference between the speech of the poet and that of the scribe. Facts that seem to point to a different conclusion, such as the more frequent use of *o* for OE. *ā*, and the frequent change of *ware* into *were*,

---

[1] G. Paris, in *Rom.* XI 151—2; see also Herrtage, p. ix.
[2] *Sege of Melayne.*   [3] Cf. Dannenberg, 3.
[4] Dannenberg, 5—6.   [5] Dannenberg, 15—51.
[6] Ed. § 5, 8.   [7] pp. 46, 47.

can be easily explained by the difference in time between the poet and the scribe; some of Herrtage's statements in regard to the dialect of the scribe, such as the wholesale change of the Northern *a* to the Southern *o*, are incorrect.

7. Date.[1] The second half of the 14th century. The influence of Chaucer cannot be traced, and old words, such as *blee* 1359, *lede* 1532, *molde* 843, *brenys* 1182, appear, words which, in the North at the beginning of the 15th century, were already probably obsolete. Furthermore the 14 century was the golden age of the tail-rime stanza.

The evidence upon which Buss[2] assigns certain Northern poems to the 15th century at the earliest, and which, if conclusive, would assign the *Sege of Melayne* to the same period, is not convincing, as the same phonological characteristics (i. e. the riming of words like *eghe, neghe*, with *me, he*, etc., and with romance words in *ee*) occur before the 15th century in Huchown's *Susanna*[3] (vv. 271, 316, 318).

8. Author.[4] Herrtage assumes that the *S. of M.* and *Roland and Otuel*, found in the same Ms., have the same author. This view is rejected by Dannenberg,[5] who finds that the linguistic characteristics of the two poems differ markedly.

Herrtage also conjectures that these two poems 'are by the same hand as *Sir Perceval*.

9. Bibliography. *Manuscripts:* Addit. 31042, Brit. Mus., *ca.* 1430—40;[6] desc. in ed., pp. viii—ix.

Editions: Herrtage, *EETS. E. S.* No. 35, 1880; for some textual emmendations, see *E. St.* V 467, 494, and XIII 156.

General References: Brandl, p. 669; *Rom.* XI 151—2.

Monographs. Dannenberg, *Metrik und Sprache der ME. Romanze The S. of M.*, Göttingen, 1890, diss.

---

[1] Dannenberg, 48.   [2] *Angl.* IX 497.
[3] Printed in *Angl.* I 93 ff.   [4] pp. xii—xiii.   [5] pp. 49—51.
[6] Date of the Thornton MS. Both MSS. were compiled for Robert Thornton; see ed., p. xiii.

XII. Otuel.

1. Subject. The Saracen knight Otuel: his combat
with Roland, his conversion, and his deeds in Lombardy
against the heathen.

2. Specimen. Vv. 581—594. After the dove has lighted
upon Otuel:

> & otuwel, þat douȝti kniȝt,
> Wiþ-drouȝ him anoon riȝt
> Fram roulond, & stod al stille,
> To fiȝte more he ne hadde wille,
> & seide, 'Roulond þou smitest fol sore,
> Wiþ-drau þin hond & smiȝt na more.
> Ȝef þou wolt holden þat þou me het,
> Þat i sschal wedde þat maiden swet,
> Þe kinges douȝter, belesent,
> For soþe, þan is mi wille went,
> Ȝef i sschal wedden þat faire may,
> Ich wille bileuen oppon þi lay,
> And alle myne godes forsake,
> And to ȝoure god ich wille take.'

3. Story. Otuel, a messenger from Garcy, the heathen
king of Lombardy, appears before Charlemagne in Paris.
He addresses the king insolently, kills a French knight
who attacks him, and refuses to give his sword to Roland.
Garcy, he says, summons Charlemagne to renounce Christianity upon penalty of forfeiting his possessions. Roland
tells Otuel that if they ever meet in battle, Otuel shall
never despise a Frenchman. Otuel, being ready to fight any
moment, a combat is arranged for the next day. The
French knights indignantly call upon Charlemagne to march
upon Garcy. Charlemagne promises Otuel riches if he will
turn Christian. Otuel refuses. Charlemagne learns that he
is a king's son, cousin to Garcy and nephew of Vernagu,
whose death he wishes to avenge upon Roland.

5*

The next morning after Mass, Otuel awaits Roland at the palace gate. The fighting place is a field surrounded by water, except in one place, at which Otuel enters first. Roland, in his hurry to meet his foe, swims across, and they charge at once. After hard fighting, Roland offers Otuel Belesant, the king's daughter, if he will become a Christian, but Otuel will listen to no 'preaching' so long as he holds his sword. The fight is resumed. While Charlemagne and his knights are fervently praying for Otuel's conversion and Roland's victory, a dove from the Holy Ghost flies down upon Otuel. He stops fighting, and says that, if he may really wed the king's daughter, he will become a Christan. The combatants embrace. Otuel is baptized by Turpin, but refuses to be married until Garcy is captured or slain.

The next spring, Charlemagne leads an army into Lombardy. One day, Roland, Oliver, and Ogier, riding in search of adventure, encounter four heathen kings, three of whom they kill; the fourth, Clariel, is taken prisoner, but, a thousand Saracens coming up, is by the advice of Oliver released, though Ogier suggests killing him. The knights make great havoc among the Saracens. Ogier is in danger, but is saved by Clariel, who advises him to surrender. He is sent to Clariel's lady, the daughter of Garcy, who cares for his wounds. Ten thousand Saracens appearing, Roland and Oliver are obliged to fly. They are met by Otuel, who with seven hundred knights, has started to their rescue. The French attack and defeat the Saracens.

The next day Clariel comes with a flag of truce, and challenges Otuel, because he has turned Christian. In their encounter Clariel is slain; Garcy vows vengeance, and the two armies meet in battle. Ogier, hearing the noise of battle, kills his guards and escapes. Garcy flies, but is captured by Otuel. He cries for mercy, and offers to do homage to Charlemagne. At Otuel's wish, his life is spared, and Otuel presents him to the king as a submissive vassal.

. . . .

[MS. incomplete.]

4. Origin. The original of both *Otuel* and *Roland and Otuel* is the OF. *Otinel*, a 'chanson de geste' of the end of the 12th or the beginning of the 13th century.[1] The story soon found its way from France to England and to Scandinavia.[2] Through the version in the *Karlamagnùs-Saga* it passed, in the 15th century, into Danish, and, in the 17th century, into Icelandic literature.

No source for the romance is known. Its plot is no part of the old Charlemagne legend. 'Almost all the particulars', remarks Gröber,[3] 'are derived from the *Chanson de Roland*, from which many of the names were borrowed, from *Aspremont*, and from the pseudo-Turpin.' The author has connected his work with the legend of Charlemagne's wars in Spain by placing the action in an interval (unknown to the other Charlemagne legends) in the Spanish war, during which interval Charlemagne is supposed to have returned to France. Otinel was further connected with the existing legend by making the Saracen hero the nephew of the giant Ferracutus, who appears in the pseudo-Turpin.

In the opinon of Gautier, *Otinel* was invented solely to satisfy the ardent love of novelty that tormented the poet's hearers, and is, therefore, a purely literary work, a 'chanson de geste' of the decadence. Wülker considers it as wholly a romance of adventure, one that might as easily have been connected with Arthur as with Charlemagne. Treutler,[4] however, places it in the first period of the ancient epic poetry of France. Although it is not specially rich in genius, novelty of invention, nor in true poetry, he yet finds it distinguished from most of the 'chansons de geste' by its greater age, and by a simplicity of treatment and of form characteristic of the epics of the first period; even the redactions of it do not show the characteristics that G. Paris has assigned to the second and third epic periods.[5] As to the poem being an invention merely, the poet was

---

[1] See *Hist. Poét.*, 150; Treutler, 149.
[2] Treutler, 101, 123, 126, 146 (stemma).
[3] p. 545.   [4] p. 149.
[5] *Hist. Poét.*, pp. 73—75.

far more likely to have invented the 'geste' of some ancestor
of a known hero, than the history of a hero and of a battle,
of which no one knew anything.[1]

In England, the poem enjoyed a geat success. It was
the earliest of the English Charlemagne romances;[2] three
versions are known: the Auchinleck *Otuel, Roland and Otuel,*
and the version of the Fillingham MS.[3], known only through
the analysis of Ellis. In the second part[4] of this last
version, the name of Otuel occurs but two or three times;
the real object being to finish the history of the Spanish
War, and, particularly, to give an account of the battle of
Roncesvalles.

Of the extant English versions, *Roland and Otuel* is,
according to the editor,[5] a tolerably close translation of its
original, while *Otuel* is a free reproduction[6] of a slightly
different version. As compared with the French poem,
Treutler[7] finds that *Otuel* is, in a still greater degree, exclusively a description of battle and death. The greater
battle scenes are given with relatively the most faithfulness,
while all the lighter or romantic elements are rejected.
Treutler makes no mention of *Roland and Otuel.*

5. Metre. 1738 verses, in short couplets, divided, in
Herrtage's edition, into 209 paragraphs of unequal length.

6. Dialect.[8] S. E. Midland. Herrtage's conclusion[9] is
that both *Roland and Vernagu* and *Otuel* 'were written by
an E. Midland scribe, who for some reason or other was
acquainted with Southern literature'.

7. Date. Not later than the first quarter of the four-
tenth century, since found in the Auchinleck MS.

8. Author. Unknown.

---

[1] Cf. *Zs. f. rom. Phil.,* IV 583.
[2] Brandl, § 37.   [3] See X 4.
[4] Ellis, pp. 373—79; *Otuel* (EETS.), pp. vii—xii.
[5] *Otuel,* p. xiii.   [6] Cf. Treutler, 129, 142.
[7] pp. 129, 132.   [8] Brandl, § 37.   [9] p. xvi.

9. Bibliography. *Manuscripts:* Auchinleck, see II. 9.
Editions: Nicholson, for the Abbotsford Club, Edin.,
1836. Herrtage, *EETS. E. S.* No. 39, L. 1882, p. 65.

The OF. *Otinel,* edited by Guessard and Michelant, in
Les Anciens Poètes de la France, P. 1859.

General References: Ten Brink, I 245—6; Brandl, § 37;
G. Paris, *Hist. Poét.,* 150, 155 and *Rom.* XI 151; Ellis, 357—
373; *Hist. Litt.* XXVI 269—78.

Monographs: Treutler, *Die Otinelsage im Mittelalter,*
E. St. V 97—149. Gragger,[1] *Zur ME. Dichtung Sir Otuel,*
Graz, 1896, and in *Festschrift d. deutsch. Akad. philol. Vers.*
in Graz.

XIII. Duke Rowlande and Sir Ottuell of Spayne.

1. Subject. See XI..

2. Specimen. vv. 577—588:

And als þᵒ kynge thus prayed faste,
A dofe come fro the holy gaste,
   & one þᵉ Saraȝene lightes:
And þaw was he fułł sore agaste,
And vnuto sir Rowlande saide he in haste:
   "Sesse, sir, of thi fighttes,
For I ame broghte in siche a wiłł,
Þat I ȝoure lawes will fulfiłł,
   And be-come a Cristyw knyghte."
Þaw douw þay layde þaire wapyns stiłł,
And aythere wente othire vntiłł,
   A Saughtillynge was þer dighte.

3. Story. See XII.

[The following are the principal points in which the
story of *Roland and Otuel* differs from that of *Otuel* as
told above. *Roland and Otuel,* though the more literal

---

[1] I have not seen this.

translation, is one hundred and forty lines shorter.] Charlemagne, in Paris, is preparing to make war against King
Merthill (v. 46). Otuel comes out of Spain from the emperor,
Sir Garcy, who, as we learn from Otuel's talk, has recently
been in Lombardy (st. 12). Otuel agrees to give his sword
in charge to Roland until his message is delivered. The
demand of the French knights to march against Garcy, the
overtures of Charlemagne to Otuel, and the information
concerning Otuel's rank are not found. Roland is armed by
the eleven 'douzeperes', Otuel by the king's daughter Belesant, assisted by two 'maydens smale'. The place of combat is not described. Charlemagne watches the duel from
the castle, and bids Roland fight 'hardely' in the name of
Mary of Heaven. Otuel, aghast at the sight of the dove,
consents unconditionally to become a Christian. Belesant's
beauty is dwelt upon, and Otuel asks if she is pleased
with him, then says that he has made a vow to 'mylde
Marie', whom he has chosen as his lady, that for Belesant's
love, and to destroy God's enemies, he will fight against
the heathen. Clariel is released by advice of Ogier, not of
Oliver. Clariel's lady is not said to be Garcy's daughter.
Otuel is armed for the combat with Clariel by the twelve
peers, assoiled by Turpin, and kissed thrice by his 'lovesome lady', who commends him to the dear Lord. Otuel
captures Garcy, and sends him to Charlemagne. Otuel is
married to Belesant, and is made lord of Lombardy.

4. Origin. See XII.

5. Metre. 1596 verses, written in the twelve-line tail-
rime stanza (class II).

6. Dialect. N. E. Midland (?). Herrtage[1] assigns the
poem to the North, but with a Southern scribe; Wilda,[2] to
the South of N. England. Dannenberg[3] concludes that the
poem probably arose not in the North, but in the N. E.
Midland.

---

[1] Ed. p. xii.   [2] pp. 17—26.
[3] p. 51 (*op. cit.* under *XI*, 9).

7. Date. The beginning of the 15th[1] or end of the 14th[2] century. The first date is assigned by Wilda upon phonological grounds that Kölbing[3] considers convincing.

8. Author. Unknown.[4]

9. Bibliography. *Manuscripts:* Addit. 31042. Brit. Mus. *Editions:* Herrtage, *EETS. E. S.* NO. 35, L. 1880, p. 53. *General References:* See XII.

XIV. The Song of Roland.

1. Subject. The destruction of Charlemagne's rear-guard by the Saracens in the mountain passes of Spain.

2. Specimen. Vv. 559—67. Roland refuses to call for help:

> And to them said he ther:
> 'ye knyghtis, for shame shon ye neuer.
> haue ye broken eny bone, or eny harm tid?
> may ye schew in your sheld eny strokis wid?
> Is not your compony hole as they come?
> Flee fast þat is afferd, þat he wer at home;
> I will fight with them that vs hathe sought.
> And or I se my brest blod throughe my harnes ryn
> blow neuer horn for no help then.'

Vv. 759—68. Oliver joins Roland in the fight:

> bothe man and horse he fellid to the ground.
> he ridis to Roulond, his broder, that stound.
> he strikis fulle sternly strokis full many,
> And he criethe to the cristyn, 'be manly!'
> they went to sadly, And set þer dyntis
> In the worship of hym that fedithe seintis.

---

[1] Wilda, 20.   [2] Ed. p. xiii.
[3] *Arthour and Merlin*, p. lvii.   [4] See XI 8.

then they to-gedur with a sad will,
Schaftis scheuered, and scheldis did spille,
riche thingis to-rof, rest they ne wold,
hewen helmes, and cleve scheldis, þat stound.

3. Story. [1][King Marsile of Saragossa, the last un-
conquered Spanish city, sends ambassadors to Charlemagne,
asking upon what conditions he may keep his kingdom.
Ganelon, nominated as messenger by Roland, carries the
answer that he shall surrender the keys of Saragossa, embrace
Christianity, and pay homage to Charlemagne. Marsile
induces Ganelon, who hates Roland, to turn traitor. To
blind Charlemage,] he sends by Ganelon a present of fair
maidens and good wine, with the message that if Charlemagne will return to France, he will soon follow for baptism. The rejoicing army starts for Gascony. Encamping
for the night, the Sultan's present causes the knights to
sin sorely.

Charlemagne dreams that Ganelon treacherously tries
to kill him; also that a wild boar pulls off his right arm,
and that a leopard from Spain tears off the boar's right ear.

In a council called to guard against Saracen treachery,
Ganelon proposes that Roland with picked knights shall
guard the rear, the post of danger. The king unwillingly
consents, and the main army passes on. If Roland's knights
are beset, they are to cry loudly to Charlemagne for aid.
The Portuguese prince, Amaris, with forty thousand Saracens, attacks Roland's advance divison under Sir Gauter, and
kills all but the leader. Gauter, wounded, flies to warn
Roland. Meanwhile Charlemagne becomes alarmed at the
long absence of his knights. Ganelon is accused of
treachery, but indignantly asserts his innocence, and tells
Charlemagne that Roland must be hunting.

Amaris advances again against the French with a
hundred thousand men. Oliver begs Roland to blow his
horn for help, but Roland refuses. At sunrise Turpin cele-

---

[1] From the French.

brates Mass. In view of twenty square miles of Saracens, Roland prays for victory, and cheers his companions with hopes of heaven and of vengeance. The battle begins. Roland, Oliver, and the other knights perform prodigies of valor. At sunset no Saracen is left, and the French return thanks to God. Thrice do fresh hosts of Saracens advance against the undaunted French. Finally, overpowered by numbers, Roland proposes to send a messenger to Charlemagne; Oliver objects.[1] [Soon but sixty of the French survive. Against Oliver's wish, Roland blows his horn for aid. It is heard by Charlemagne. A reinforcement of fifty thousand Saracens arrives. All the French are slain except Roland and Archbishop Turpin, who are mortally wounded. Roland dies after bidding a touching farewell to his dead companion Oliver and to his trusty sword Durindal. Charlemagne arrives, takes vengeance on the Saracens, and puts Ganelon to death.]

4. Origin. The original of this fragment is the famous *Chanson de Roland,* the national epic of France. The historical fact forming the nucleus of the legend, briefly chronicled by contemporaries, was the destruction of Charlemagne's rear-guard, August 15, 778, by Basque mountaineers in the pass of Roncesvalles. Songs commemorating the disaster must soon have arisen. Their earliest home, according to G. Paris,[2] was probably in Brittany, of which Roland was count.[3] In time, the historical event, greatly changed as to actual fact, magnified in its proportions, and deepened in significance, became the expression of the national and religious spirit of France.

The most famous version of the legend of Roland, the *Chanson,*[4] goes back to the last third of the 11th century.[5]

---

[1] End of MS.

[2] Einhard (*Vita Caroli,* ch. ix) speaks of him as merely 'Hruodlandus, Britannici limitis praefectus.'   [3] p. 54.

[4] MS. *ca.* 1170 in Bodl. Libr., Oxford: 4002 assonanced decasyllabic verses.

[5] G. Paris § 34. The versions of the pseudo-Turpin and that of the *Carmen de proditione Guenonis* are somewhat more ancient.

Gautier [1] thinks its author was probably a Norman of the Conquest. It is interesting to remember that a poem upon Roncesvalles was chanted at the battle of Hastings by the Norman minstrel Taillefer. [2] The English fragment is a very free reproduction of its original. The incident of the women and the wine, with which it opens, is taken from the pseudo-Turpin, either directly, or from some version of the *Chanson* into which the incident had already been incorporated. Wichmann favors the former view, [3] for if, as he believes, the author was a cleric, the attempt to represent the overthrow at Roncesvalles as a punishment from God would find favor with him.

The English version corresponds in general with that of the oldest MS. of the *Chanson,* though in some instances it agrees with later MSS. Schleich, therefore, concludes [4] that the poet used as the basis of his work a MS. of the β class, the so-called French rime redaction, his MS. being most similar probably to Vz. [5] and Vs. [6] Wichmann [7] thinks that the author cannot have drawn directly from one of these versions, since, of all the known versions, the English alone agrees with O [8] in the statement that, in the dream of Charles, he was attacked by a boar instead of by a bear.

Where the author follows the version of O, he does so with great freedom; for the most part abridging the narrative, especially of the battles, though sometimes expanding, noticeably in the speeches, changing the order of events, and altering names, incidents, and speeches. Wichmann's final conclusion [9] as to the origin of the poem is that the author, probably a monk, did not draw directly from any extant version, nor from the original, but that, having at hand in the cloister different versions of the *Chanson,* representative of both the assonanced and the rimed versions, as well as the pseudo-Turpin, he used them all

---

[1] See Julleville, 91, 92; cf. G. Paris, § 36 (p. 61), Gröber, p. 463.

[2] See ed., p. xix.

[3] p. 72; so also G. Paris, *Rom.* XI 151, n. 1.

[4] *Proleg,* 35.   [5] Venetian MS. VII.   [6] Versailles MS.

[7] p. 77.   [8] Oxford MS.   [9] p. 79—80.

in an independent manner. G. Paris[1] remarks that it is to be regretted that, to an independence rare in his time, the author did not join more talent.

The difference between the two, both in delineation of character and in general spirit, is marked.[2] The English poem cannot, of course, bear comparison with the *Chanson*. The characters are less impressive, less passionate, more talkative and didactic. Charlemagne is less majestic and noble; Roland, equally valiant, but far less warlike, and more devout; Ganelon is an 'entirely black traitor',[3] while in the OF. he is a very human character, a valiant knight and loyal subject, who is conquered by the passion of revenge. In its general spirit, the English fragment is distinguished from the OF. poem in two respects. It is more decidedly religious, or perhaps, to speak more exactly, shows more piety, and it entirely lacks the patriotic and warlike inspiration of the French poem.

5. Metre. A fragment of 1049 verses, rimed in couplets. The metrical structure is extremely irregular[4]: the number of stressed and unstressed syllables in a verse being frequently and irregularly extended; the alliteration, often very deficient, often entirely lacking; the inner structure of the verse, not that of the alliterative long-line; the rimes, poor, and sometimes lacking altogether. The scheme of the verse, Schleich, in his *Prolegomena*,[5] seems to regard as that of the alliterative long-line, but later[6] he concludes that we have to do with the short couplet, and that the alliteration was added as an ornament. Upon the style and metre of the poem, Ten Brink[7] remarks: 'The power with which the form and import of the grand composition[8] affected the English author, is plainly evident. He strove for a terse, pregnant diction, and with some success, but he

---

[1] *Rom.* XI 151.   [2] Wichmann.   [3] Brandl.
[4] See Schleich in *Proleg.* pp. 14—28, *Anglia* 315—17; Herrtage, pp. xxii—xxv. Brandl, § 113.
[5] p. 22.   [6] *Angl.* IV 315 - 17.   [7] I 245.
[8] The French original.

was not able to give his verses an even, epic movement. His short couplets are often lengthened under the influence of the French ten-syllabled line, and the epic spirit in his original involuntarily moves him to adopt the ancient ornament of the national poetry, alliteration, which he uses without definite rules.'

6. Dialect. The S. W. Midland; the scribe belonged to the N. E. Midland. This, the conclusion of Schleich,[1] is disputed by Wissmann, who, upon phonological grounds, concludes that the N. E. Midland was the home of the poet. Schleich[2] defends himself against the objections of Wissmann and of Herrtage,[3] in regard to the dialect of the scribe, citing, in support of his view, numerous examples from ME. literature.

7. Date. The poem has been assigned by G. Paris[4] to the 13th, and by Ten Brink to the 14th century. Since in many cases the final *e* must have been silent, and since there are no cases where, of necessity, it must have been pronounced, Schleich[5] would place the poem in the period, 1400—1450.[6] As shown by the poems of Chaucer and by *Sir Firumbras,* which arose in the S. W. about 1350, before 1400 the final *e* was still pronounced in the South. Upon this point, Herrtage,[7] who fixes the probable date at 1400 or even earlier, says that in *William of Palerne,* which was composed about 1350 'in very nearly the same dialect' as the *Roland,* the final *e* has lost its value. S.[8] however, denies that the dialects of the two poems are 'very nearly the same'; (e. g. the ending es in pres. pl. ind. and in the imp. is not at all unusual in *WP* but is not found in the *Roland.*) The MS. could hardly have been written before 1450.[9]

---

[1] *Proleg.,* 6.   [2] *Angl.* IV 307—13.   [3] Ed., p. xxix.
[4] *Hist. Poét.,* 155.
[5] *Proleg.,* 3—5, and *Angl.* IV 313—15.   [6] p. xxxi.
[7] Brandl also, § 113, gives the 15th century.
[8] *Angl.* IV 313.
[9] Upon the date of poem and MS., cf. Wülker (*Hist.*) p. 112.

8. Author. The poem gives no direct information concerning its author, but suggests that he was a monk or cleric.[1] The incident from the pseudo-Turpin, the Biblical allusion to Moses and the Ten Commandments (v. 840—1), the learned allusion to the battle of Troy (v. 844), the frequent use of religious motives and moments, a certain devotional tone sometimes noticeable, all point in this direction. The fact of a clerical authorship may also, perhaps, account largely for the spinning out of the laconic speeches of the heroes of the *Chanson* and for the brief treatment of the warlike elements.

9. Bibliography. *Manuscripts:* Lansdowne 388, Brit. Museum.

Editions: Herrtage, *EETS. E. S.* No. 35, 1880, p. 107; text criticism, Schleich, *Angl.* IV 317—41.

La Chanson de Roland, ed. Gautier, 1897; see Gröber, p. 463, n. 1.

General References: Ten Brink I 244—45; Brandl § 113; *Hist. Poét.,* 155; W. Grimm, *Ruolandes Liet,* Göttingen, 1838, pp. xci—ii, n. 9, xcix; see further Schleich, *Proleg.,* 1—3.

Monographs: Schleich, *Prolegomena Ad Carmen de Rolando Anglicum.* Burg, 1879, (Berlin, diss.); revs. — Wülker, *Angl.* III 401—4; Wissmann, *Litbl.* 1880 (9) 334. — Schleich, *Beiträge zum ME. Roland. Angl.* IV 317—41. Wichmann, *Das Abhängigkeitsverhältnis des altengl. Rolandsliedes zur altfr. Dichtung,* Münster, 1889, diss.

XV. The Taill of Rauf Coil჻ear.

1. Subject. Charlemagne, incognito, in the home of a peasant: the peasant at the court in Paris; his fight with a Saracen.

---

[1] See Wichmann, 65—69, 71—2, 79—80; Brandl.

2. Specimen. Vv. 157---169. Rauf again orders the king 'to begin the board':

He start vp stoutly agane—vneis micht he stand—
For anger of that outray that he had thair tane.
He callit on Gyliane his wyfe, "ga, tak him by the hand,
And gang agane to the buird, quhair ʒe suld air haue gane."
"Schir, thow art vnskilfull, and that sall I warrand;
Thow byrd to haue nurtour aneuch, and thow hes nane;
Thow hes walkit, I wis, in mony wyld land,
The mair vertew thow suld haue, to keip the fra blame!
Thow suld be courtes of kynd, and ane cunnand Courteir.
                Thocht that I simpill be,
                Do as I bid the,
                The hous is myne, pardie,
                And all that is heir".

3. Story. During a storm in the mountains, Charlemagne is separated from his retinue. At night fall he meets a peasant, Rauf the collier, driving a mare, and begs to be directed to a place of shelter. Rauf, though somewhat surly, says that the stranger is welcome to his home seven miles away. Arrived there, Rauf peremptorily bids his wife kindle a noble fire and cook two capons. On the threshold, the king stands aside to let the collier enter first, but Rauf politely pushes him in by the neck. When supper is ready, Rauf orders his guest to take the dame by the hand, and 'begin the board'. The king hesitating, Rauf fells him to the floor, repeating the order. At the table Rauf boasts how he has slain the royal deer. He bids his wife pass round the cup. Supper over, they sit by the fire and Rauf tells many tales. He asks his guest where he lives, and is told 'with the queen; I am called Wymond of the Wardrobe'. The king urges Rauf to come to court, promising him a good sale for his fuel. At bedtime, Rauf and his wife see their guest to bed. The next morning the king departs.

The day following is Christmas. Charlemagne commands Roland to go to the moor-road and bring to court whomever he may meet. Rauf appears, but refuses to accompany Roland. He finds his way to the palace. Inquiring for Wymond of the Wardrobe, he pushes his way into the hall where the king and queen are dining in state. Rauf recognizes Wymond, but is abashed at his splendor. The king tells of his treatment by Rauf, at which the lords laugh loudly, and advise that Rauf be hung. The king, however, dubs him knight, assigns him a revenue, and promises him the next vacant fief.

At the king's desire, Rauf rides out to win his spurs. Upon the moor-road he meets a mounted Saracen; they fight until separated by Roland, who secures the conversion of the Saracen by promising him riches and a beautiful wife, Lady Jane of Anjou. Sir Rauf is rewarded for his valor by being made marshal of France. He sends for his wife to share his good fortune.

4. Origin. For this 'charming little poem'—such G. Paris [1] finds it—no French source is known, and none has been ascribed to it. It is connected only externally with the Charlemagne legend. Of the literary movement in Scotland of which it is an example, Brandl [2] speaks as follows: 'In the middle and second half of the century, the popular tone pressed into the form and motive circle of the Art poem so that a mixture characteristic of Scotland arose, in which Chaucer's humor throve far better than with his English disciples'.

Brandl regards the poem as a parody upon the knightly romance. If such were intended, it perhaps is most apparent in the conflict between Rauf and the Saracen, which reminds us of similar scenes in the Charlemagne romances, particularly in *Otuel*. In both *Otuel* and *RC* the motive inducing the Saracen to accept Christianity seems the same.

---

[1] *Rom.* XI, 150.

[2] p. 135, where Arthur instead of Charlemagne is, by mistake, spoken of as entertained by Rauf.

The subject[1] of the poem, the meeting of a king, incognito, with a subject, is thoroughly popular. 'The underlying motive of all narratives of this kind', says Tonndorf, 'can be traced to the East, although here the rudeness characteristic of the subject in the English version is lacking'. The stories told concerning Haroun al Raschid are, of course, the most famous examples from the Orient.[2]

Similar stories are also found in German literature.[3] One, *Der hartgeschmiedete Landgraf,* shows the same rudeness in the character of the peasant as does *RC.* Tonndorf remarks that in German mythology it is said that Wodan loves to come among men as an unrecognized traveller. The motive of *RC* seems to have been especially popular in English ballad poetry. Tonndorf enumerates ten ballads illustrating it, seven of which are found in Bishop Percy's *Reliques,* these divided into two groups according as the encounter takes place by accident or through the intention of the ruler. To the first class belong *King Henry II and the Miller of Mansfield* (which, of all the ballads, resembles *RC* most closely), *King Henry and the Soldier, James I and the Tinker, William III and the Forester.* To the second belong *King Edward and the Shepherd, Edward IV and the Tanner of Tamworth, Henry VII and the Cobler.* To these may be added *John the Reeve,*[4] *King Edward and the Hermit,*[5] and *Henry II and the Cistercian Abbot.*[6]

5. Metre.[7] 975 verses in the favorite thirteen-line stanza of the Gawain School,[8] showing, with only an occasinal modification, the rime order *ab ab ab ab cd dd c.* The first nine lines are long, the last four, short.

As a rule, the long lines are regularly alliterative, though about fifty long lines show no alliteration. Of the

---

[1] Tonndorf pp. 8, 9.   [2] See further Tonndorf, p. 9.

[3] Grimm, *Deutsche Sagen,* 1816. Nos. 550, 565, 563, 566.

[4] *PF. MS.* II 550—594, see ed. of *RC.* pp. v—vi.

[5] *Hartshorne,* pp. 293—315, also *Hazlitt, Remains of the Early Popular Poetry of England,* I pp. 11—34.

[6] *Rel. Ant.* I p. 147.   [7] Tonndorf, 45—49.   [8] Brandl, § 135.

short lines, about one-third only are alliterative, and by far the larger proportion of these have but two alliterative letters.

The long lines are unequally divided by a cesura, masculine or feminine; each half of a long line must be read with two stresses, though the first half line sometimes seems to have more. Of the short lines, the first three have three stresses, the last line, but one.

6. Dialect.[1] The dialect is clearly Scotch: Its linguistic peculiarities are those of the transition stage between Old and Middle Scotch in S. Scotland.

7. Date.[2] The last quarter of the 15th century. In 1500 the poem is mentioned by the poet Dunbar. Linguistic considerations assign it to the period given above, and the evidence derived from this source is confirmed by historical considerations that permit us to entertain no reasonable doubt. In vv. 930—36 we read:

The gentill Duches, Dame Jane, that claimis be hir kin
Angeos and vther londis, with mony riche toun.
. . . .
> In all France is nane so fair
> Als scho is, appeirand air
> To twa Douchereis.

This lady, Tonndorf discovers, was Jeanne de Laval, second wife of René II, titular king of Naples, duke of Anjou, and count of Provence. By her beauty and grace, Jeanne won the heart of her future husband when only thirteen years old. She survived him eighteen years, receiving by his bequest several estates, a castle, the family jewels, etc. A year after René's death in 1480, by the death of his brother and only direct male heir, his possessions passed to the king, Louis XI. Jeanne was the only person who could have opposed the claim of the king. The

---

[1] Tonndorf, 12.   [2] Tonndorf, 13—16.

poem, therefore, must have arisen between 1480 or 1481 and the death of Jeanne in 1498.

8. Author.[1] Unknown.

It has been conjectured[2] that *Rauf Coilzear, Golagrus and Gawain, The Aunters of Arthur* and the *Pystyl of swete Susane,* because of resemblance in age, dialect, and form, may have had the same author. But Trautmann[3] has shown that the three last mentioned poems cannot have had the same author, and Tonndorf, after comparing *RC* with each of these as regards metre and style, concludes that it cannot be assigned to the author of *GG, AA,* or *SS.*

The author of *RC* seems not have been a cleric, and may have been of knightly rank.

9. Bibliography. *Manuscripts*: None is known; cf. Tonndorf, p. 7.

Editions: Old print, by Robert Lekpreuik, St. Andrews, 1572, — the only copy is in the Advocates' Libr., Edin., where it was discovered in 1821.

David Laing, in *Select Remains of the Ancient Popular Poetry of Scotland,* 1420—1580, Edin., 1821.

Herrtage, *EETS. E. S.* No. 38.

John Small, in a new ed. of Laing's *Remains,* with additions, Edin. and L., 1882.

Amours, *Scottish Allit. Poems in Riming Stanzas,* Part. I, *Sc. T. S.* No. 27, 1892.

Monographs: Tonndorf, *Rauf Coilyear,* Halle, 1893, diss.

---

[1] Tonndorf, 17—22.
[2] D. Irving, *History of Scottish Poetry,* ed. Carlyle, 1861, p. 89.
[3] *Anglia* I 129 ff.

The Arthurian Legends.

General References. The bibliographies in Gröber, 485, 495; G. Paris; Julleville, 340—44. G. Paris, in: *Litt. Franç.*, Ch. IV; *Hist. Litt.*, XXX; *Rom.* X 464—70. Gröber, 485—492, 590—99 (on the *lais* and Marie de France). Clédat, in Julleville, 255—340. Ten Brink I 134—6, 140—2, 164—5, 171—80, 187—93. Sommer's ed. of Malory's *Morte Darthur* (1890), III. Wülker, *Die Arthursage in der engl. Litt.*, Leipsic, 1896, diss. Rhŷs, *The Arthurian Legend*, Oxford, 1891. Saintsbury, *FlR.*, Ch. IV. Ker, Ch. V. Maccallum, *Tennyson's Idylls and Arthurian Story*, N. Y., 1894. The views of different scholars in regard to the origin of the Arthurian legend are summarized in: *Rev. Celt.* XIII 475 f.; Saintsbury, *op. cit.*, 133—40; Rhŷs, *op. cit.*, Ch. XVI.

XVI. Sir Tristrem.

1. Subject. The love between the hero and his uncle's wife, awakened before her marriage by a magic potion, recognizing no barriers, and strong until death.

2. Specimen. Vv. 1024—1034 (st. 94).

Þe yland was ful brade,
Þat þai gun in fiȝt;
Þer of was Moraunt glade,
Of Tristrem he lete liȝt.

Swiche meting nas neuer non made
Wiþ worþli wepen wiȝt;
Aiþer to oþer rade
And hewe on helmes briȝt
Wiþ hand.
God help Tristrem, þe kniȝt!
He fauȝt for Ingland.

3. Story. Tristrem is the son of Rouland of Ermonie and Blanchefleur, sister of king Mark of England. Rouland is treacherously slain in battle against his unjust lord, Morgan. Blanchefleur dies after giving birth to Tristrem. Rohand, Roland's steward, for fear of Morgan, brings up Tristrem as his son. Tristrem studies diligently, and at fifteen is skilled in minstrelsy and venery. Carried to sea while playing chess on board a Norwegian ship, he is landed upon the coast of England. Conducted to the court, he becomes a favorite of king Mark.

Rohand, after a long search, finds his foster-son, and reveals his parentage. Tristrem returns to Ermonie, conquers Morgan, makes Rohand ruler, and returns to England to give timely aid to Mark against Moraunt, who claims the yearly tribute due from England to Ireland. (Every fourth year three hundred noble youths must be given.) Tristrem kills Moraunt, leaving a bit of his sword in the wound, and is himself severely injured. His wound refusing to heal, after three years of suffering he puts off to sea in a ship, with his harp and one attendant. The wind bears him into Develin, an Irish haven. Queen Ysonde, sister of Moraunt, cures Tristrem's wound; Tristrem gives the princess Ysonde instruction upon the harp. After a visit to England, Tristrem returns to Ireland to request Ysonde as his uncle's bride. Here he kills a dragon, the reward promised for the deed being the hand of Ysonde. Ysonde, discovering in Tristrem through his jagged sword the slayer of her uncle, wishes to kill him, but is appeased by his promise to make her a queen. On their voyage to England, Tristrem and Ysonde by mistake drink a love-

potion intended for Mark and his bride. Henceforth they
are united by a love that, even after Ysonde has become
the wife of Mark, knows no barriers. Many are the
dangerous intrigues in which the lovers are involved.
Their guilt being finally revealed to the king, Ysonde is
obliged to take an oath of purification at Westminster,
holding a hot iron. By an ingenious device of Tristrem's
that makes her oath no lie she passes the ordeal triumphantly. Again discovered, the lovers are banished by Mark,
and live happily in the forest for nearly a year. Mark,
while hunting one day, finds them asleep with a sword
between them, willingly believes them innocent, and permits
their return to court.

Once more the king is apprised of their relations;
Tristrem flees, but Ysonde is pardoned. After a visit to
Spain, Tristrem goes to Brittany, where, not without much
hesitation, he weds the duke's daughter, Ysonde the White-
Handed. Reminded by the ring of Ysonde the queen of
his love already pledged, Tristrem turns from his bride.
He accompanies his brother-in-law Ganhardin to England
upon a love adventure of the latter's, and once more meets
queen Ysonde.

In Brittany, Tristrem engages in battle in behalf of a
knight whose lady-love has been stolen from him, and
carries away an arrow in his old wound.[1] [Lying at the
point of death, he knows that queen Ysonde alone can
heal him, and sends Ganhardin to bring her from England.
White sails on Ganhardin's returning boat will announce her
presence, black sails, her absence. The vessel comes with
white sails. Tristrem's wife, having learned of the arrangement, reports that the sails are black. Tristrem dies
of grief. Ysonde lands, learns of Tristrem's death, and dies
embracing her lover.]

4. Origin. The romance of *Tristan* is but loosely
connected with the cycle of the Round Table, and is

---

[1] End of the MS.

generally considered[1] to have been originally independent
of it. A seemingly early connection of Tristrem and Arthur
is pointed out by Rhŷs[2] in one of the Welsh Triads,[3]
where Arthur tries to take some of king Mark's swine,
which Tristan is watching.

To the nucleus of the legend, or at least to some of
its elements, a mythological origin has been assigned. The
story of Tristan, in more than one point, recalls that of
Theseus,[4] both perhaps having come from 'a common source
in quasi prehistoric times'. In Welsh mythology, according
to Rhŷs,[5] 'one of the chief names of the Celtic Pluto was
Morc or Marc in Irish, and March ab Meirchion in Welsh,
which might be rendered into English by Steed son of
Steeding or the like'. The name, and the horses' ears
attributed to him seem to point to an anthropomorphic
treatment of the Welsh conception of the devil in the form
of a black steed.[6]

In its most essential features, the legend, according to
the most generally accepted but not unquestioned theory,
is of Celtic origin. Evidence of such an origin has been
pointed out in the derivation of many proper names,[7]
Tristan,[8] Marc, Morholt, Iseut (according to a recent authority[9]), and others; in the scene of the story laid in Cornwall,
Ireland, and Brittany; in the domination[10] of the Irish over

---

[1] Ten Brink, I 174; G. Paris, § 56, 57; Kölbing, I, p. LV; Golther,
1887, 2, 3.

[2] *op. cit.*, 378; cf. *Rev. Celt.* XV 408.

[3] *The Myvyrian Archeology of Wales*, L., 1801, II 1—22, 57—80,
Triads i. 30; ii. 56; iii. 101.

[4] G. Paris, § 56. *Rom.* XV 485.   [5] *op. cit.* p. 70.

[6] Rhŷs, 69, 70. For a probably mythological origin assigned to
Tristan, equating him and Lancelot with Heracles, see pp. 154, 362.

[7] In general, see Golther, pp. 3—6; Zimmer, in *ZsfFSp.* pp. 58,
73—82, rev. in *Rev. Celt.* XII 397—9; Lot, in *Rom.* XXV 14—31.

[8] See note 7; Loth in *Rom.* XIX 455 f.; *ZsfRPh.* XII 351—3, 524;
Rev. Celt. XV 405—6; *Rom.* XVI 295; XVIII 323.

[9] Loth, *op. cit.*; cf. Golther, p. 3, n. 1, p. 6 n. 1 and in *ZsfRPh.*,
op. cit.

[10] *Rom.* XV 598.

Cornwall, suggested by the tribute laid upon it by Morholt;
and in features[1] of the poem that show a society more
primitive or more barbarous than that reflected by the
French texts of the 11th and 12th centuries, and to some
of which parallels may be found in the Irish epics. As
examples of such features may be mentioned: the horses
ears attributed to Marc, whose name in Celtic signifies
horse; the rôle of Minotaur played by Morholt, originally
a sea monster, the first element of his name (*mor*) signifying
sea; the episode of the lepers, which, says Muret,[2] 'surpasses in horror the most barbarous scenes of the chansons
de geste'; the chamber of Iseut traversed by a brook; the
prodigious leaps of Tristan. Finally, much in the spirit[3]
of the story, above all the conception of love[4] forming its
chief motive, is claimed as Celtic.

The birth place of the Tristan, like that of the
Arthurian legend, has not been definitely fixed. G. Paris[5]
declares in favor of Celtic England; Rhŷs seems to have
reached a similar conclusion. Zimmer[6] thinks that the
name Tristan is Pictish, and traces the legend to an historical
origin in Scotland at a time when there were dealings
with the vikings of Ireland; Bretons who went North with
the Normans in 1072, hearing the story, then changed the
character and setting to suit themselves. For the story in
its present form, an exclusively Celtic origin can hardly be
claimed. Sarrazin[7] sees in many features of the legend,
in the fight with the dragon, the island duel, the iron-test,
the magic potion on the bridal night, the separation by a
sword, — a surprising resemblance to German legends and
tales. According to Golther,[8] this resemblance is due, for
the most part, to the influence of the widely spread

---

[1] *Rom., op. cit.* and XVII 605 f.   [2] *Rom.* XVII 605.
[3] Saintsbury, *FlR.*, 117—18.
[4] G. Paris, *Tr. et Is.*; cf. *Rev. Celt.* XV 407—8.
[5] *Rom.* VIII 425, XIV 604; see also Gröber, 471.
[6] *ZsfFSp.*, 1890. Cited from Maccallum, *op. cit.*, 65.
[7] *Zs. f. Vergl. Ltgesch.* I 265 f.; *Rom. Forsch.* IV 329 f.
[8] p. 11, n. 1.

Märchen' and 'Novellen' literature [1] of the Middle Ages, which became united with native traditions. As a whole, the story of Tristan is not, he maintains,[2] a Celtic tale. The outline of a legend, perhaps the love of Tristan for his uncle's wife, some data of the introductory history, some individual features, especially those of a marvellous nature,[3] and many of the proper names are doubtless of Celtic origin; but in its present form the story is composed of different, rather loosely united episodes, the origin for a large number of which is the popular literature already referred to.[4]

The earliest extant versions of the Tristan legend, two [5] in number and both incomplete, are the work of Anglo-Normans [6] in the second half of the 12th century. Redactions and translations of these poems carried 'the incomparable epic of love' [7] into every language of Mediaeval Europe.[8] The many allusions [9] to the story in Mediaeval literature witness to its fame.

Of the two 12th century versions, the long fragment known by the name of Béroul cannot, according to Golther,[10] be considered the work of one poet. It represents an only slightly individualized redaction of a widely spread and many-sided minstrel version, built up during the 12th century. The poem of Thomas [11] on the contrary, representing a version different from that of Béroul, though, as regards subject matter, not radically so, is the work of a creative artist.

Upon the poem of Thomas are based the poem of

---

[1] In this literature, classical influence is not unimportant. The motives of the tales and 'Novelle', in their final origin, go back to Oriental sources. Golther in *ZsfRPh.* XII 349, 51; cf. Golther, 1887, pp. 24—7.

[2] p. 42.   [3] pp. 20—21.
[4] Cf. Muret, *Rom.* XVII 603 f.
[5] The version of Chrétien de Troyes is lost.   [6] G. Paris, § 56.
[7] G. Paris, *Rom.* XV 599.   [8] Michel I i—xxviii.
[9] See n. 8 and *Rom.* XV 534—57.   [10] pp. 75, 81, 86.
[11] Golther, *op. cit.*, pp. 101—104.

Gottfried von Strassburg, a Norse saga, and the English
Sir Tristrem.

Kölbing, in his comparative study of the three versions
and the fragments of the original, reaches the conclusion
(which confirms and completes the earlier one of Bossert[1])
that each version represents, essentially, the version of
Thomas, the saga being the closest reproduction; divergencies
and contradictions between the versions show, however,
that each must have been based upon a different redaction[2]
of the original. Before Kölbing, Heinzel[3] maintained that
the lost French romance, the source of Gottfried's *Tristan*,
did not represent essentially the work of one author, but
had arisen from a union of the poem of Thomas, who
treated only a large division of the legend, with other
independent redactions of the Tristan material. The conclusion now accepted by scholars is that of Kölbing.

Sir Tristrem is a condensed but more or less faithful
translation of the original. Although in many passages
the translation is almost literal, the character of other
passages points to the conclusion that the poet did not
have before him a written source, but composed from
memory.[4] He seems to have expended most of his effort
upon his metrical form,[5] and his meaning is often obscure.
Although based upon the so-called courtly version of the
French *Tristan,* and written in a 'difficult, courtly, ambitious'
metre, the poem is popular in its general tone, its style[6]
recalling that of the folk-song and of the old epic.

5. Metre.[7] 3344 verses in stanzas of eleven lines,
having, in all but ten stanzas, the rime order *ab ab ab ab c bc.*

---

[1] pp. 101, 106—7.
[2] Kölbing's ed., pp. xxiii, xxv; Norse version, p. cxlii.
[3] *ZsfdAlt.* XIV 272; *Anz. f. d. Alt.* VIII 212.
[4] Kölbing, I, p. cxlvii; cf. Vetter, p. 34, and *E. St.* VII 357.
[5] See Ten Brink and Brandl.
[6] Brandl, § 51, and *Anz. f. d. Alt.* X 348. See the interesting
comparison made by Bossert, pp. 88—100, between *ST.* and the poem
of Gottfried.
[7] Kölbing's ed., pp. xxxii—lx.

Vv. 1—8, 10—11 always have three stresses; v. 9, but one. Alliteration, according to a somewhat elaborate system, is used as an ornament. In many stanzas it is intentionally used to unite vv. 8 and 9.

In the view of Ten Brink [1] and of Schipper,[2] the metre is of Romance origin, the verse-unit being an Alexandrine of six accents, divided by the middle rhyme into two short lines. Kölbing [3] says that the verse is constructed more on Germanic than on Romance principles.

In the use of alliteration,[4] *ST* in some respects resembles *King Horn*,[5] but Wissmann's conclusion that the latter poem most probably rests upon 'alliterative songs of like content' is rejected by Kölbing; *ST*, with like characteristics as regards alliteration; goes back as we know to a French source.

6. Dialect. Northern (Kölbing [6]); N.W. Midland (Brandl[7]). The reference (vv. 1—2) to Thomas of Erceldoune as the poet's authority points, Kölbing thinks, to N. England or to S. Scotland as the home of the poem. The use of alliteration also points decidedly to the North. S. England is excluded by the explanatory statement in regard to the Thames, *þat is an arm of þe se* (2246), and Scotland, by the prayer for Tristrem because *He fauȝt for Ingland* [8] (1034). Against the conclusion in favor of N. England, the linguistic investigation brings, Kölbing thinks, no really weighty considerations and much that seems to support it. The poem cannot be assigned to Yorkshire, from whose dialect its own differs in several not unessential points. It is naturally very tempting to assign the author to the vicinity of Erceldoune, where Brandl would place the poem of *Thomas of Erceldoune*;[9] and, indeed, considering that about one hundred years separate the two poems, the

---

[1] I 240; cf. Kölbing, p. LI.   [2] In *P. G.* II. 1. 1068.
[3] p. LXXVI.   [4] Kölbing, p. LII.   [5] See I 5, p. 9.
[6] pp. LX—LXXVIII.   [7] *Anz. f. d. Alt.* X 332—3.
[8] Brandl, *op. cit.*, p. 332.
[9] See *TE.* (*op. cit.* on p. 93, n. 8) p. 42.

dialects show a surprising resemblance. The scribe belonged to the South.

Brandl[1] claims that the linguistic evidence adduced by Kölbing in favor of the North speaks equally for the W. Midland. Some assured forms in *ST*, unknown in the North, but occurring in the South, and in the W. Midland, show that the dialect, if Northern, was changed in copying with a consistency that seldom occurs. Brandl, therefore, is inclined to assign *ST* to the boundaries of the N. and W. Midland.

7. Date.[2] Probably the last decade of the 13th century. The poet's false[3] citation of Thomas of Erceldoune as his source of information could hardly have been made previous to the death of the latter, shortly before 1294. The presence of the poem in the Auchinleck MS., and the reference to the poem by Robert Mannyng,[4] who wrote about 1330, shows that *ST* cannot have arisen after the first quarter of the 14th century.

8. Author. In the opening lines of *ST,* the author tells us that he was at Erceldoune and there spoke with Thomas, from whom he heard the history of Tristrem. References to Thomas as his authority are also found in verses 397, 412, 2787. Robert Mannyng[5] in his *English Chronicle* (*ca.* 1330) also refers to a Thomas as author of Sir Tristrem, though, judging strictly from the context, it is uncertain whether Thomas of Erceldoune or Thomas of Kendale is meant. In another passage Mannyng[6] refers to a tale about two brothers by Thomas of Kendale.

Walter Scott[7] concluded that the author of the poem was 'Thomas of Erceldoune,[8] called the Rhymer, who flourished in the 13th century'. This view is also supported

---

[1] *op. cit.*   [2] Kölbing, p. XXXI.   [3] See **8.**
[4] Kölbing, p. XXVII.
[5] Quoted by Kölbing, p. XXVII; by Mac Neill, p. XXXV.
[6] See Kölbing, p. XXX; Mac Neill, p. XL.
[7] Introduction, p. 63 f.
[8] See Kölbing, p. XXVII; Brandl, *Thomas of Erceldoune*, Berlin, 1880, p. 15.

by Mac Neill,[1] principally upon the authority of Robert
Mannyng as representative of the belief of the age in which
Thomas of Erceldoune lived, and in which *ST* was composed. The authorship of Thomas of Erceldoune is, however, generally denied by modern scholars.[2] Kölbing gives
no weight to the testimony of Mannyng, derived as it
probably was simply from the romance. The French fragments, the poem of Gottfried, and *ST* all refer, and always
in the third person, to a Thomas as the authority for the
history of Tristrem. The conclusion, therefore, seems to be
that the unknown author of *ST*, finding repeatedly in his
French source the name of a certain Thomas, in order to
ensure for his poem a livelier interest among his country-
men, cited as his authority the famous Thomas of Erceldoune. Brandl[3] is inclined to favor Thomas of Kendale
(Westmoreland) as the possible author. The man[4] appears
to better advantage in the poem than does the artist.

9. Bibliography.

Manuscripts: Auchinleck, Edin.; see II. 9.

Editions: Walter Scott, Edin., 1804, '11, '19, '33, '68;
see Kölbing, pp. xiv—xviii.

Kölbing, *Die Nordische und die Englische Version der
Tristan-Sage*, I, II, Heilbronn, 1878—82. Cf. *E. St.* II 533;
VI 463; VII 189; XIII 133. *Revs.:* I. Behagel, *Ltbl.* 1880,
pp. 93—7; Brenner, *Anz. f. d. Alt.*, V 405—13; Lambel, *Mag.
f. d. Lt. des In- u. Auslandes*, Jahrg. 50, p. 455 f.; Löschern,
Jen. Ltzt., 1879, p. 351; *Arch.* LXIV 201; Paul, *Lt. Cbl.* 1879
(23), 738 f.; Schipper, *Zs. f. öst. Gymn.* 1884, p. 210—16;
Stengel, *ZsfRPh.* IV 170 f.; Stratmann, *Angl.* VI, *Anz.*,
48—50; Vetter, *Rom.* VIII 281—4; *L'Athenaeum*, Belgian,
1880, no. 2; *Germ.* 1878, 345; *GGA.* 1879, 447; *Jen. Belege*
1880, 16; *Rev. des langues romanes*, III ser. III 131; *Rom.
St.* IV 192. — II. Zupitza, *Lt. Zt.* 1883 (23), 813; Brandl,
Anz. f. d. Alt., VIII 331—50.

---

[1] p. xliv.

[2] See Kölbing, pp. xxviii, xxx, n. 1, xxxi; *E. St.* X 289.

[3] § 51.   [4] See Brandl, in *Anz.*, pp. 348—9.

Mac Neill, *Scot. TS.*, Edin. and L., 1886. *Revs.:* Kölbing, *E. St.* X 287 f.; *Ath.* 1887, No. 3090, p. 92.

The fragments of the OF. source: F. Michel, *Tristan, Recueil de ce qui reste des poèmes relatifs a ses aventures,* L., 1835—9; Villemarqué in *Arch. des Missions scient.,* V 97; Novati, in *Studj di fil. rom.,* 263 f. See Vetter, *La Légende de Tr. d'après le poèm frçs. de Th.,* Marburg, 1882, diss., cf. *E. St.* VII 349; Röttiger, *Der Tr. des Th., ein Beitrag zur Kritik und Sprache desselben,* Göttingen, 1883, diss. (pp. 3—5 outline the contents of the fragments).

Specimens: Spr. P. I 234 (sts. 70—102 of Scott's ed. of 1833); Ten Brink I 239—40 (vv. 1809—1914 in prose).

General References: Ten Brink I 237—41; Brandl, § 51. Analyses of the legend may be found in the editions of Kölbing and of Mac Neill, and in: *Hist. Litt.* XIX 687—704; Julleville, 259—80; Bossert, (the poem of Gottfried) 51—76; Jusserand (according to Bossert), 135—9. Mac Neill, pp. xiv—xxviii, gives the literary history of *Tristan* down to modern times.

Monographs: ST. has been treated by: Michel, *op. cit.,* I xxxiv—xlvi; Heinzel, in *ZsfdAlt.* XIV 272—447; *Anz. f. d. Alt.* VIII 212—17; Bossert, *Tr. et Is., poèm de Gotfrit de Strassburg, comparé à d'autres poèms sur le même sujet,* P., 1865, pp. 88—108; Vetter, *op. cit.,* 32—6. On the Tristan legend: Golther, *Die Sage von Tristan und Isolde, Studie über ihre Entstehung und Entwicklung,* Munich, 1887; *revs.:* Muret, *Rom.* XVII 603—9; Singer, *Anz. f. d. Alt.* XIV 233—41; Bechstein, *Zs.f.Vergl.Ltgesch.* 1890, 161—4. Bartsch, *Germ.* XXXIII 119 (brief); *ZsfdPh.* XXII 245; *Oest. Lt. Cbl.,* 1888, (15) 177; *Moyen Age,* 3, 1. Golther, *Zur Tristan-Sage, ZsfRPh.* XII 348 f.; rev. by G. Paris, *Rom.* XVIII 322—4. G. Paris, *Tristan et Iseut,* Bouillon, 1894, and in *Rev. de Paris,* 1894, p. 138 f.; rev. in *Rev. Celt.* XV 407—8, cf. *Rom.* XXIV 154. *Rom.* XV 481—602 (several monographs). Röttiger, *Der heutige Stand der Tristanforschung* (1897). See, further, Gröber, 470, 492—5, 593, and the foot-notes under **4.**

XVII. Joseph of Arimathie.

1. Subject. Joseph of Arimathea, the guardian of the Holy Grail, at the court of the king of Sarras.

2. Specimen. Vv. 258—66, 295—8:

Þenne he seos Ihesu crist · in a sad Roode,
and his fyue Angeles · þat forþ wiþ him stoden,
As red as þe fuir · and he hem bi-holdes.
¶ Þat on beres in his hond · a cros of queynte hewe;
¶ Þat oþer beres in his hond · þreo blodi nayles;
¶ Þe þridde þe Coroune · þat his hed keuerde;
¶ Þe Feorþe, þe launce · þat lemede him wiþ-Inne;
¶ And þe Fyfþe a blodi cloþ · þat he was inne i-braced,
whon he lay after slauht · in þe sepulcre.

· · · · · · · · · · · · · · · · · · · ·

HE seiȝ an Auter I-clothed · wiþ cloþes ful riche;
Vppon þat on ende lay · þe launce and þe nayles,
And vppon þat oþer ende · þe disch wiþ þe blode,
and a vessel of gold · geynliche bi-twene.

3. Story.[1] [2][A monk, who doubts the Trinity, has his faith confirmed by a vision in which a radiantly beautiful man presents him with a book of four treatises, which he is told to copy. He begins with the history of the Holy Grail.
Joseph of Arimathea, secretly a Christian, collects the blood from the wounds of the Crucified into the dish used by Christ at the Last Supper. Seized by the Jews, he is kept for forty-two years in prison, whither Christ brings him for company and comfort the dish containing the blood. He is released by Vespasian, who has been cured of the leprosy by the sight of a cloth stamped with the Saviour's likeness, owned by Marie la Venissienne.]

---

[1] The narrative of *Joseph of Arimathie* is continued by that of Lonelich's *Holy Grail*. In the portion common to the two, the leading incidents are the same.

[2] Supplied from the French text.

In obedience to a voice, Joseph, with his converts, leaves Jerusalem, carrying with him in an ark the sacred dish. They come to Sarras (whence the Saracens have sprung), whose king, Evelak, Joseph tries to convert, unfolding to him, much to his perplexity, the mysteries of the Christian doctrine. At night the king has two visions symbolical of the Trinity and of the Incarnation. A voice bids Joseph beget Galahad. Josaphe, Joseph's son, is appointed by Christ guardian of the dish, and is consecrated as bishop. Looking into the ark, he sees a vision of the Passion. Joseph disputes concerning the Trinity with a Saracen clerk, who is struck dumb. The heathen idols are discomfited.

[1] Evelak prepares to oppose Tholomes, an Egyptian invader. Joseph marks Evelak's shield with a red cross, bidding him, in need, look upon it and pray to Christ. In the battle that follows, Tholomes has the advantage. Evelak is reinforced by his brother-in-law, Seraphe, who, at first partially victorious, is finally overpowered. Evelak, taken prisoner, uncovers his shield, and sees upon it a child streaming with blood. In answer to his prayer, a white knight appears, who turns defeat into victory.

Evelak, upon his return to Sarras, blesses Joseph's God. Seraphe is baptized as Nasciens, and then Evelak as Mordreins (a 'late man' in truth). Five thousand [2] of Evelak's subjects also receive baptism. Queen Sarracynte has long been a Christian in secret. (Lonelich then tells of Joseph's missionary-visit to Orcanz.) After appointing two men to remain in charge of the blood,[3] Joseph's company leave Sarras.

[End of *Joseph of Arimathie*.]

Mordreins, after a dream prophetic of the future, which no one can interpret, is borne away by the Holy Ghost. Nasciens, accused of killing Mordreins, is imprisoned.

---

[1] Lonelich begins just before this point.

[2] Lonelich, Ch. XV, v. 257 says over 500 000.

[3] Lonelich mentions this upon Joseph's departure for Orcanz.

Mordreins is brought to an island, 'the Rock Perilous', on the way from Scotland and Ireland to Babylon. He is visited daily by a shining man in a silver ship, who confirms his faith, and is tempted by a fair woman. Nasciens is freed by a fair white hand, and his son Celidoine is snatched from destruction by nine hands. The white hand bears Nasciens to 'Yl Torneawnt', 'Turning Island'. Nasciens ventures on a ship that he is warned not to enter unless full of faith. The ship, which typifies Holy Church, contains various symbolical objects. Celidoine is carried to another isle, where he converts its king, Label. After Label's death Celidoine is put to sea in a boat with a lion, who turns harmless at the sign of the Cross. Celidoine, Nasciens, and Mordreins are finally reunited upon one ship. Messengers from Sarras, seeking for Nasciens, find Label's daughter, whom an enemy has put to sea in a ship full of corpses. They finally join Nasciens' party. A white clad priest comes walking over the sea, who orders Celidoine into a ship apart, and takes the others to Sarras.

By divine command, Joseph, Josephes, and their company, after many journeys, cross the sea to Britain. The Grail-bearers go first, walking barefoot as upon dry land. The others cross upon Josephes' shirt, except two sinners, who drop off into the sea. In Britain they are later joined by Nasciens, who there finds Celidoine. By means of the Grail, five hundred people are fed from twelve loaves.

Joseph and Josephes proceed to convert the 'Paynims' of Britain (including Scotland); their first convert is the Saracen duke, Gaanort. Later they meet with persecution. Mordreins, Nasciens' wife, and Label's daughter come to Britain, Christ having commanded Mordreins to avenge Him on king Crudelx of North Wales, who has imprisoned Joseph and his company. Mordreins, approaching too near the Holy Grail, is struck blind, and has power neither 'to stand nor go'. He turns hermit, founds the abbey of White Monks, and lives there two hundred years, as promised, until Galahad comes, as Robert of Borron says, who translated this from Latin into French at the command of Holy Church.

Celidoine marries Label's daughter. Moys, having taken a seat at the Grail table, left vacant by Josephes for a holy man typifying Christ, is carried to a far, burning castle. He is later found by Joseph, at whose prayer the fire is quenched, but Moys must remain where he is until Galahad comes. The twelfth of Brons' sons, Aleyn the Gros, choosing virginity, is promised the keeping of the Grail. Aleyn catches a fish, with which he feeds the entire company. He is therefore called the 'Rich-Fisher'. Galas, Joseph's younger son, born in Britain, is made king of Hotelise.

Joseph dies. His body is later transferred from its first resting place to the abbey of Glays, henceforth called 'Glaystyngbery'. Josephes, dying, gives the Grail to Aleyn, and castle Corbenie is built for it. From Aleyn's brother Joswe, descends Pelle, the mother of Galahad. Nasciens, Flegentyne, and Sarracynte all die in a day. Celidoine reigns and dies. From him descends Lancelot of the Lake.

4. Origin. Under this section will be discussed the origin of that part of the Grail legend represented, in Middle English verse, by *Joseph of Arimathie* and by *The Holy Grail*[1] of Lonelich. Both poems are versions, the one partial, the other, originally, nearly complete, of the French prose romance known as the *Grand St. Graal,* which, in its presents form, dates from about 1240,[2] and is, probably, the latest portion of that great body of French romance dealing with the Grail legend, which began with the *Perceval* or *Conte du Graal* of Chrétien de Troyes about 1175. The *Grand St. Graal* treats of that portion of the Grail legend known as the Early History.[3] An older version of the Early History, which has been used in the present redaction of the *Grand St. Graal,* is the metrical *Joseph d'Arimathie* (ca. 1215[4]) of Robert de Boron. Robert's poem ends where Brons, Joseph's brother-in-law, with Joseph's

---

[1] See XVIII.   [2] G. Paris.
[3] Nutt.   [4] G. Paris.

7*

company, and with the Grail in charge, departs by divine command for the West, Joseph remaining in the East.

The English *Joseph* is an abridgment of a part only of the *GSG*. According to Skeat,[1] rather less than 100 lines have been lost at the beginning of the poem. There is nothing to show that the MS. is incomplete at the end.[2] The poet follows, in the main, his French original, but in his effort at compression does not always escape being obscure.[3]

The origin of the Early History of the Grail cannot be studied satisfactorily apart from the origin of the whole legend. Though the Quest, the second portion of the legend, may offer in itself a consistent whole,[4] yet even its earliest version presupposes[5] the Early History, and nearly all the versions refer to it directly. The question then arises, Is the Quest a development from the Early History, or is the Early History, as Nutt says, an 'explanatory and supplementary after thought' to the Quest?

The views upon the origin of the Grail legend as summarized by Nutt,[6] show, in the main, three theories. (1) That the story of the Quest is of Celtic origin, the Grail itself being but the Christianized form of a pagan feature. A definite opinion on the origin of the Early History is not usually reported, but the inference clearly is (this seems also to be the view of Nutt[7]) that the Early History, based probably upon a nucleus of Christian legend on the conversion of Britain by Joseph of Arimathea, or, perhaps, merely upon the accounts concerning Joseph in the canonical and apocryphal gospels,[8] was developed principally by the French poets in the interests of the further Christianization of the Celtic story. (2) The Grail legend, in all fundamental features, is the development of Christian legend,

---

[1] pp. viii—ix. [2] See Skeat, 66. [3] Skeat, pp. xvi, 53.
[4] Nutt, 93. [5] Nutt, 95; Heinzel, 186. [6] Ch. IV.
[7] pp. 218—224.
[8] For the legendary sources on Joseph known to de Boron, see Birch-Hirschfeld, 241; Gröber, 522.

though, in the Quest portion, some features of less importance may be of Celtic origin.[1] (3) Between these two
theories stands another, that of Birch-Hirschfeld (1877):
The Early History was the invention of Robert de Boron
(who knew the apocryphal writings on Joseph of Arimathea)
for the purpose of connecting the Arthurian legend with
the Christian past. The table prepared by Joseph in the
East and the Round Table of Arthur and his knights represent that at which Christ ate the Last Supper with his
disciples, the Grail being the symbol of the Saviour's bodily
presence at the Supper, and also commemorating his death.
Joseph, who laid his body in the grave, was the natural
guardian of the Grail. Both Joseph and the Grail came
necessarily to England, for where the third wondrous table
and the third Grail guardian were to be, there must the
Grail also be.

As the latest and most fully developed representatives,
respectively, of the first and second theories, the work of
Nutt (1888) and that of Heinzel (1891) deserve, so far as
they bear upon the Early History, some attention in detail.

Nutt's theory of the Celtic origin of the Quest does
not necessitate his view of the Early History as an 'explanatory and supplementary afterthought'. Such, however,
he considers it, for the following reasons. (1) The English
Sir Perceval and the Welsh *Peredur,* which do not know
the Grail, also know nothing of the Early History;[2] a fact,
which of itself gives no uncertain hint as to which portion
of the romance is the original, and which the accretion.
(2) The later in date the versions of the Quest, the more
strongly marked is the influence of the Early History, 'and
pari passu the increasing prominence given to the Christian

---

[1] The view of Paulin Paris does not fall exactly under this head.
While holding that the Early History is a British legend, between
whose lines 'may be read a long struggle between heretic Britain and
orthodox Rome', he assigns a large share of influence to Celtic traditions;
the Grail itself and the lance being originally pagan symbols. See
Nutt, pp. 103—4.

[2] p. 68.

mystic side of the Grail'.[1] (3) As the emphasis of the Quest upon the Early History increases, its own leading motive becomes confused.[2] (4) The Grail itself is believed to be originally a feature of Celtic legend. In a number of Celtic 'quest' tales, the hero accomplishes his purpose by means of three magic talismans, sword, lance, and food-producing vessel;[3] in other tales, the vessel contains a healing or life restoring balsam.[4]

(5) The romances afford a clue by which we may explain the transformation of the pagan vessel of increase and healing into the Christian sacred vessel. Of the two accounts of the conversion of Britain in the Early History, the Brons version, though later in form, clearly represents an older and purer form of the Quest than does the Joseph version.[5] According to this account,[6] Brons is the guardian of the holy vessel and, in one version, fisher of the mystic fish, whilst in another his son Alain takes this part. In this Brons legend we notice the Celtic names of the personages and their connection with the Celtic paradise, Avalon. There is repeated insistence upon the connection between the Grail host and Avalon. Finally, Brons is the possessor of 'secret words' and may not die until he has revealed them to his grandson. But the name Brons suggests to students of Celtic legend that of Bran, the representative of an old Celtic god of the otherworld, and owner of the cauldron of renovation. He is also the hero, in later Welsh tradition, of a conversion legend, where he is known as Bran the Blessed, and according to which he first brought the faith of Christ to the nation of the Cymry from Rome, where he was seven years a hostage. In a confusion between Bran, Lord of the Cauldron, and Bran the Blessed lies the first step in the transformation of the *Peredur*-saga into the Quest of the Holy Grail. As hero of a conversion legend, Bran the Blessed was supplanted by Joseph of

---

[1] pp. 92, 93.   [2] p. 90.   [3] pp. 181—6.
[4] pp. 186—7, 202.   [5] p. 218. See pp. 76—80, 93—4.
[6] See pp. 218—220.

Arimathea, a familiar and favorite legendary figure[1] on British soil. The connection between the two perhaps was made at Glastonbury, where Cymric myth locates the Celtic paradise, Avalon,[2] and where one of the earliest of Christian churches in Britain was established. Then into the Quest tale, where the king of the bespelled castle corresponds to Bran, Lord of the Shades, was introduced a Christian feature: through the natural association of Joseph of Arimathea with the story of the Passion, the spear and the lance, part of the gear of the old Celtic gods, became transformed, respectively, into the spear with which the side of Christ was pierced, and the dish used at the Last Supper.

The Bran-Joseph hypothesis just stated is Nutt's 'connecting link'. G. Paris,[3] who says that he is in accord with Nutt upon all essential points, remarks, however, that his hypotheses upon the British origin of the early history of the Grail lack solidity. Rhŷs,[4] while not attaching importance to the conversion legend concerning Bran the Blessed on account of its probably late date, points out some additional resemblances in the legend of this hero to that of the Grail, his conclusion being that 'the origin of Brons' Grail is to be sought in a Welsh story about Bran the Blessed, though no such is extant in the precise form which that of the Grail would seem to postulate'.

Heinzel, the most thorough-going advocate of the Christian legendary origin of the Early History and of the leading features of the Quest, in his detailed consideration of the different Grail romances, aims to show the conception of the Grail legend held by its different redactors—that is, their conception of the Grail and of the persons and things in direct connection with it—and, where possible, to explain the origin of the various features of the legend. The conclusions drawn from the study of the romances he frequently supports by other legends from sources certainly or probably

---

[1] pp. 220—222.

[2] Cf. Rhŷs, *Arthurian Legend*, Ch. XIV.

[3] *Rom.* XVIII 588.   [4] *op. cit.*, pp. 308—311.

uninfluenced by them. The following seem his most important points on the development of the Early History.

The Grail was originally a blood relic, a vessel containing the blood from the wounds of Christ. It attracted to itself other blood relics and holy objects,[1] such as the bleeding lance—which is the spear wherewith the centurion pierced the side of Christ—and the Veronica-cloth upon which was imprinted his likeness. The Grail was not originally identified with the dish used at the Last Supper. This had its own history,[2] which originally was not connected with that of the Grail. The identification was, however, an important step in the development of the Grail legend, since with this identification is connected[3] probably the power of satisfying hunger ascribed to the Grail, and certainly the power to distinguish the evil from the good at the Grail table, as well as the formation of the table itself. The Grail is also related to the sacrifice of the Mass, to Transubstantiation, and to the Trinity, as something perhaps similar to the chalice containing the wine.[4]

Joseph of Arimathea, who had received and entombed the body of Christ, was naturally associated with the Grail. But, since Joseph was not himself present at the Crucifixion, the conception[5] that represents the blood as caught and preserved by certain believers (Nicodemus, or James, or the Virgin Mary with other women) may be older. According to the version of one of Chrétien's continuators,[6] which Heinzel believers older than that of Chrétien or de Boron, while Joseph was imprisoned on account of the honor that he paid the Grail, it was not with him in prison. Certain legends, not connected with the Grail romances, point to the conclusion that, before de Boron, there existed a legend in which appeared the forty years imprisonment and the wonderful sustainment of Joseph without food and drink, not by means of the Grail, but merely by divine

---

[1] See p. 180.   [2] p. 47; Birch-Hirschfeld, 223.   [3] p. 46.
[4] p. 179.   [5] p. 49.
[6] 2nd interpolation in pseudo-Gautier, Potvin's ed., p. 343 ff., vv. 1—229.

help, as, in the gospel of Nicodemus, he was freed by divine help. This conception of the maintainance of Joseph's life in a supernatural manner was united with that of Joseph as possessor of the Grail. Nothing would be more natural than the use of the Grail in order to give him food and light in prison.

In the legends of the conversion of Britain by Joseph and others, the blood relics, according to old English accounts,[1] do not appear at all, and in some later accounts they differ entirely from the Grail. Features[2] in the romances, also, point to an old legend on the conversion of Britain, without the Grail. It therefore seems that the real English tradition of the blood of Christ and the vessel in which it was preserved is, like the legend of the conversion of Britain by Joseph, different from that of the French romances.

Next to the Holy Grail, the most important feature of the Early History is the figure of Joseph of Arimathea. The short imprisonment, from which he was released by Christ, the version of the gospel of Nicodemus and of the second interpolation of the pseudo-Gautier, represents doubtless the original legend. The long imprisonment of forty years, from which he was freed by Vespasian, arose from a confusion between Joseph of Arimathea and the learned author Josephus Flavius, who in 69 A. D. was released by Vespasian from a two years' imprisonment, and, after the conquest of Jerusalem, went with him to Rome. (Manessier makes Joseph of Arimathea go to Rome with Vespasian, and from there to Britain.)

According to de Boron, Joseph does not go to Britain, but remains in the Orient. This undoubtedly represents the earlier version. The legend of the conversion of Britain by Joseph is of a kind with the legends ascribing the conversion of different countries of Europe to disciples of Christ.[3] The oldest accounts[4] of the conversion of Britain

---

[1] pp. 49, 179.   [2] See, especially, pp. 134, 176.
[3] See pp. 38, 41.   [4] Gildas, Nennius, Bede.

say nothing of the mission of Joseph. The *Carta S. Patricii* (before 1135 [1]) makes the first converters twelve disciples of Philipp and James, the builders of the oldest church in Glastonbury. William of Malmesbury [2] mentions Joseph and twelve others sent by Philipp as the builders of a chapel of the Virgin. The English legend [3] connects Joseph not only in life but in death with Glastonbury, while the French romances know nothing of this relation. In the oldest version of the French legend, [4] Joseph and his friends or relatives, among whom are Nicodemus and Joseph's sister, are banished by the Jews, and come, probably in a rudderless vessel, to England. The passage in the ship was later [5] transformed to one upon Josephe's shirt.

The origin of Josephe, Joseph's son, is found in the union of the accounts concerning Joseph and Josephus Flavius, who has also been conceived of as a Christian priest. Josephe, as a priest, and as, therefore, a holier man than his father, supplanted Joseph as the real converter, in Britain as in the Orient.

Brons, who appears in two of the romances [6] as the converter of Britain, Joseph remaining in the East, was originally Nicodemus and the hero of a separate conversion legend. [7] The name Brons supplanted that of Nicodemus, from the fact that Nicodemus, who had made an image of Christ, was conceived of as the husband of Veronica, the owner of another likeness. Brons comes from [8] *mulier Veronica* (Veronica = Fronica; *mulier Veronica* =, in French, *femme de Vron, Bron, or d'Ebron*, which, at first meaning woman from Vron etc., became later understood

---

[1] p. 41.

[2] *De antiquitate ecclesiae Glastoniensis* (Gale's *Hist. Britann. Script.* I 292). Heinzel, pp. 43—4, in opposition to Zarncke (Paul u. Braune's *Beiträge* III 331 f.) maintains the genuineness of this passage. Cf. *Zs. f. rom. Phil.* XIX 329—32.

[3] pp. 42—45, and Skeat's ed., pp. 68—71.

[4] 2nd interpolation of pseudo-Gautier.   [5] *Grand St. Graal.*

[6] De Boron's *Joseph* and the Didot-*Perceval.*

[7] p. 92.   [8] p. 94.

as wife of Vron, Bron, or Ebron). Veronica, being a missionary to the West—according to another legend[1] she and her husband Amator converted Provence—, her husband also became such; then the figure of the woman as missionary retreated into the background, and, through the connection[2] of Joseph of Arimathea with Nicodemus, England became the field of his mission. It is also probable that there was once a tradition of the conversion of England by Nicodemus independent[3] of his connection with Joseph. Was Brons perhaps Bran the Blessed, the apostle of Wales?[4]

The wife of Nicodemus became also the sister of Joseph. In the romances she is called, not Veronica,[5] but Eniseus.[6] In the 2nd Interpolation of the pseudo-Gautier, the sister of Joseph is unnamed, but possesses the likeness of Christ. The conception of the owner of this relic as the sister of Joseph was effected through several influences: the attraction between two such relics as the Grail and the likeness of Christ; the connection of her husband, Nicodemus, with Joseph; and the relationship of Lazarus to Martha and Mary Magdalene, also owners of a likeness and missionaries to the West.

Brons through his Fish, which, like the Grail, by its mere presence possessed the power of satisfying hunger, became the 'Rich Fisher', which title, or that of 'Fisher-King' was transmitted to his descendants through the line of Alain. How the Fish came to be ascribed to Brons is not at all clear. It seems most probable[7] that, originally belonging to Peter, who also appears as a converter of England,[8] it was later transferred to Brons, before the union of the Brons with the Joseph legend. The presence of the Fish upon the Grail table beside the Grail is evidence of the fusion of two conversion legends.[9]

---

[1] p. 95. [2] p. 45. [3] pp. 45, 46.

[4] pp. 93, 95, 98. On Bran, see also pp. 97, 192.

[5] See p. 93.

[6] This name also indicates the ownership of the likeness. For derivation, see p. 95.

[7] p. 97. [8] p. 41. [9] p. 92.

The story of the conversion of Evelach and Seraphe was suggested by the apocryphal story of Simon and Judas, for which there seems to be some historical background. The name of Galaad comes from the Old Testament.[1]

5. Metre. 709 alliterative long lines. The divergencies of the poem from the general metrical scheme of the 14th century alliterative verse are, according to Luick,[2] more numerous and significant than in the case of the *Alexander* fragments. It is especially distinguished from the other poems of its class by the fact that, in each half line, there is usually but one alliterating letter.[3] Skeat[4] finds the verse structure rugged; Rosenthal[5] speaks of it as extremely correct and standing, seemingly, not far from that of the *Alexander*; Luick[6] thinks the judgment of Skeat more correct.

6. Dialect. S. W. Midland, according to Brandl; W. Midland, according to Skeat.[7] The forms have been frequently altered by a Southern scribe.[7]

7. Date. *Ca.* 1350.[8] Ten Brink[9] considers this poem and the *Alexander* fragments the oldest of the 14th century alliterative poems. Skeat[10] thinks that the poem may safely be dated not later than 1360, but prefers *ca.* 1350, since the metre is of a 'more rugged and earlier character than even that of *William of Palerne*.' The 'earlier character' of the metre, is shown by the fact that each line has but two alliterating letters. Luick,[11] while not considering this argument weighty, yet, upon phonological grounds, supports Ten Brink's conclusion.

8. Author. Unknown.

9. Bibliography.
Manuscripts: Vernon, Oxford.

---

[1] Numbers 26 : 29 etc. (Vulgate).   [2] *Angl.* XI 569.
[3] Cf. Skeat, p. x; Rosenthal, in *Angl.* I 437, n.
[4] p. x; see under 7.   [5] p. 417.   [6] p. 569.   [7] p. xi.
[8] Ed. p. x.   [9] I 32.   [10] p. x.   [11] *Angl.* XI 571—2.

Editions: Skeat, *EETS. ES.,* No. 44, 1871. In his edition, Skeat prints also a prose *Lyfe of Joseph of Armathy,* printed by Wynkyn De Worde; a prose *De Sancto Joseph Ab arimathia,* printed by Pynson, 1516; a religious legend, *Here begynneth the lyfe of Joseph of Armathia,* concluding with *A praysing to Joseph,* (456 vv. in all) followed by an 'Officium', printed by Pynson, 1520.

For the editions of the OF. original see XVIII 9.

General References: Ten Brink I 332—3, 171—4 (Grail legend); Brandl, § 73. For analyses of de Boron's *Joseph* and of the *Grand St. Graal,* see Birch-Hirschfeld, pp. 150—8, 9—28; Nutt, pp. 64a—d, 52—64. On the conceptions and ideals of the Grail legend, see Nutt's last chapter.

Monographs: (The following works are those on the Grail legend that are referred to under 4.) Birch-Hirschfeld, *Die Sage vom Graal,* Leipsic, 1877; Nutt,[1] *Studies on the Legend of the Holy Grail,* L., 1888 (cf. G. Paris, *Rom.* XVIII 588—901); Heinzel, *Ueber die französischen Graalromane, Denkschriften der kaiserl. Akad. d. Wissenschaften, phil.-hist. Cl.,* XL, Vienna, 1892: rev.[2] by Golther, *Ltbl.,* 1892 (2), 50 ff. (gives a good idea the work); Martin, *Anz. f. d. Alt.,* XVIII 253—61; Suchier, *Zs. f. rom. Phil.,* XVI 269.—On Glastonbury and its Abbey, see Paul u. Braune's *Beiträge* III 326 ff.; Skeat's *JA.,* p. xxiii; Rhŷs, (*op. cit.,* on p. 85) Ch. XIV; Baist, *Zs. f. rom. Phil.,* XIX 326—45 (on Wm. of Malmesbury's *De antiquitate Glastoniensis ecclesiae).*

XVIII. The Holy Grail.

1. Subject. The history of the Grail and its first guardians, from its consecration until after the conversion of Britain.

---

[1] This and the manual of G. Paris, are the most convenient books for general reference on the Grail legend.

[2] In the case of works not bearing directly upon the English poems, the reviews are not given unless it seems specially advisable.

2. Specimen. Vv. 273—78, 285—92. Mordreins prays that he may not die

'Tyl that þe goode knyht of þe Nynthe degre
Of Sire Nasciens that I Myht se,
whiche þe Merveilles of Seint Graal schal do,
that I mowe sen hym to-foren me go,
that I myhte hym boþe Clippe & kisse,
And that were mochel of my worldly blisse'.

A voice promises:

'For deyen schalt þou nowher here
Tyl that knyht to-foren the Apere;
and what tyme he Cometh to the,
thy sihte Aʒen schal ʒolden be
that thou schalt se ful Openly,
Alle Manere Of thing þat is the by;
Ek thanne Of thy woundes heled schalt þou be,
and not to foren, sire kyng, Sekerle'.

3. Story. See XVII.

4. Origin. As already stated,[1] *The Holy Grail* of Lonelich is a translation of the long French prose romance known as the *Grand St. Graal,* which, according to Skeat,[2] the translator follows with tolerable closeness. The only MS. of Lonelich's translation has lost its beginning, nearly eleven chapters being missing. The MS. begins with the last twenty two lines of Chapter XI. In Chapter XXVII v. 26, the English omits the account of the nature and origin of 'Turning Island'. On the origin of the 'Early History' of the Grail, see XVII 4. In Chapter XXIV, v. 185, Furnivall points out the omission of a long passage on the miraculous visit of Salustes to Mordreins.

5. Metre. *Ca.* 23 794 verses, in 4-stressed couplets.

6. Dialect.[3] That of the South or of the S. Midland, or, more exactly, in an English that was more or less vulgar, but without a trace of the Northern dialect.

---

[1] XVII 4.   [2] *Joseph of Arimathie,* p. xxxiii.   [3] *Brandl,* § 113.

7. Date. *Ca.* 1450, according to the editor.

8. Author. Herry Lonelich, skynner (Ch. LVI, v. 533).

9. Bibliography.

Manuscripts: 80, Corpus Christi Coll., Cambridge.

Editions: Furnivall, *Seynt Graal or The Sank Ryal*, printed for the Roxburghe Club, 1861—63, 2 vols.

Furnivall, *The History of The Holy Grail, EETS. ES.* Nos. 20, 24, 28, 30, 1874—78.

The OF. original is printed in Furnivall's ed. of 1861—3.

General References: Brandl, § 113. See XVII.

XIX. Arthour and Merlin.

1. Subject. Merlin, the Wizard: his direction of the fortunes of Britain in the reign of Uther Pendragon and of Arthur.

2. Specimen. (1) Vv. 2195—2214:

    & afterward, wiþ outen fable,
    Our king bigan þe rounde table,
    Ðat was þurch Merlines hest,
    Of kniʒtes, þat men wist best
    In þis warld þurch out,
    Ðat table schuld sitte about;
    At þat table non sitt miʒt,
    Bot he were noble & douhti kniʒt,
    Strong & hende, hardi & wise,
    Certes & trewe wiþ outen feyntise;
    Her non oþer schuld faile
    No neuer fle out of bataile,
    Whiles he on fot stond miʒt,
    Bot ʒif hem departed þe niʒt.
    At bataile & at bord al so
    Bi hem selue þai schuld go,

So monkes don in her celle;
Bi hem selue þai eten, ich telle;
Wher wer were alder mast,
Þai were þider sent on hast.

3. Story.[1] Constans, king of Britain, has three sons:
Constans, a monk, Aurelius Ambrosius, and Uther Pendrgon.
The king, dying, appoints the monk his successor. Fortiger,
Constans' powerful steward, though pledged to aid 'king
Moyne', refuses his help when Angys of Denmark invades
England. Messengers from the British princes, when assured
of Fortiger's help if Moyne were dead, murder Moyne, and
make Fortiger king.

Fortiger tries to build on Salisbury plain a castle,
whose foundations are twice mysteriously razed. Astrologers
announce that the work must be besmeared with the death
blood of a child born without man's intervention. Fortiger
sends to find this boy, Merlin, whose birth was on this
wise. Certain rebel angels, who, instead of falling into Hell
remained in mid-air, wishing to defeat the results of the
Incarnation, determined that a demon should beget a child
upon an earthly maiden. This was finally accomplished,
though without the maiden's knowledge. When her preg-
nancy was discovered, she was condemned to death, but
finally granted a two years' respite.

The child, when born, was immediately baptized as
Merlin by Blaise, a hermit, the fiends thus losing their
power over his nature. When two and a half years old,
Merlin saved his mother at her trial by declearing his
supernatural origin, and by proving the justice's own ille-
gitimate birth.

The history of Merlin's origin and of his later deeds
are, in time, told by Merlin to Blaise, who writes them all
in a book.

Merlin, brought before Fortiger, declares that the foundations of the citadel have been destroyed by earthquakes

---

[1] According to MS. A.

caused by the fighting of a red and a white dragon beneath the ground. When the dragons are discovered, Fortiger makes Merlin his chief counsellor. Merlin declares that the dragons symbolize the coming contest of Fortiger with Aurelius and Uther Pendragon. The prophecy is soon confirmed. Fortiger, though aided by Angys and his 'Saracens', perishes; Aurelius, by Merlin's counsel, defeats Angys, who is slain; later, Aurelius is slain, and Uther Pendragon becomes king.

Uther Pendragon falls in love with Igerna, the beautiful duchess of Cornwall. Assuming her husband's appearance by means of Merlin's magic, Uther gains access to Igerna's chamber Arthur. The duke is slain that night. After some time, Uther Pendragon formally marries Igerna, who remains ignorant of the identity of her seducer. Merlin demands that their child be delivered to him. The child is baptized as Arthur and given to the knight Antour, who educates him in ignorance of his parentage. After Uther Pendragon's death, while men are praying for a sign by which his successor may be designated, a miraculous stone with a sword, Escalibor, driven into it, is found before the church. Arthur alone can draw the sword from the stone, and is proclaimed king.

At the coronation, Arthur's true parentage is revealed by Merlin, and six rival claimants for the throne are defeated. More kings now form a confederacy against Arthur. By Merlin's magic and counsel they are finally routed, though not entirely subdued. Saracens invade the land. Galachin and Gawain, seeing the lack of unity among the Britons, resolve to reconcile their uncle Arthur to their respective fathers, king Nantes and king Lot. Going to London to seek Arthur, they conquer three Saracen armies. They find Arthur, under Merlin's guidance, gone to assist king Leodigan—whose daughter he wishes to marry—against one Rion. Victorious in his attack upon the enemy, Arthur is conducted triumphantly to the bath by Guenever, and declares his love to her. Various Christian victories follow, in which Gawain and Ywain, counselled and magically

8

aided by Merlin, play an important part. Arthur is betrothed to Guenever, and, with Merlin's magic aid, defeats Rion with great slaughter.

4. Origin. The Merlin legend [1] is represented in Middle English, by *Arthour and Merlin,* a poem of the 13th century, and, besides the version found in Sir Thomas Malory's famous compilation, by two other 15th century versions, one in verse by Lonelich, and one in prose.

All these versions go back to the French Merlin romance. In considering the origin of this romance, its two parts must be clearly distinguished. The first part, ending with the coronation of Arthur, is the work of Robert de Boron. Of his poem we now possess only a fragment, [2] but his entire narrative has been preserved in French prose redactions. [3] The second part is a continuation of Robert's narrative by his redactors.

Robert's poem is based upon Geoffrey of Monmouth, while the nucleus of the legend is still older. Jewish sources and parallels for the earlier part of the legend have been pointed out by Gaster, who, Kölbing [4] thinks, has given irrefutable evidence that at least the history of Merlin's youth represents the fusion of different Jewish legends on the building of Solomon's temple, and on Ashmedai and Ben Sira. The first trace [5] of the Merlin legend in European literature is found in the British historian Nennius (end of the 8th century), [6] who tells how king Vortigern, unable to build his citadel because the materials collected in the daytime disappear at night, receives from his wise men the revelation concerning the child born without a father. When the child is found, its mother swears that she never knew a man.

---

[1] For the different versions, see Kölbing, pp. cvii—xi.

[2] 504 verses.

[3] The prose account is much interpolated, and contains more details than de Boron's poem. Sommer, III 6, n. 2.

[4] p. cvi.

[5] The extant references to Merlin in Welsh literature are later than Geoffrey of Monmouth. *DNB.* XXXVII 286.

[6] pp. 31—4.

The sequel is as narrated above. The child's prophecy concerning the meaning of the dragons and their contest is brief. Questioned as to his name and origin, the boy answers that he is called Ambrosius or, in British, Embriesguletic (king Ambrosius), and that a Roman consul was his father.[1] The king assigns to Ambrosius the city in which they now are and all the western provinces of Britain. Ambrosius does not again appear in Nennius.

It is evidently the story of Nennius that Geoffrey of Monmouth[2] has amplified, and connected with Arthur. Geoffrey gives the history of Constantine's three sons and the treacherous Vortigern. Merlin's mother is a princess and a nun, who confesses to Vortigern that, as she was once with her companions in their chambers, there appeared to her a most beautiful young man, who often embraced her eagerly, and kissed her; then, after a little, suddenly vanished. But many times after this he would talk with her when she sat alone, without appearing visibly. After a long time, he came again several times in the form of a man, and became the father of her child. One of the king's wise men, when consulted, said, referring to Apuleius on the Demon of Socrates, that Merlin's father might have been one of those spirits, called incubuses, who inhabit between the earth and the moon, and who are of the nature partly of men, partly of angels. When brought before the king, the supernatural child has become a youth. His name is Merlin,[3] or, in full, 'Merlinus Ambrosius'. He says nothing concerning his parentage, but predicts the history of the island to the death of Henry I and for an indefinite period beyond. Geoffrey's most interesting addition to the

---

[1] San Marte (ed. of Geoffrey of Monmouth's *Historia,* p. 331) speaks of this passage of the child's answer as apparently corrupted. On a possible confusion between Ambrosius the king and Ambrosius the enchanter, see *DNB. op. cit.* p. 286, and the ME. prose *Merlin,* I p. ii ff.

[2] Bk. VI, Ch. 17 ff.

[3] On the origin of the name, see G. Paris, § 54. On the two Merlins cf. *DNB. op. cit.* p. 286 ff.

legend of Merlin is the story of the love of Uther Pendragon for Igerna.[1] Arthur's legitimacy and his right to
the throne are unquestioned.[2]

Geoffrey's account of Merlin is repeated by different
chroniclers[3] in prose and in verse; but, with the exception
of the notable lines in Wace which tell us that, for his
noble barons,

> ' Fist Artus la roonde table,
> Dont Breton dient mainte fable:
> Iloc seeient li vassal
> Tuit chivalment et tuit ingal,'[4]

no features of importance for the Merlin romance are added
until Robert de Boron introduced Merlin into romance,
making the story of which he is the central figure the
connecting link between the legend of Joseph of Arimathea
and that of Perceval.[5] The leading features of de Boron's
romance are those of the 'story' given above. The
changes and additions made by Robert are discussed
by G. Paris[6] in the Introduction to the Huth *Merlin*.
Only a few of his points can here be noted. The
feature of the council of the demons was taken, evidently,
from the gospel of Nicodemus. The manner of Merlin's
conception, though based upon Geoffry, seems to have
been influenced by the ideas in circulation upon the
manner in which Antichrist was to come into the world.[7]
The happy idea of the defeat of the plan of the demons
owing to the innocence[8] of Merlin's mother is Robert's own.
The figure of Blaise, though entirely unnecessary to the
narrative, is very important in the general plan of the work

---

[1] Dunlop (I 153) thinks that the disguise of Uther was suggested
by the story of Jupiter and Alcmena; cf. p. 152, n. 1.

[2] The features of the romance drawn from Geoffrey will not be
noted beyond this point; they deal principally with the wars of Arthur.

[3] See Kölbing, pp. cvii—viii.   [4] *Brut*, v. 9998 f.

[5] See ed. of the Huth *Merlin*, by G. Paris and Ulrich, 1886, p. ix.

[6] pp. x—xxiii.   [7] See p. xiii, n.

[8] Cf. *Arthour and Merlin*, vv. 988—990.

of which the *Merlin* is a part. This imaginary scribe appears again in Robert's *Perceval*.[1] Kölbing[2] thinks that Blaise may have been suggested to Robert by a hermit that appears in Layamon (v. 18762 ff.). Robert's 'capital' invention, for the general plan of his work, is his connection of the Round Table, which Wace (v. 9998) expressly says was instituted by Arthur,[3] with the two holy tables of Jesus and Joseph of Arimathea. His account of the loves of Uther Pendragon and Igerna differs considerably from that of Geoffry, especially in regard to the birth of Arthur, Robert's object in the changes made being, evidently, to increase the prestige and to aggrandize the rôle of Merlin. Though not expressly stated, it seems clear that the sword-test[4] was arranged by Merlin.

The second part of the romance, the continuation of de Boron's narrative, has been variously called *Livre du roi Artus*,[5] *Livre d'Arthur, La Suite de Merlin*,[6] its object being to fill in the gap in the narrative of the Arthurian romances between the coronation of Arthur and the arrival of Lancelot at court. This the author does, 'either by developing the indications of the Lancelot, or by returning to Geoffrey of Monmouth or to the *Perceval* of Robert, or by compiling narratives of diverse origin'.[7]

Turning now to our Middle English *Arthour and Merlin*, we find that there are two versions of the poem, designated by Kölbing as *A* and *y*.[8] *A* is the older, *y*, the younger version.[9] Both are derived from an older and more complete

---

[1] The Didot-*Perceval*. Nutt, 94, and Heinzel, 187, do not ascribe it to Robert.

[2] p. cxii, n.

[3] Cf. *Arthur, EEIS*. No. 2, vv. 43—52.

[4] For origin, see Paris, p. xx, and Kölbing, p. cxiii, n. 2.

[5] P. Paris, V 356.   [6] G. Paris' ed. of the Huth MS., p. xxiii.

[7] The Huth *Merlin*, p. xxiv.

[8] See under 9. *Manuscripts*. For differences in the narratives, see Kölbing, pp. clviii—lxi, clxv—vii, clxviii—lxxi.

[9] Bülbring, *op. cit.*, 259, holds the reverse relation the more probable.

text *a.* Kölbing's study of the poem, which he designates
as *E,* gives the following results as to sources: The versions
of the Merlin legend before Robert de Boron, Kölbing
designates as redaction I; Robert's version and those after
him, as redaction II. Of the two parts of the Merlin legend,
that preceding and that following the coronation of Arthur,
the second part undoubtedly belongs to red. II. The first
part, although as a rule it agrees with red. II, the resemblance between *E* and *RB*[1] being especially significant,
shows, nevertheless, features that diverge from red. II and
agree with red. I;[2] the two most important being (1) the
names given to the sons of king Constans, and (2) the way
in which the poem opens, with the history of Constans and
his sons, instead of, as in red. II, with the circumstances
connected with the birth of Merlin, who in *E,* as in *RB,* is
to be the central figure. *E,* therefore, does not belong to
red. II, but represents a transition between I and II. Its
source must have been either the lost first version of Robert's
poem,[3] or the work of a predescessor of his, which Robert
must have known, for the resemblance between *E* and *RB*
is too significant to admit of any doubt upon this point.
In case such a predescessor for *RB* be accepted, the degree
of originality ascribed to Robert, already none too great,
will be considerably diminished.

Kölbing's conclusion in regard to the source of *E,* is
disputed by Bülbring.[4] In the first place, if Kölbing's view
be correct, and *E* does not belong to red. II, it seems strange
that the first and second parts of *E* should be connected
exactly as in the French prose redactions of *RB.* Furthermore, the two reasons of any weight in favor of Kölbing's
view may be set aside: the first,[5] as being an arbitrary
change made by the author of *A* (*y* follows red. II) and
inconsistently carried out, as *A* still shows traces of the

---

[1] de Boron's *Merlin.*   [2] pp. cxxii—iii.
[3] See the Huth *Merlin,* p. ix, n. 1.   [4] *E. St.* XVI, 257 ff.
[5] Kölbing does not ascribe great weight to this argument; see
p. cxxvi.

version of red. II; the other, the circumstances with which
the narrative begins, as being overweighed by positive
evidence that the source of E had originally an introduction
treating of Joseph of Arimathea and a continuation treating
of Perceval. This evidence consists of allusions,[1] occurring
in the same connection as the corresponding but fuller
passages of Robert, to the Round Table, to the empty seat
at the Table, and to the knight who should fulfil the
'meruails of þe greal'. The clear allusions to the Perceval
legend, would, if G. Paris' view[2] of the purpose of *Merlin*
be correct, of themselves argue that the source of E originally contained the Joseph legend. To a similar conclusion points the important part played by Blaise. If the
French source of E began with the *Joseph,* it could not
have contained the history of the sons of Constans, with
which E, in divergence from red. II, begins. This must
have been introduced by the English translator (or, less
probably, by a French scribe), who was more interested in
the deeds of the British kings than in the wonders of the
Grail; we observe that he knew of the 'Bruyt' and that,
while he frequently condenses the history of Merlin, he
occasionally makes additions to the history of Constans,
and seldom omits anything when telling of the warlike
deeds of the British kings. Bülbring therefore concludes
that the first as well as the second part of E belongs to
red. II.

The second part[3] of E, from the coronation of Arthur,
is based upon the *Livre d'Arthur.* The course of the
narrative in the two is, in general, entirely similar, and
there are numerous verbal correspondencies. E, notwithstanding its 'very respectable' length of almost ten thousand
verses, is incomplete, the last half of the French original
not being reproduced in the Auchinleck MS. When compared
with the French romance, E is found to be only a much
shortened translation of its source. Even some of the intro-

---

[1] Vv. 2195, 2220—2, 2750; see also v. 8891—3.
[2] *Merlin,* p. ix.   [3] Kölbing, p. cxxviii.

ductory landscape pictures, which Ten Brink has ascribed without reserve to the English poet, are suggested in his source.[1]

The aesthetic and poetical worth ascribed to the poem by Kölbing is slight. In the latter respect, it cannot compare with romances like *Alisaunder, Richard Coer de Lion,* or *King Horn.*

The three romances of *Arthour and Merlin, Alisaunder,* and *Richard Coer de Lion,* all of which Kölbing assigns to the same author, composed as they probably were in the reign of Edward I, are regarded by Brandl[2] as an expression of the national self consciousness aroused in England by the brilliant military achievements of that monarach, and expressing itself in the desire to hear the deeds of the greatest conquerors, extended heroic romances, in which love and exile at the most appear as episodes.

5. Metre.[3] *A* contains 9938 4-stressed verses, rimed in couplets. Often four successive verses have the same rime; six successive rimes (*e. g.* vv. 6439—44, 8799—8804) occur but seldom. In many cases, this repetition of the rime is used, undoubtedly, to heighten the effect of the verse, as at the beginning or the end of a division of the narrative, in a specially emphatic speech or at the close of a speech, in the lyrical nature-verses, and, finally, in vividly presented scenes of combat and of battle (*e. g.* v. 8799 ff.). Assonance is relatively frequent. A large number of verses show alliteration, the cases of which are elaborately classified by Kölbing.[4]

6. Dialect. Kölbing concludes[5] that *A* arose in S. E. England, in the vicinity of Kent.

7. Date.[6] Version *A* cannot be later than the first quarter of the 14th century, the period to which the MS. has generally been assigned. The relatively numerous cases

---

[1] See p. lxvii.   [2] § 35, 36.   [3] Kölbing, xxxiii—lii.
[4] pp. xxxix—lii.   [5] pp. lv—ix; see also Kaluza's review.
[6] Kölbing, lx.

of assonance point to a rather early period, perhaps the middle or third quarter of the 14th century.[1]

8. Author.[2] Kölbing concludes that the author of *Arthour and Merlin* is identical with the author of the romances of *Kyng Alisaunder* and *Richard Coer de Lion*; he is also somewhat inclined to ascribe to the same poet the romance of *The Seven Sages*.[3]

The common authorship of the three romances first mentioned is witnessed to, first of all, by the resemblance in the material and by the lyrical pieces serving as introductions to different divisions of the poems. The likeness of material is seen in the important feature, common to all three romances, of the mysterious origin of the hero; in the feature, common to *Alis.* and *A. and M.,* of the spear or sword that only the future world-conqueror or the rightful king can pluck from the earth or stone. Both Alexander and Merlin are credited with being able to speak as soon as they are born; and both have to bear the imputation of a dishonorable birth, in this case the corresponding couplets showing a marked verbal resemblance. Again, all three poems are principally composed of descriptions of battles, either between Christians and heathen, or between civilized Europeans and uncivilized races.

'Of all the ME. epic poems', says Kölbing,[4] 'only these three show the peculiar but very pleasing ornament of the introduction of some of the larger divisions of the poem by descriptions of nature or by mottoes.' These lyrical passages[5] celebrate the different months or seasons, especially the 'merry month of May'; sometimes they dwell on the occupations belonging to the season, or, occasionally, on its effect upon the appearance and feelings of men. In *Alis.,* sometimes, and once in *Richard,* these descriptions of nature are connected with proverbs and mottoes, thus imparting to the whole, a lyrical-didactic character. In *A. and M.* the

---

[1] For the later versions, see 9, *Manuscripts.*
[2] Kölbing, lx—cv. [3] p. civ. [4] p. lxii.
[5] See Ten Brink I 242.

lyrical passages are independent of what follows, though sometimes there is a correspondence between the season of the year celebrated and that in which the events following take place. Occasionally, in the other two poems, a connection of this kind is formally made by the author, as where in *Alis.* v. 145 f., after a description of April, the author continues: 'In this tyme, I understonde, etc.' As regards the originality of these passages, Kölbing [1] concludes that, in a few places, the passage was suggested by the original, but that the others were added independently.

The evidence in favor of a common author is further strengthened by resemblances in metre and in style as well as by the fact of a common dialect. It seems to be generally admitted by scholars in ME. that, in the case of *Alis.* and *A. and M.*, Kölbing has proved his point. [2] The evidence that *Richard* has the same author is not so strong.

Kölbing [3] finds some lines in the poems that suggest the religious profession of the author.

9. Bibliography. *Manuscripts:* [4] I. Version *A.* Auchinleck; see II. 9.

II. Version *y.* L. 150, Lincoln's Inn Library, beginning of the 15th century; [5] see *E. St.* VII 194 f.

P. Percy Folio, pp. 145—178, beginning of the 15th century. [5]

H. 6223 Harl., *ca.* 1650; [6] the first 62 verses.

D. 236 Douce.

Editions: Of *A.* Turnbull, for the Abbotsford Club, L. 1838; for correction of the text, see Kölbing's ed. pp. ix—xv.

Kölbing, in *Altengl. Bibliothek,* Leipsic, 1890; on the text, see ed., pp. xvi—xvii, and the reviews, *infra,* (except Wülker's and Bülbring's). Revs.: Zupitza, *Arch.* LXXXVII

---

[1] p. lxviii.

[2] Cf. the reviews of K.'s ed. Wülker remarks that none of the proofs are exactly compelling.

[3] pp. civ—v.   [4] Kölbing's ed. pp. xvii f.

[5] Kölbing, p. clxxii.   [6] Ward I 385.

88—94; Wülker, *Lit. Cbl.*, 1892 (16), 573—4; Kaluza, *Ltbl.*, 1891 (8), 265—71; Bülbring, *E. St.* XVI 251—268; Koeppel, *Mittheil.*, 1891 (4), 105—7; Schröer, *Zs. f. Vergl. Ltgesch.*, 1890, 409—412.

L. *PF. MS.* I 420 (first 16 vv.), 479 (last 28 vv.); Kölbing, *op. cit.*, pp. 275—359, 1980 vv.

D. Kölbing, *op. cit.*, pp. 275—355, 1278 vv.

Lonelich's *Merlin* (MS. 80 Corpus Christi Coll. Cambr.). The first 1638 verses are printed by Kölbing in *A. and M.*, p. 374 ff.; see The ME. prose *Merlin*, edited by Wheatley, with an introduction by D. W. Nash, *EETS.*, 1865—69.

General References: Ten Brink, I 244, II² 10. Brandl § 35, 36. Dunlop I 146—159. Ed. of the ME. prose *Merlin* I i—xvi. Translations of Geoffrey of Monmouth's *Historia* and of Nennius, in *Six Old English Chronicles*, ed. Giles, L. 1848. Analyses: Of *Arthour and Merlin*, Ellis, pp. 77—142: Part I according to MS. *L*, supplemented by *A*, Part II according to *A*; of Robert de Boron's *Merlin*, P. Paris, II 3—97,—Birch-Hirschfeld, (*op. cit.* on p. 109) 166—70; of *Le Roi Artus*, P. Paris, II 101—389.

Monographs: Gaster, *Jewish Sources of and Parallels to the Early Engl. Metrical Romances of King Arthur and Merlin*, a lecture delivered at the Anglo-Jewish Hist. Exhibition, Royal Albert Hall, June 23, 1887. L. 1887; *Die Sagen von Merlin*, San Marte, 1853, (contains the *Prophetia Merlini* and the *Vita Merlini*, cf. Ward I 207—9, 278 ff.) on Geoffrey of Monmouth's *Historia*, see Ward I 203 ff.; Ward on *Lailoken (Or Merlin Silvester)*, *Rom.* XXII 504—26.

XX. Merlin.

1. Subject. See XIX.

2. Specimen. Vv. 1616—1630.

Thanne Blayse anon, so god me save,
Dide ordeynen alle thinges, him nedid to have,

> And whanne that al thing redy was,
> Thanne cam Merlyn into that plas
> And anon began him telle,
> Of Cristes deth how it befelle,
> Also of Josep of Armathye,
> How of hym it happede, trewelye
> And of Aleyn and of Perown also,
> & of his compenye, how they departid tho;
> And thus endyd he of Josep there
> & of al his feleschepe also in fere
> And gan to tellen hym furtheremore
> Of þe parlement of þe develis thore,

Very little has as yet been published upon Lonelich's metrical version of the romance of *Merlin*.[1] Lonelich himself declares that his versified narrative is a translation of de Boron's work;[2] Kölbing concludes[3] that it is an independent translation of the French prose redaction of Robert's *Merlin*. Although consisting of about 28 000 verses, rimed in couplets, the poem is unfinished.

For the few facts that can be reported on the date, dialect, and author, see the section on Lonelich's *Holy Grail*.[4]

The MS., no. 80, is preserved in Corpus Christi College, Cambridge. The poem has never all been printed. Kölbing,[5] however, announces an edition by himself and Miss Mary Bateson to appear, 'in course of time', as a publication of the *EETS*. Extracts from the poem have been printed by: (1) Furnivall, *Seynt Graal,* Roxburghe Club, 1861—3, end of Vol. II; (2) Furnivall, *The History of The Holy Grail,* *EETS.*, 1874—8, 146 vv. on *The Birthe and Engendrure of Mordret*; (3) Kölbing, in *A. and M.,* vv. 1—1638. The extract begins with the parliament of the devils; for its end, see under 2.

---

[1] See Kölbing's *Arthour and Merlin,* (*A. and M.*) pp. xviii—xix, clxxx ff. For the sake of greater compactness, the usual form of presenting the material is, from this point, not followed.

[2] *A. and M.*, p. clxxx.   [3] *Op. cit.,* pp. clxxx—clxxxix.

[4] XVIII.   [5] *Op. cit.,* p. xix.

XXI. Sir Perceval of Galles.[1]

1. Subject. A youth brought up by his mother in a forest goes out into the world, avenges his father's death, rescues and weds a royal lady, and is finally reunited to his mother.

2. Specimen. Vv. 225—40:

> Evene whenne he wolde hym have;[2]
> Thus he wexe and wele thrave,
> And was reghte a gude knave
>   With-in a fewe ȝere;
> Fyftene wynter and mare
> He duellede in those holtes hare,
> Nowther nurture ne lare
>   Scho wolde hym none lere:
> Tille it byfelle on a day,
> The lady tille hir sone ganne say,
> Swete childe, I rede thou praye
>   To Goddez sone dere,
> That he wolde helpe the,
> Lorde, for his poustee,
> A gude mane for to bee,
>   And longe to duelle here!

3. Story. Perceval's father, brother-in-law to king Arthur, in a tournament given at Perceval's birth is slain for revenge by the Red Knight. Perceval's mother, 'Acheflour', brings up her son in a forest, in ignorance of the practices of chivalry. At fifteen, Perceval one day starts out to find the great God of whom his mother has told him. He meets Gawain, Iwain, and Kay, mounted and clad in green. Perceval asks which one is the great God who made the world. Gawain answers courteously that they

---

[1] The title in Halliwell's ed. The poem is usually referred to as *Sir Percyvelle.*

[2] The last three lines of the preceding stanza say that it was useless for any wild beast to flee from him 'Whenne that he wolde him have'.

are only knights of Arthur's court. The next day Perceval,
mounted upon a wild mare that he has caught, sets forth
to ask Arthur to make him a knight. His mother gives
him a ring as a parting token of remembrance, and advises
him to be 'of measure' in hall and in bower. He stops
at night at a hall where he sees only a sleeping lady, from
whom he takes a ring, placing his own ring upon her finger.
He rides rather rudely into Arthur's hall, but is courteously
received by the king, who notices his likeness to the late
Sir Perceval. Arthur promises to make Perceval a knight
if he will regain the king's gold cup, which the Red Knight,
who comes in after Perceval's arrival, has just carried off.
Perceval, destined to avenge his father, pursues the Red
Knight, demands the cup, and, upon being insultingly
answered, kills him by a skilfully aimed cast of his spear.
Unable to unlace the knight's armor, Perceval builds a fire
to burn him out of it. Gawain, coming up, removes the
armor. Perceval throws the corpse into the fire, puts on
the armor, and delivers the cup to Gawain, saying that
since he is now as great a knight as Arthur, he will not
return to the court. Meeting a witch, the mother of the
Red Knight, who would have restored him to life had not
his body been burned, Perceval kills her. While spending
the night with an old knight, really his uncle, he learns
from a messenger from 'Maydene-land' on his way to
Arthur's court of Lady Lufamour, now besieged by a Sultan
who wishes to marry her. Perceval starts for Maidenland
to slay the Sultan. Arriving there, he kills all the Saracens
before the castle. The grateful lady invites him into the
castle.

Arthur, who has learned of Perceval's undertaking
through Lufamour's messenger, and with three knights has
started to his assistance, arrives. The Sultan challenges
Perceval, who, after being knighted by Arthur, kills the
Sultan, weds Lufamour, and rules her land for a twelvemonth. Then he starts to find his mother. In a wood he
meets the lady from whom he took the ring, bound to a
tree by her lord, the Black Knight, who believes her guilty

of an intrigue with some stranger. Perceval overthrows the Black Knight, swears he never did the lady harm, returns her ring, and demands his, which has been given to a giant, the brother of the Sultan. After killing the giant, Perceval enters the castle and regains his ring. The porter tells him that the giant once offered it to a lady whom he loved. Upon seeing it she cried, 'Hast thou slain my son?' and ran to the woods distraught. After searching seven days, Perceval finds his mother. He carries her to the castle, where a draught is administered that causes a long sleep. She wakes sane. Perceval with his mother returns to his queen. Afterwards he goes to the Holy Land, where he wins many cities and is finally killed.

4. Origin. Among the Perceval romances, *Sir Percyvelle* [1] occupies a place of interest, not because of intrinsic poetical merit, but because of the place that has been claimed for it in the history of the origin of the Perceval legend.

A comparison [2] with the *Conte du Graal* of Chrétien de Troies—as regards date of actual composition the oldest of the Perceval romances and the point of departure in any study of them—discloses the following facts in regard to *SP*: (1) Though *SP* is more condensed, the two narratives correspond, important incident for incident, to the end of the adventure with the Red Knight. [3] (2) *SP* is much the shorter and simpler poem. After the adventure with the Red Knight, it has but two principal incidents, the rescue and winning of Lufamour and the reunion of the hero with his mother. Of the most famous incident of Chrétien's poem, namely Perceval's adventure in the Grail castle, of Perceval's subsequent history in quest of the Grail, and of the adventures of Gawain, features all found in Chrétien's poem, it knows nothing. In the absence of any features pertaining to the Quest, *SP* is unique among the Perceval

---

[1] = *SP*.   [2] See Steinbach.
[3] v. 821 of *SP*.

romances.[1] Its specially archaic character is illustrated by
Nutt,[2] who, in giving examples of the *Aryan Expulsion
and Return Formula* in Celtic legend, mentions several
features of the Perceval legend peculiar to *SP* and others
that are found only in *SP* and in *Peredur,* nearly all being
paralleled in the Celtic *Lay of The Great Fool,* prose
opening. The most striking are: Perceval's playing in the
forest with wild beasts, v. 176; his fleetness of foot,
vv. 221—4;[3] his catching the wild mare for a steed, v. 341;
his threatening Arthur with death if he be not knighted,
vv. 527—8; the prophecy that he is to avenge his father's
death,[4] vv. 567—8; his doing this; reunion with his mother.
Nutt remarks[5] also that in *SP* the details of the adventure
of the ring *i. e.* Perceval's kissing the sleeping lady and
leaving her a ring in exchange, vv. 473—6, are more in
accord with popular tradition than elsewhere.

The characteristics of *SP* just mentioned have led to
two very different theories in regard to its origin. On
account of its correspondence with the *Conte du Graal,* its
editor, Halliwell (1844), concluded that it was but an
abridgment of Chrétien's poem. This theory, slightly modified, is held by some modern scholars, and will be noticed
later.[6]

The poem's simplicity of plot and its specially archaic
features, have, however, led others to a very different conclusion. Before Halliwell, San Marte (1841) had already
claimed *SP* as 'the representative of an early Breton
jongleur poem, which knew nothing of the Grail legend';[7]

---

[1] In the Welsh version, *Peredur,* there is no Grail. The wondrous
objects seen by the hero are a mighty spear with three streams of
blood flowing from the point, and a salver, in which a man's head
swims in blood.

[2] *Folk-Lore Record,* IV 9—11; see also Nutt's *Studies,* 153—7.

[3] The text says that he learned to shoot so well (with his spear)
that no beast could escape from him. Peredur is also fleet of foot.

[4] *Peredur* has a revenge motive.

[5] Folk-Lore, *op. cit.,* 9, n. 3.   [6] pp. 131—32.

[7] Cited from Nutt's *Studies,* 99.

and the majority of scholars who have since expressed
their views on the origin of *SP* favor or maintain the
theory that *SP* represents an earlier version of the Perceval
legend than that known to Chrétien.[1] This theory is most
fully stated by Gaston Paris[2] (1888), according to whom
the *Conte du Graal* and *Peredur,* the Welsh version, go
back to an Anglo-Norman poem, which in turn was based
upon a Breton *lai.* *SP* stands nearer the Anglo-Norman
poem than do the other two. Speaking of Chrétien's source,
Paris says: 'It is probable that it came from a very
defective[3] transmission of a poem like the original of ours,
mingled with the tale of the "graal", or mysterious dish,
and of the bleeding lance: the narrative thus amplified
seems to be the source of the poem of Chrétien, and, for
a great part, of the Welsh *mabinogi* of Peredur, which is
not more original than the copy of this poem . . .'

A theory combining the two already stated was advanced by Steinbach (1885) as the result of his detailed
comparison of *SP* with the *Conte du Graal.* He maintains
that, while *SP* makes use of Chrétien's poem, it is not a
mere abridgment of the *Conte du Graal,* but that[4] 'into a
frame-work originally of Breton origin, with the use of
some popular features, partly of more ancient, partly of
later origin, perhaps invented by the Celts of Britain, and
with the addition of some parts recalling the description
of battles in the " chansons de geste", the English poet has
woven, in a free, abridged redaction, the *Conte du Graal*
to about v. 6000 '.[5] Nutt[6] accepts Steinbach's views as
'meeting the difficulties of the case fairly well', and that[7]

---

[1] For views expressed previous to 1871, favoring the 'early
version' theory, see Nutt's *Studies,* pp. 101. 102; see also Gervinus,
Geschichte der deutschen Dichtung, 1871, I 577; Hertz (Nutt, p. 125);
Kaluza, *E. St.* XII 91.

[2] *Hist. Litt.* XXX 12, 13, 260.

[3] 'It knew neither the true rôle of the Red Knight, nor the
meaning of the adventure of the ring.'

[4] p. 41.   [5] Cf. Kölbing, *Germ.* XIV 180.

[6] p. 150.   [7] p. 151.

'Sir Perceval like the Mabinogi has been influenced by Chrestien'. Heinzel [1] declares that neither Steinbach nor Golther [2] has shown the dependence of *SP* upon Chrétien, and that *SP* has alone preserved for us the original Perceval legend. Schofield, while concluding, [3] as the result of his comparison of the legend of the *Fair Unknown* [3] with *Peredur,* that the latter 'is not a mere working over of the *Conte du Graal,* but is based to a large extent upon some earlier version of the Perceval story, which, we may add, went back in all probability (though not necessarily directly) to a Celtic story', says [4] of *SP* that it 'is strikingly like Chrétien's narrative', remarking also that it cannot be said to show any agreement of importance with the interpolated introduction to that narrative. Here perhaps two facts may be mentioned which I do not remember having seen stated anywhere, namely, that the English and the Italian [5] version of the *Fair Unknown* story have one feature in common with *SP* not found in the *Peredur,* the reunion of the hero with his mother; also, Carduino is the avenger of his father, as is Sir Percyvelle.

From the opinions cited above, it is clear that the theory of *SP* as representing an early version of the Perceval legend seems to involve, or to depend upon, the theory of the Celtic origin of the legend. This theory has been elaborately defended by Nutt. From a comparison [6] of the different versions of the Grail romances he concludes that there was an older version of the legend than that known to Chrétien; and from parallels [7] found to incidents and features of the romances in Celtic (principally Irish and Scotch) legends and folk-tales, he concludes that Chrétien drew from a Celtic legend. The Celtic legends [8] of greatest interest in connection with *SP* are those of Fionn, Cuchulinn, and the Great Fool (in the prose narrative). These all contain

---

[1] *Op. cit.* (on p. 109), p. 22.   [2] See *infra.*
[3] *Op. cit.* (under XXII), p. 153.   [4] p. 194.
[5] *Carduino.*   [6] Chs. I—III, V and part of VII.
[7] Chs. VI—VIII.
[8] See Nutt, in *Studies,* 152—9; *Folk-Lore Record,* IV 1—33.

elements corresponding to the story of the boyhood of Perceval and illustrative of the *Aryan Expulsion* and *Return Formula.* The hero grows up in the wilderness, under the care of his mother or his nurse, strong and hardy; he goes out into the world, avenges his father's death,[1] and regains his lands.

The methods of Nutt have been severely criticised by Zimmer,[2] who supports the theory of the Celtic origin of the Arthurian Legend, in two respects: (1) His parallels are drawn principally from Gaelic literature, whereas the Arthurian Legend is wholly of British, especially of British-Armorican origin; (2) The Gaelic literature from which he cites has, for the most part, been profoundly affected by non-Celtic influences,[3] *i. e.* by North-German influence from the 7th to the 12th centuries, and later by the common Mediæval legendary literature.

A vehement protest against the views and methods of Paris and of Nutt has been made by Golther. All the forms of the Perceval legend,[4] he asserts,[5] are 'demonstrably derived' from Chrétien. Paris and Nutt therefore, in using *Peredur, SP* etc. in establishing the theory of a pre-Chrétien Perceval story, have fallen into a *circulus vitiosus.*[6] The history of Perceval Chrétien fashioned from circulating legendary elements, whose source is for us no longer discernible. The material, in and for itself, shows no sort of connection with Celtic legendary productions, and may just as well have reached Chrétien from another source. Chrétien brought Perceval into connection with Arthur and his heroes, and wove into the story the mysterious Grail.

---

[1] Not in the legend of Cuchulinn, whose father is a supernatural being, another *formula* element: cf. the birth stories of Merlin and of Arthur; *Folk-Lore, op. cit.,* pp. 34—6; Weston, *The Legend Sir Gawain,* L., 1897, p. 60.

[2] *Gött. gel. Anz.,* 1890, June 10, pp. 488—528.

[3] p. 495 ff.

[4] Also the introduction to the *lai* of *Tyolet,* to *Libeaus Desconus* and to *Carduino.*

[5] p. 213.   [6] pp. 208. 209.

As regards the origin of *SP*,[1] Golther thinks that the influence of Chrétien cannot be denied. The features peculiar to the poem originated with the author.[2] That he has not fully reproduced Chrétien's poem, and especially that he has omitted the visit to the Grail castle is due to his effort to make a whole out of Chrétien's unintelligible torso. He understood the meaning of the Grail as little as did the Welsh or the Norwegian redactor. He fits his story into a new frame-work, which he certainly took from the widespread, popular narrative of how a widow's son avenges the death of his father; but the folk-lore element is added to a work of literary art in only an accidental and secondary manner. The folk-lore elements of *SP* and of *Peredur* are those of their authors' own day[3] and are not safe sources from which to infer the original pre-literary, legendary form.[4] Brandl's[5] view of the origin of *SP* seems essentially that of Golther.

5. Metre.[6] 2286 verses in the 16-line 'tail-rime' stanza, with the rime-order, usually, *aaab cccb dddb eeeb* (class III). The longer verses are 4-stressed, the *caudae*, 3-stressed. The stanza is a development of that of twelve lines. As a rule, one or more words of the last line of a stanza are repeated in the first line of the succeeding stanza.

According to Luick,[7] the metre of *SP* is a development of the alliterative long line, the longer verses corresponding to the first half of that line, the shorter verses, to the second half. Luick calls the verses two-stressed ('zweihebig' not 'zweitaktig'). The alliteration is not regularly carried out.

6. Dialect.[8] The North of England. The Midland

---

[1] p. 203.   [2] p. 207.

[3] Zimmer also, *op. cit.*, p. 514—15, makes this point in regard to *Peredur*.

[4] Nutt replies to his German critics in *Rev. Celt.* XII; same article in *Folk-Lore*, June, 1891. See also Loth, *Rev. Celt.*, XIII 475–8.

[5] § 79.   [6] Ellinger, 26—36.   [7] *Angl.* XII 440—41.

[8] Ellinger, 3—26.

forms within the verses may be accounted for by supposing either that Thornton, the scribe, copied from a Midland MS., or that the Northern poet was influenced by the Midland dialect, as might naturally occur in the case of a travelling minstrel. When it is considered that the final *e* plays about the same rôle as with Chaucer, a Midland influence cannot be denied.

7. Date.[1] The second half of the 14th century. Kölbing[2] assigns the poem to the middle of the century.

On phonological grounds, Ellinger thinks that this is perhaps too early. It is certain, however, that Chaucer knew the poem.[3] G. Paris[4] says that the poem is, undoubtedly, of the 13th century.

8. Author. Unknown.

9. Bibliography.

Manuscripts: Lincoln, A. 1. 17 (Thornton MS.), Lincoln Cathedral Libr., *ca.* 1440; desc. by Halliwell, pp. xxv—xxxvi.

Editions: Halliwell, *Thornton Romances,* for the Camden Society, L., 1844.

General References: Brandl, § 79. G. Paris, in *Hist. Litt.,* XXX 254 - 61. *Analyses:* Lady Guest, in the *Mabinogion,* L., 1849, I 398—409, with many quotations; the same, transl. into German by San Marte in *Die Arthursage . . .,* Quedlinburg and Leipzig, 1842, pp. 237—45; G. Paris, *op. cit.,* 255—8; Nutt, *infra,* pp. 37—8. For analyses of the *Conte du Graal,* see Nutt and Birch-Hirschfeld (*opp. cit.,* on p. 109), and, of Chrétien's part, Harper, *infra,* 89—92.

Monographs: Steinbach, *Über den einfluss des Crestien de Troies auf die altengl. Lit.,* Leipsic, 1885, diss.; *revs..* Brandl, *Litbl.,* 1888 (5), 211—212; Kaluza, *E. St.,* XII 89—91. Ellinger, *Über die sprachl. u. metrischen Eigenthümlichkeiten*

---

[1] Ellinger, 26.   [2] *Sir Tristrem,* p. lxx.
[3] See *Cant. Tales,* v. 2106 (*Sir Thopas,* v. 205).
[4] *Op. cit.,* 254.

in 'The Romance of Sir P. of G.', Troppau, 1889, prgr.; rev. by Dieter in Mitteil., IV (12) 363.

On the Perceval legend, Nutt, Studies on the Legend of The Holy Grail, 1888; Golther, Chrestiens Conte del Graal in seinem Verhältniss zum wälschen Peredur und zum englischen 'Sir Perceval', in Sitzungsber. d. Münch. Akad., phil.-hist. Cl., 1890, II 203—212; Heinzel, in Sitzungsber. d. Wiener Akad., phil.-hist. Cl., CXXX, pp. 50, 51, 112 (on the agreement of SP with Kyot and with the common source of Kyot and Chrétien); G. M. Harper, Legend of The Holy Grail in Publications of the Mod. Lang. Assoc. of America, VIII, pp. 77—140 (contains with other matter, an outline of Parzival, in features pertaining to the Grail, and a translation in verse of the account of Parzival's youth).

XXII. Libeaus Desconus.

1. Subject. The valiant feats of a youth, who, brought up by his mother in seclusion, goes to Arthur's court, is knighted, and undertakes the mission of delivering an enchanted queen.

2. Specimen. Vv. 169—180:

> Up start þe ȝinge kniȝt,
> His herte was good and liȝt,
>   And seide: 'Arthour, my lord!
> I schall do þat fiȝt
> And winne þat lady briȝt,
>   Ȝef þou art trewe of word.'
> Þan seide Arthour: 'Þat is soþ!
> Certain, wiþ outen oþ,
>   Þer to I bere record:
> God graunte þe grace and miȝt,
> To helde up þat lady riȝt
>   Wiþ dente of spere and sword!'

3. Story. Gingelein, is a son of Sir Gawain, begotten 'be a forest side'. His mother, who keeps him 'close' lest he see a knight, calls him Beaufis because of his fair face. Once, while hunting, he dons the armor of a dead knight, goes to Arthur's court at Glastonbury, and begs to be knighted. Arthur names him Libeaus Desconus, knights him, and grants him the first fight that shall be asked of the king. While the court is at table, a beautiful maiden, Elene, richly attired, appears, attended by a dwarf. Kneeling, she tells Arthur that her lady of Sinadoun is in prison, and that she begs for a knight to free her. Libeaus claims and receives the privilege of espousing her cause. Elene and the dwarf, though displeased because Libeaus seems a mere child, ride forth, Elene continually chiding Libeaus.

Upon the third day of their journey, Libeaus defeats the redoubtable William Salebraunche, who holds the pass by the 'chapell auntrous'. William is pledged to deliver himself to Arthur. Libeaus then rides merrily on, enjoying the society of Elene, who has asked his pardon for despising him. Soon he conquers three knights, whom he pledges to go as prisoners to Glastonbury. While encamped in the forest at night, they discover two giants, who have captured a maiden. Libeaus attacks and destroys both giants, restoring the maiden, Violette, to her father, a rich earl, who offers her to Libeaus with a large dowry; but Libeaus, saying he cannot yet wed, goes on. He hears of a fair lady whose knight will give a snow-white gerfalcon to any knight who brings a fairer lady; but if the latter prove less fair, her knight must fight; if overcome, his head will be fixed upon a pole. Libeaus decides to put Elene in competition with the knight's lady, who, however, is declared by the people the fairer. Libeaus then jousts for the falcon, which after a long contest he wins and sends to Arthur. Libeaus is next engaged in a desperate fight with Sir Otis de Lile and twelve companions over a little dog to which Elene has taken a fancy. Libeaus wins and sends Otis to Arthur. Libeaus is chosen a knight of the Round Table. He next kills a giant who is besieging a

fair lady. The lady, 'la dame d'amour', invites Libeaus to
be her lord. Consenting, he lives with her more than a
twelvemonth. Through her acquaintance with sorcery, she
causes him to forget his mission. When Elene reproaches
him, he is overcome with shame, and continues his journey.
Arrived before Sinadoun, he must first joust with Sir
Lambard, steward of the queen. Lambard is overthrown,
but rejoices when he learns why Libeaus has come. The
lady is imprisoned by two magicians, brothers, until she
will give to one, Maboun, her dukedom and herself. Entering
the enchanted palace, Libeaus kills one magician and wounds
the second, who is mysteriously carried off. A serpent with
a woman's face, glides into the hall, winds about the
horrified Libeaus, and kisses him. At once she becomes a
beautiful woman. She has been thus enchanted until she
shall kiss Gawain or one of his kin. She is married to
Libeaus at Arthur's court.

4. Origin. Besides *Libeaus Desconus,* the story of the
'Fair Unknown' is extant in three other versions, all in
verse: The Old French *Guinglain* or *Le Bel Inconnu*; the
Italian *Carduino,* and the Middle-High German *Wigalois.*[1]
The author of the English romance more than once refers
to his source as French.[2] Is this 'frensche tale' the
romance of *Le Bel Inconnu* by Renaud de Beaujeu? To
this question two answers have been given: one, first advanced by Kölbing[3] (1877), and supported by the more
extended investigations of Paris (1886), Mennung (1890),
and Schofield (1895), that the original of *LD* is not *BI,*
but that both go back to an older French poem now lost;
the second theory is that of Kaluza (1890), who maintains

---

[1] The different versions will be designated, respectively, as *LD,*
BI, Car., and *Wig.*

[2] Vv. 246, 688, 2224.

[3] *E. St.* I 121—69, a comparison of *LD* (MS. N), *BI* and *Wig.*
The later investigations include *Car.,* which is believed to rest, at least
in parts, upon an older version of the story than that of *LD* or *BI*
(*Wig.* is based on *BI*); see Schofield, 183 ff.

that *BI*, though probably in a different MS., is the source of *LD*.[1]

The chief points of agreement and difference between *BI* and *LD*, as stated by Kaluza,[2] are as follows. The two poems agree in the whole course of the narrative and in the number and the essential content of the episodes;[3] but, on the other hand, the verbal correspondences are few, the details of the episodes and especially of the combats, differ widely, and in *LD* are greatly shortened. *LD*, moreover, lacks the whole second half of *BI*, namely the hero's second visit to *L'Ile d'Or* and the tournament given by Arthur; *LD* has also no trace of the personal element found in *BI*.

The difference between *BI* and *LD* in regard to the *Ile d'Or* episode is generally regarded as of primary importance in determining their relation. In *BI* the hero urged by Hélie (Elene) not to forsake his mission, remains at *L'Ile d'Or* but one night. The beauty of the lady of the castle has, however, completely fascinated him (she is not said, as in *LD*, to have practised upon him at this time any arts of enchantment); and, after his mission is performed, and the enchanted queen restored to her human shape, the hero, sending her on to Arthur's court, hastens back to *L'Ile d'Or*. Here he is at first repulsed by the indignant *fée*;[4] but, finally, having been sufficiently humiliated by the enchantments to which she subjects him, he is received fully into her favor. With her he lives a long time in joy and bliss, and Arthur only succeeds in alluring him back to court by the proclamation of a grand tournament, which the French poet describes at great length. In this tournament, Guinglain is of course the victor, and

---

[1] For the earlier similar view of Mebes and of Bethge, see Kaluza, p. clii, and Kölbing in *E. St.* IV 182 ff. For the sides taken by the reviewers, see Schofield, 3.

[2] pp. cxl—xliii.

[3] 'There are at least 150 significant points in which the two poems differ.' Schofield, 56.

[4] Thus called here for the first time.

at Arthur's request, he marries the disenchanted queen, *Blonde Esmerée.*

This ending, however, the poet clearly implies is not to his liking; for in closing, he says that, if the lady of his love[1] will show him *biau sanblant,* he will, in a new story, bring Guinglain back to his true love.

It is generally agreed that Renaud has, for his own purposes, changed the simple natural ending of the original story, which is found in *Car.* and in *LD.* Kaluza,[2] however, maintains that *LD,* as it stands, shows traces of the second visit to *L'Ile d'Or* being in its original: in the prolonged stay of the hero with the enchantress 'for twelf monþe and more' (v. 1507), he sees a fusion of the first and second visits of *BI*; and in the lines (1504—6)

> 'Allas! he nadde be chast,
> For aftirward at þe last
> Sche dede him troie and tene',

a distinct reference to the second visit. The author of *LD,* he concludes, therefore, changed the ending of *BI* in the interest of greater unity of action. Paris[3] explains 'aftirward at þe last' as referring merely to the delay in the execution of the hero's task caused by the enchantress, and remarks that a 14th century poet who could have seen that the return of the hero to the *fée* was contrary to the spirit of the romance, and have renounced voluntarily an ending as attractive for his age as for ours must have been 'un esprit attentif et réfléchi'.

That *BI* is not the original of *LD* seems to have been established beyond reasonable doubt by Schofield, who shows[4] that *BI* has made a wholesale use of the French romance of *Erec* that does not reappear in *LD.* As already pointed out by Mennung,[5] certain episodes of the *LD-BI* group have parallels in *Erec,* but in *BI* alone the use of

---

[1] Of whom he speaks at the beginning of his poem.
[2] p. cxlii.   [3] *Rom.* XX 298.   [4] pp. 60—106; 111—132.
[5] p. 49.

Erec extends to borrowings 'in the matter of phraseology, and even of long descriptions',[1] to the modification of such general features[2] of the poem, as the omission of the account of the hero's youth and the introduction of the tournament, and to many smaller changes;[3] Renaud was also acquainted with Chrétien's *Perceval* and with some form of the *Tristan* story.

Philipot,[4] in his review of Schofield, while admitting that *Erec* has had an important influence upon *BI* as regards literary expression, and that two or three episodes of *BI* can be explained only by *Erec,* thinks that on the whole it is to be regarded not as the source of material for *BI* or for the original of *BI* and *LD,* but rather as a fifth version of the story to be added to the four already noticed.

The origin of the story next claims our attention. The culminating incident is, of course, the disenchantment of the queen by means of the *fier baiser.* This legend, 'one of the most widely spread in the domain of folk-lore',[5] and according to Paris[6] apparently of Oriental or at least of Byzantine origin, is regarded by him as the true subject of the narrative. Mennung's theory of the origin of the story, is, briefly stated, that the most primitive elements, the episode with the *fée* and that with the enchanted queen, first existed amongst the Bretons as independent tales, but were later combined; then additional episodes, from different sources, were added at different times. *Car.* is a more primitive version, containing fewer episodes, than the common source (U) of *BI* and *LD.* In U, for the first time, the hero is called Guinglain and 'The Fair Unknown', and is made a son of Gawain. Paris[7] considers this theory, upon the whole, 'judicious and probable'.

---

[1] Schofield, 60.   [2] Ibid., 106, 111.   [3] Ibid., 139—45.

[4] *Rom.* XXVI 290—305.

[5] Schofield, pp. 199—208. See Child, Vol. I 306 ff., II 502, III 504, IV 454, V 213, 90.

[6] *Hist. Litt.* XXX 191. In *Car.* the hero gives the transforming kiss; this seems the more primitive version.

[7] *Rom.* XX 300.

Schofield,[1] however, finding in the Welsh *Peredur,* 'in continuous narrative, a series of adventures bearing close resemblance to those of the poems of our cycle, relating them in exactly the same order in which they occur in the English poem; which is the least artistic and seems to best represent version A of the *Desconnu* group', holds that the nucleus of the adventures in the 'Fair Unknown' story is not the tale of the disenchantment of the queen, but that of the boy who grows up in the woods. Not that *Peredur* and the 'Fair Unknown' stories are directly related, but that 'they both are to some extent based on one original, from which they have developed independently of each other, worked over for different purposes by different hands'.[2] *Peredur* explains unique features in *BI, LD,* and especially in *Car.* The principal steps by which the story of the Fair Unknown was developed from the Perceval legend into a separate narrative are not difficult to trace. Under the influence of the widespread *Märchen* of the *fier baiser,* the serpent killed by Peredur and the beautiful woman who aids him are merged into one. This 'easy combination' once made, other changes in the framework of the story, such as the disenchantment being the special mission on which the hero leaves Arthur's court, etc., naturally followed. The two castles ruled over by women became united, the result being the episode with the *fée.*[3]

Both Lot and Philipot regard Schofield's identification of the Fair Unknown story with that of Perceval as mistaken: Lot[4] upon the ground that narratives concerning a hero whose youth was obscure and wild were found everywhere and influenced one another reciprocally; Philipot[5] thinks that beyond the story of the *enfances* the comparison is forced. Moreover the version of the hero's youth is rather that of the *enfances féeriques* of Lancelot than of the

---

[1] p. 179.   [2] p. 153.

[3] See further, pp. 152—79.

[4] *Le Moyen Âge,* Oct. 1896; cited from Miss Weston's *Legend of Sir Gawain,* L., 1897, Ch. IX.

[5] *Op. cit.,* pp. 296—300.

enfances humaines of Perceval. Miss Weston favors Scho-field's view.

5. Metre. [1] Kaluza's critical text contains 2232 verses, in the 12 line 'tail-rime' stanza, the rime-scheme being *aab aab ccb ddb* (class I). In fourteen stanzas the rime-order is that of class II, *aab aab ccb ccb*. As a rule, the verse has three stresses or rather measures ('dreitaktig' not 'drei-hebig'). [2] In vv. 1—42 and 1705—1752, the *caudae* are 3-stressed, the others, 4-stressed. According to Kaluza, these verses, which occur in this metre in all the MSS., are the work of an early redactor of the original English poem, the leaves upon which they were written being missing in the MS. before him. G. Paris, [3] however, believes the verses genuine. Luick [4] pronounces the verse of *LD* to be, as a rule, 'zweihebig' and that, in the poem, 'zwei-hebige und vier- resp. dreitaktige Verse sind bunt ver-mischt'. This view is contested by Kaluza. [5]

Alliteration occurs not less frequently than in most of the other romances written in the tail-rime stanza. [6]

6. Dialect. [7] That of Kent or of a neighboring county. Although *LD* shows some isolated linguistic expressions characteristic of the North or Midland, Kaluza does not agree with Wilda [8] in assigning the poem to the S.E. Mid-land, nor with Sarazin that, on account of a rather long residence in N. England, the author had appropriated some Northern speech-forms. He holds [9] rather that the Northern and Midland forms are due to the author's use of poems belonging to these regions; for the poet was very well read in romantic literature, and was especially well acquainted with the romances belonging to the North and to the N.

---

[1] Kaluza, pp. xlii–lxxiv.   [2] p. lx; cf. Schipper, I 258.
[3] *Rom.* XX 299.   [4] *Angl.* XII 442, 443.
[5] p. lxix ff.
[6] For classification, see Kaluza, pp. xlviii—lvi.
[7] Kaluza, lxxiv—lxxxviii.   [8] p. 17.
[9] pp. xci—ii; cf. *J. B.*, 1886, no. 1567.

Midland; *Sir Tristrem, Rouland and Vernagu, Amis and Amiloun*, etc.

7. Date. About the second quarter of the 14th century. Since the author knew the romances in the Auchinleck MS., *LD* cannot have arisen earlier than the first quarter of the 14th century. Neither can it be later than *Sir Thopas* [1] (between 1380 and 1400), in which it is mentioned; indeed, it must have been written considerably earlier, since it is cited in the *Squyr of lowe degree*, which Chaucer also knew, [2] though he does not call it by name.

8. Author. In his edition of *Octavian*, Sarrazin [3] concludes that both *Oct.* and *LD* were written by Thomas Chestre, the author of the *Launfal.* This is also the final conclusion of Kaluza, although he expresses a different opinion in his edition of *LD.* There, after bringing forward parallel passages, in addition to those mentioned by Sarrazin, between *Oct.* and *LD* and between *LD* and *Launfal*, which exclude the possibility of 'accidental resemblance', [4] he concludes that *Oct.* and *LD* have the same author; but that, since verses in *Laun.* resemble verses in the first four stanzas, *i. e.* vv. 1—42, of *LD*, which are not genuine, [5] this author was not Thomas Chestre. Chestre, however, probably supplied vv. 1—42, 1705—52 in *LD*, and may have made many other slighter changes. [6] *LD* is earlier than *Laun.*, [7] and was much used by Chestre in its composition. Later (1893), upon new evidence afforded

---

[1] v. 189.   [2] See Kölbing, *E. St.*, XI 509.

[3] *Op. cit.* on p. 144.

[4] Sarrazin's conclusion was rejected by most of his reviewers upon the ground that the resemblances are either accidental or represent the use of purely typical minstrel formulae: Hausknecht, *Ltbl.*, 1886, p. 138; Breul, *E. St.*, IX 459—466; Wülker, *Lt. Cbl.*, 1887 (5), 150; *JB.*, 1886, 1887. S.'s view is favored by Bülbring, *E. St.*, XVII 120.

[5] See under 5.

[6] Bülbring, in his review of Kaluza's edition of *LD*, thinks a close comparison of *LD* and *Oct.* necessary.

[7] pp. clxi—iii.

principally by the publication of *Landavall*,[1] which Chestre has freely used in the composition of his *Launfal,* he is led to decidedly reverse this opinion.[2] And, since the expressions in *Lan.* paralled in *LD* nearly all occur in the verses by Chestre, and not in the verses borrowed by him from *Landavall,* Kaluza concludes that Chestre was the author of *LD* and *Oct.,* the latter being his latest and best work.[3] Kaluza assigns to Chestre a prominent place among the English romance poets of the 13th and 14th centuries.[4]

9. Bibliography.

Manuscripts:[5] I. 150 Lincoln's Inn Libr., beginning of the 15th cent.; desc. *E. St.* VII 194 ff.; 1107 vv. (about half is lost).

C. Brit. Mus., Cotton Calig. A II, 15th cent., 2nd quarter.

N. National Libr., Naples, 1457; desc. by D. Laing in *Reliquiae antiquae,* L., 1847; cf., Kölbing in *E. St.* I 121.

A. Ashmole 61, Bodl. Libr. Oxford, 15th cent., 2nd quarter (see Kaluza, p. x).

L. 306 Lambeth, end of 15th cent.; desc. by H. J. Todd in *Cat. of the Archiepiscopal Manuscripts in the Library at Lambeth Palace,* L., 1812.

P. *PF. MS.,* middle of the 17th cent.

Editions: The first ed. appeared probably in the 16th cent.; see Kaluza, p. x—xi. MS. P is in all probability a copy of this old print.

C. Ritson, *AEMR.,* II 1—90; collation, Kaluza, pp. xii-xv; re-ed., Goldsmid, Edin., 1885, II 35 — 98.

C. Hippeau, *Le Bel Inconnu,* Paris, 1860, pp. 241—330 (text unreliable).

P. Furnivall, *PF. MS.,* II 405—97.

A critical text, Kaluza, *Altengl. Bibl.,* Leipsic, 1890: revs., Bülbring, *E. St.* 17, 118—122; G. Paris, *Rom.* XX

---

[1] See under XXIII, p. 150.   [2] *E. St.* XVIII 185—7.

[3] Sarrazin's judgment, p. xxviii, is the reverse of this.

[4] On Chestre personally, see XXIII 8.

[5] Kaluza's ed. ix—xvii.

297—299; Schröer, *Zs. f. Vergl. Ltgesch.*, V 412—14; Suchier, *Lt. Cbl.*, 1891 (23), 792—3; Varnhagen, *Lt. Zt.*, 1895 (6), 172 (a few lines).

Ed. of the OF. version, Hippeau, *op. cit.*

General References: Brandl, § 70.

Monographs. Origin: Kölbing, *E. St.* I 121—69. G. Paris, *Guinglain ou Le Bel Inconnu, Hist. Litt.*, XXX 171—99 and *Rom.* XV 1—24. Mennung, *Der Bel Inconnu des Renaut de Beaujeu in seinem Verhältniss zum Lybeaus Disconus, Carduino, und Wigalois*, Halle, 1890—revs: Paris, *Rom.* XX 299—302; Kaluza, *Ltbl.*, 1891 (3), 84—6. Schofield, W. H., *Studies on The Libeaus Desconus, Harvard Studies in Philol. and Lit.*, Boston, 1895—revs: Lot, *Moyen Âge*, Oct. 1896; Philipot, *Rom.* XXVI 290; *Rev. Crit.*, 1897, 1. p. 258.

Author: Sarrazin, *Octavian*, Kölbing's *Altengl. Bibliothek*, Bd. III, Halle, 1885, p. xxv ff., and in *E. St.* XXII 331 (a few lines on the name 'Chestre' as an appellative); Kaluza, *E. St.* XVIII 165—190.

XXIII. Sir Launfal.

1. Subject. The love of a fairy for a poor knight, his disobedience to her injunction, his punishment, her interference to save him, his departure with her for fairyland.

2. Specimen. (1) From Chestre's poem, vv. 1009—1020:[1]

> Þe lady lep an hyr palfray
> And bad hem alle haue good day,
>   Sche nolde no lengere abyde;
> Wyth þat com Gyfre all so prest
> Wyth Launfalys stede out of þe forest
>   And stod Launfal besyde.

---

[1] Erling's text.

Þe knyʒt to horse began to sprynge,
Anoon wythout any lettynge,
   Wyth hys lemman away to ryde;
Þe lady tok her maydenys achon
And wente þe way þat sche hadde er gon,
   Wyth solas and wyth pryde.

(2) From *Landavall*,[1] vv. 498—525:

Landevale saw hys loue wold gone,
Upon hir horse he lepe anone
And said, 'Lady, my leman bright,
I wille with the, my swete wight,
Whedir ye ride or goo,
Ne wille I neuer parte you fro.'
'Landevale,' she said, 'with-outyne lette,
Whan we ffirst to-gedir mete
With dern loue with-outen stryfe,
I chargyd you yn alle your lyffe
That ye of me neuer speke shulde;
How dare ye now be so bolde
With me to ride with-oute leve?
Ye ought to thyng ye shuld me greue.'
'Lady,' he said, 'faire and goode,
For his loue that shed his blode,
For-yefe me that trespace
And put me hole yn your grace.'
Than that lady to hym can speke,
And said to hym with wordys meke:
'Landevale, lemman, I you for-gyve,
That trespace while ye leue.
Welcome to me, gentille knyghte;
We wolle neuer twyn day ne nyghte.'
So they rodyn euyn ryghte,
The lady, the maydyns, and the knyghte.
Loo, howe love is lefe to wyn
Of wemen that arn of gentylle kyn!

_____

[1] Ms. *R*.

3. Story. Launfal, owing to his great bounty, has been Arthur's steward for ten years. Grieved because at Arthur's wedding feast the queen in her distribution of gifts passes him by, Launfal, accompanied by two knights, leaves the court at Carlisle, and takes up his abode at Caerleon, the unwelcome guest of the mayor, formerly a servant of his. Before the end of the first year he is so much in debt that the two knights return to Arthur (now at Glastonbury).

One day Launfal rides out 'with lytyll pride' into the forest, where he dismounts and rests under a tree, very sorrowful. Soon he sees two beautiful, richly dressed maidens approaching,[1] whom he greets courteously. They say that their lady, Dame Tryamour, bids him come speak with her. Going with the maidens, he finds within a rich pavilion a surpassingly beautiful woman. She is the daughter of the king of Olyroun, who is

'king of fayrye,
Of Occient, fer and nyʒe.'

The fairy offers Launfal her love, which he willingly accepts. She then tells him that, if he will forsake every other woman for her, she will make him rich, and keep him from harm in tournament or in war. She also promises to come to him secretly whenever he wishes, but he must never boast of her love. After Launfal's return to Caerleon, the fairy fulfills her promises. Launfal is now more generous than ever with his gifts. At a tournament proclaimed in his honor by the knights of Caerleon, he wins the prize over the Constable of Caerleon, the Earl of Chester, and many Welsh knights. Challenged by a giant, Sir Valentine of Lombardy, Launfal goes to that country, and meets and slays the giant.[2]

---

[1] The older version, represented by *R, H,* and *P,* begins by saying that Landavale is renowned at Arthur's court for his generosity, that he falls into 'grete dette', and one day rides away into the forest, where the maidens appear to him.

[2] In *R, H,* and *P* Landavale returns from the fairy's pavilion (her

Arthur, hearing of Launfal's 'noblesse', sends for him to return to the court to a great feast which is to be held at Saint John's mass. At the close of the feast (which lasts forty days), the queen and her ladies dance with Launfal and the other knights upon the green. The queen soon draws Launfal aside, and tells him that she has loved him more than seven years. He replies that he will never be a traitor; and when she calls him a coward, saying that he loves no woman or no woman him, he declares that he has loved for seven years a fairer woman than she ever set eyes upon, and that his love's homeliest maid is more fit to be queen than is she. In revenge, the queen accuses him to the king of wishing to dishonor her, and tells of his boast. The king swears that Launfal shall be slain. Launfal, meanwhile, is distracted with sorrow; for Tryamour will not appear to him, and all that she has given him has disappeared or is changed. Bound and brought before the king, Launfal is sentenced to die, unless by the end of a twelvemonth and a fortnight he can substantiate his boast. The queen says, 'If he bring a fairer thing, put out my grey eyes'. Sir Gawain and Sir Percival become Launfal's bondsmen, but he can do nothing; and when the time allotted him has expired, he is again brought before Arthur and his knights.

At this moment ten[1] beautiful maidens come riding to the hall, who ask Arthur to prepare a room for their lady; these maidens are soon followed by ten others, and then there appears alone, riding upon a white palfrey, Tryamour herself. Upon seeing her, Launfal cries, 'Here cometh my sweet love!' Tryamour tells the king the truth concerning Launfal and the queen, and Arthur declares that the knight was justified in his boast. Tryamour, after blowing such a breath upon the queen that she never sees again, prepares to depart. Launfal leaps upon his steed, which has

---

name is not given) to Carlisle. There is no mention of victories in tournament.

[1] In *R*, *H*, and *P*, two.

been brought by Tryamour's 'knave', Gyfre, and rides away
with his lady far into the island of Olyroun. [1]

4. Origin. The original of *Launfal* is the *Lai de
Lanval* of Marie de France. In the lai of *Guingamor*—also
assigned to Marie [2]—to whose story that of *Lanval* is closely
related, G. Paris [3] sees 'a variant of the well known legend
that has found in the popular German songs relating to
Tannhäuser its most famous expression ... The place where
Guingamor passed three centuries like three days is evidently
the happy land, where death comes not, "the place of
eternal youth" of the Irish traditions.' The principal
traits of the *lai,* he says, [4] 'separated or united, sometimes
much effaced and altered, but always recognizable, mingled
often with histories very different, are found in *Graelent,
Lanval, Partenopeus, Guigemar, Oger le danois.'*

The simplest and most ancient form of the theme is
found in the Irish literature of the 7th century, in the
Voyage of Bran. [5] Here we read that [6] Bran and his companions on a journey came to the Land of Women, where
they lived a long time in great happiness. At last, home-
sickness seizing one of their number, his companions sailed
with him for Ireland. The women told them that they
would rue their going, and directed that no one should
touch the land; but as they neared the shore, the home-
sick man leaped from the boat. 'As soon as he touched
the earth of Ireland, forthwith he was a heap of ashes.'
Bran related his wanderings to the people on the shore,
and then, bidding them farewell, sailed away and was
never heard of more.

---

[1] Cf. *R* quoted under **2.** In *P,* Launfal leaps up behind the fairy,
after having entreated her in vain to forgive him.

[2] G. Paris, § 55, *Rom.* XXVII 323; Schofield, 221.

[3] *Rom.* VIII 50.   [4] *Rom.* XXVII 323.

[5] K. Meyer, *The Voyage of Bran,* L., 1895, I xvi. In this work
numerous other Irish traditions on the same theme are summarized by
Nutt, I 115 ff.

[6] The following account is condensed from Schofield, p. 223.

To this Irish tradition the lai of *Guingamor* 'offers a striking resemblance'.[1] Guingamor, who has rejected the proffered love of the queen, finds, while hunting in the forest, a *fée* bathing in a fountain, becomes her *ami*, and dwells with her in her castle for three hundred years, which seem to him but three days. Returning home in order to relieve the anxieties of his friends, he learns from a woodcutter, to whom he tells his story, that they are all dead. Unheeding the command of the *fée* to take no food while in his own land, he eats some wild apples. Immediately he becomes a shrivelled up old man, and falls from his horse as if dead. Then two maidens come and bear him gently back to the *fée*.

Another lay, that of *Graelent*,[2] agrees closely in its first part, as regards both the principal incidents and their sequence, with *Guingamor*; but after the hero receives the love of the *fée*, the version is essentially that of *Lanval*.[3] In regard to the relation of the three lays, Schofield[4] concludes that 'the induction in *Guingamor*, and perhaps other features, are due to the influence of the *Graelent* saga,' and that 'if the author of *Guingamor* was, as is suggested, Marie de France, then the prefixing of this account is not remarkable. Marie doubtless knew the *Graelent* version of the story, of which she has given us such a charming rendering in *Lanval*; but in the latter poem she wisely brought about the knight's meeting with the *fée* at the beginning of the poem so that his action later in the presence of the queen might be more satisfactorily explained.' The story of the depravity of the wife in high

---

[1] Schofield, 222.

[2] Roquefort, *op. cit. infra*, I 486—541. The lay is not now ascribed to Marie.

[3] Between *Lanv.* and *Grael.* there are some verbal agreements; see Kolls, pp. 2—4 and Schofield, 228—9. Kolls therefore concludes that the two lays have a common source in a Breton folk-legend. Kittredge, p. 17, has no confidence in 'any results reached by so summary a process'.

[4] p. 238; cf. Gröber, 594—7.

station, Schofield [1] considers as originally extraneous to the legend. [2]

According to Zimmer, [3] Brittany was the original home of the *Lanval* legend.

The different *ME.* texts of a romance on Launfal or Landavall fall into two groups [4]—the poem of Chestre on the one hand, and *R, H,* and *P* on the other. [5] *R, H,* and *P* 'are, on the whole, identical not only in content but in phraseology and rhymes'. Chestre's poem is twice as long as any of the others, and has a different rime-scheme. The two groups do not, however, represent two independent translations of the French lai; but, exclusive of the additions in C from other sources, one earlier ME. translation (*x*), which, judging from *R, H,* and *P,* seldom departed further from its original than the liberty of a translator allowed. In essentials, Chestre's poem also agrees pretty closely with the *Lai de Lanval.* It is an amalgamation of *Lanval* 'with the anonymous *Lai de Graelent,* and contains, in addition, two long episodes [6] drawn from the author's imagination, or rather from the common stock of mediaeval romances.' *P* and *H,* Kittredge [7] finds, have a common source, *z,* this side of *x. H* and *F* come from *w,* this side of *z. D* is, in all probability, a reprint of *H.*

5. Metre. [8] Chestre's poem consists of 1044 verses in the twelve line 'tail-rime' stanza, the rime-scheme being *aab ccb ddb eeb* (class III). The long lines are always four-stressed, the *caudae,* three-stressed. Alliterative combinations are frequent. [9]

Landavall (MS. *R,* 535 vv.) and *Sir Lambewell* (MS. *P,* 632 vv.) are both rimed in couplets.

---

[1] p. 237.   [2] Cf. Gen. XXXIX.

[3] *GGA.,* 1890 (no. 20), p. 798.

[4] Kittredge, p. 5 ff.   [5] See **9.**

[6] The tournament at Caerleon, vv. 433—492, and the combat with Valentine, vv. 505—612.

[7] pp. 9—13. For further details concerning the *stemma,* see pp. 13—16.

[8] Münster, 6—8.   [9] Ibid., p. 35.

6. Dialect. For Chestre's poem, that of S.E. England. This is the view of Sarrazin,[1] Münster,[2] and Kaluza.[3] The S. Midland is preferred by another scholar.[4] According to Brandl, Chestre's poem[5] belongs to 'südlicherem England'; *Landavall*[6] is written in an 'English more or less vulgar but without a trace of Northern dialect', and version *F*,[7] in the Scottish dialect.

7. Date. Chestre's poem is assigned by Brandl to the first half, and by Münster,[8] to the last quarter of the 14th century. Münster, adopting the opinion of Sarrazin, that *Launfal* and the SE. version of *Octavian* have the same author, and that the latter poem is, 'with great probability', to be assigned to the middle of the 14th century, concludes that Chestre's *Launfal* was written between 1375—1400. The latter date is given as the *terminus ad quem* on account of linguistic peculiarities not found later; 1375 is the earliest date under which M. finds any mention in England of the term 'Olyroun' (from the French island of Oléron), used by Chestre, vv. 278, 1023, instead of Avalon, to designate the island-home of the fairy. But Kittredge[9] points out that *La Charte D'Oleroun des Juggementz de la mièr,* in an early 14th century hand, is found in the *Liber Memorandum* of the London Corporation. If Kaluza's conclusions[10] in regard to the date of *Libeaus Desconus* and to the relative dates of *Libeaus* and *Launfal* be correct, the latter must have been written before 1350, and probably belongs to the second quarter of the century.

8. Author. *Launfal, miles* is one of the few ME. romances whose author is known. In v. 1039 we read, 'Thomas Chestre made þys tale'. From the knowledge of knightly combats displayed by Chestre, and from his fond-

---

[1] *Octavian (op. cit.* on p. 144), p. xxviii, cf. xvi.
[2] pp. 11—32.   [3] See XXII 6 and 8.
[4] *JB.,* 1886, no. 1567.   [5] § 70.   [6] § 113.
[7] § 133.   [8] pp. 8—11.   [9] p. 13.
[10] *E. St.* XVIII 185; see pp. 142—143 of this work.

ness for describing them, Sarrazin [1] conjectures that he may
have been a herald at such combats.

9. Bibliography.

Manuscripts: [2] C. Cotton, Caligula, A ii, Brit. Mus.,
15th cent.; on graphical peculiarities, see Kolls, *infra,*
pp. 5, 6.

R. Rawlinson, C. 86, Bodleian, Oxford; late 15th cent.;
desc. by Sir F. Madden, *Syr Gawayne,* p. lxiv.

P. PF. MS., now Addit. 27, 879, Brit. Mus., *ca.* 1650;
desc. by Furnivall, *PF. MS.,* I, p. xii—xiii.

H. Halliwell fragment, Malone 941, Bodleian; 16th cent.
probably; see Kittredge 3—4.

D. Douce II 95, Bodleian, one printed leaf (61 lines),
probably a reprint of H; see Kittredge, 4.

F. Kk. 5. 30, *Cambr. Univ. Libr.,* 90$^1/_2$ lines, 1612. [3]

Editions: [4] (1) C. *Launfal Miles*: Ellis, in *Way's Translations from the Fabliaux of Le Grand d'Aussy,* 1800, II
298—340; 1815, III 233—287.

Ritson, *AEMR.,* 1802, I 170—215; 1885, ed. Goldsmid,
II 2—33.

Halliwell, *Illustrations of the Fairy Mythology of A
Midsummer Night's Dream,* Shakespeare Soc., 1845, pp. 2—34.

W. C. Hazlitt, *Fairy Tales, Legends, and Romances,
illustrating Shakespeare,* 1875, pp. 48—80, Halliwell's text.

Erling, *Li Lais de Lanval,* etc., Kempten, 1883,
pp. 17—46; revs.: Rhode, *E. St.* VIII 378—9,—cf. *E. St.*
IX 182; Kaluza, *E. St.* XVIII 168—84.

(2) R. *Landavall,* Kittredge, *Am. Jour. Philol.,* X 1—33.

(3) P. *Sir Lambewell,* Hales and Furnivall, *PF. MS.,*
I 144—164; reprinted by Kolls, *infra.*

---

[1] *Octavian, op. cit.,* p. xxviii; see also Sarrazin on 'Chestre' as
an appellative in *E. St.* XXII 331.

[2] Kittredge's ed. of R, pp. 1—5.

[3] Zupitza, *Arch.,* LXXXVIII 68—72, says that this date is on
p. 26 of the Ms., whose first part, containing other matter, is of the
15th century, the date (1460—70) given by Kittredge, 4.

[4] Kittredge, 2—5.

(4) H. *Sir Lamwell, PF. MS.*, 1867, I 522—32, whence most of it was reprinted by Kolls.

(5) D. Printed in: the Douce Catalogue, Bodleian, p. 311; *PF. MS.*, I 533—35; thence by Kolls, pp. 39—43.

(5) F. Furnivall, *Captain Cox, his Ballads and Books,* 1871, p. xxxi; also in *Robert Laneham's Letter* etc., printed in 1890 for the New Shakespeare Society.[1]

The OF. *Lais de Lanval:* Roquefort, 1820, I 202; Warnke, Halle, 1885; Erling, *op. cit.*; beautifully translated into German by W. Hertz, *Spielmannsbuch,* 1886, pp. 25—44 (with valuable notes, pp. 323—9).

The related lai of *Graelent:* Roquefort, *op. cit.*, pp. 486 —540; Barbazan, *Fabliaux et contes,* tome 4, pp. 57—80; Le Grand d'Aussy, *Fabliaux et contes,* tome 1, pp. 16—23.

General References: Brandl, § 70. Bédier (on the lays of Marie de France), *Rev. des Deux Mondes,* 1891 (5), pp. 835—63. Summaries of *Lanval:* Julleville I pp. 291—294; Bédier *op. cit.,* 856—7; Roquefort (abridged translation), *op. cit.,* I 202 ff.

Monographs: Kolls, *Zur Lanvalsage, eine Quellenunter- suchung,* Berlin, 1886; revs.: Wülker, *Lt. Cbl.,* 1888 (14), 491; Varnhagen, *Ltzt.,* 1888 (29) 1092; *Rom.* XV 644. Münster, *Untersuchungen zu Th. Chestre's Launfal,* Kiel, 1886, diss.— Schofield, *The Lay of Guingamor* in Harvard *Studies and Notes on Philol. and Lit.,* V (1896), pp. 221—43; rev. by G. Paris, *Rom.* XXVII 323.

XXIV. Ywain and Gawain.

1. Subject. A knight, who marries the widow of one slain by him in single combat, is separated from her through his forgetfulness of her command; but, after great sorrow and many noble deeds, is reunited to her.

---

[1] Cited from Zupitza in *Arch.* LXXXVIII 68.

2. Specimen.   Vv. 619—632: [1]

> Than to the well he rade gude pase,
> And doun he lighted in that place,
> And sone the bacyn has he tane,
> And kest water upon the stane,
> And sone thar wex, withowten fayle,
> Wind, and thonor, and rayn, and haile.
> When it was sesed, than saw he
> The fowles light opon the tre,
> Thai sang ful fayre opon that thorn,
> Right als thai had done byforn;
> And sone he saw cumand a knight,
> Als fast so the fowl in flyght,
> With rude sembland, and sterne cher,
> And hastily he neghed nere.

3. Story.   In order to avenge the defeat of his cousin, Sir Colgrevance, by a mysterious knight, Ywain, a knight of Arthur's court, rides forth into the forest until he reaches a well near a chapel. Following directions, he dips water from this well into a golden basin and pours it upon a stone near by. A tempest at once arises. After its subsidence, the knight appears, engages Ywain in combat, and receives a mortal wound. Ywain pursues the knight into a castle, whose portcullis falls killing Ywain's steed.

A damsel, Lunet, to whom Ywain once showed courtesy, saves him from the vengeance of the knight's vassals by the gift of a ring of invisibility. From his hiding place, Ywain sees the lady of the castle, as in great sorrow she follows her lord to his grave, and Love wounds him sorely. Lunet persuades the lady to marry Ywain in order that he may protect her lands from Arthur. Ywain is visited by Arthur and his knights. Yielding to the persuasions of Gawain, he craves permission of his wife to return to Arthur's court, in order to win more fame in 'chivalry'. She consents, giving him a ring that will protect him from

---

[1] Ritson's text.

harm, but commands him to return in exactly a year. The year is spent in riding about engaging in many tournaments. Saint John's day, the time for return, is past when Ywain remembers his wife's command. A messenger from her denounces his falseness, and takes away the ring. Ywain goes mad from sorrow and leads a wild life in the woods. He is finally cured by a damsel who anoints him with magic ointment.

Going forth into the forest, Ywain saves from a dragon a lion, who henceforth follows him devotedly and in his subsequent adventures gives [1] him indispensable aid. Coming again to the chapel, he finds Lunet confined there. Unless she can find a champion, she is to be burned the next day on the charge of treason to her lady. Ywain offers to fight for her. He goes that night to a castle, and the next morning kills a giant who comes against it. He then hastens back to the chapel, where he arrives barely in time to save Lunet.

Ywain next becomes the champion of a maiden whose elder sister refuses her her share of their inheritance. As the knight, the lion, and the damsel journey to Arthur's court, they pass a night at the castle of "Heavy Sorrow". Before setting forth the next morning, Ywain is obliged to fight two champions, whom he overcomes after a terrific combat, thus freeing many noble maidens, hostages who are toiling as silk-weavers. After Ywain's arrival at court, Ywain and Gawain, each unknown to the other, fight as champions of the two sisters. Ceasing their strokes when the light fails, each learns the other's name, and each declares before the king that he has been overcome. Arthur decides that the younger sister shall hold her lands as a fief under the elder, thus decreeing the first division of land ever made in England.

Ywain, feeling that if he is not reconciled to his lady he must go mad or die, returns to the well, and raises such a storm that Alundyne in her castle feels great terror.

---

[1] Except in the combat with Gawain.

Lunet tells her that they greatly need to defend them one like the famous Knight of the Lion. This knight and his lady, Lunet says, have quarreled, and he will not fight for anyone who will not swear to do her utmost to effect a reconciliation. This Alundyne swears upon holy relics to do. Lunet brings Ywain to her and tells her his name. They are finally reconciled, and Ywain, Alundyne, Lunet, and the lion live happily until their lives' end.

4. Origin. In *Ywain and Gawain* we have the only *ME.* romance that is certainly [1] a translation or adaptation from the most famous of the Old French romance writers, Chrétien de Troyes. [2] *Yvain, ou Le Chevalier au Lion,* is considered by Foerster Chrétien's masterpiece and the highest point in the development of the French court-epic. Contrary to his usual practice, Chrétien mentions in *Yvain* no oral or written source for his story. He has however, according to Foerster, [3] freely changed and combined episodes from different sources in order to realize his own independent conception, which consists of two fundamental ideas very skillfully combined: in the first half, the eternally old and ever varied theme—*Mutabile semper femina;* [4] to which is opposed in the second half the constancy of true love. [5]

Sources for many of the different episodes have been pointed out. The first adventure in the wood of Brocéliande (already mentioned by Wace [6]) is, Foerster says, [7] clearly a Breton (Armorican) place legend, which Chrétien has used as a means of bringing together the hero and heroine. F. Lot [8] gives an account of an Irish legend,

---

[1] See *Sir Perceval,* pp. 128—32.

[2] According to G. Paris, pp. 247, 8, Chrétien flourished *ca.* 1160-1175.

[3] *Yvain,* p. xii.

[4] See Foerster's interesting remarks, p. x, upon the irony intended in *Yvain* against the ideal heroine of the day, whom Chrétien had just delineated in his *Lancelot* or *Conte de la Charette.*

[5] On the significance of the poem, see also Brandl, and Gröber, 501.

[6] *Rou* II 6395 ff.   [7] p. xii.   [8] *Rom.* XXI pp. 67—71.

whose antiquity [1] is attested both by the substance of the narrative and by details; and which, while as a whole absolutely different from *Yvain,* presents the 'most striking analogies' with the story of the marvellous fountain in Chrétien. In this legend we find a fountain, closely resembling that described in *Yvain.* [2] When the hero, who is thirsty, stoops to touch his lips to the water, he hears a noise like that of a body of warriors on the march; when he arises, the noise ceases. Seeing on the top of a great stone near the fountain a richly decorated drinking horn, he secures it and again tries to drink. A giant now arises from the fountain, who, after reproaching the hero for troubling his fountain, engages him in combat. The hero, getting the better of his adversary, pursues him into his subterranean kingdom. Here all resemblance to Chrétien's narrative ceases.

G. Paris [3] sees in the central incidents a more altered form of the theme that we find in *Guingamor, Oger le danois, Tannhäuser,* [4] etc. Laudine, [5] he thinks, was certainly a *fée* originally. The legend of the fountain, whose waters when agitated produced a storm, did not belong to the primitive *fonds* but was added to explain the name of 'lady of the fountain' which had become incomprehensible. [6] In the character of Laudine as the easily consoled widow, Foerster [7] sees a direct imitation of the Widow of Ephesus.

In the Welsh version of the romance, Rhŷs [8] finds many points of resemblance to the last part of the *Peredur* legend, beginning especially with the adventure at the castle of the Arrogant Black Fellow. The death of the

---

[1] No MSS. before the 18th century are known.

[2] For details, see Lot, *op. cit.,* 70.   [3] *Rom.* XVII 334—5.

[4] See under *Sir Launfal* (XXIII) p. 148.

[5] Alundyne, in the English romance.

[6] Cf. Foerster, *op. cit.,* p. xiv, n., xv. Philipot, *Rom.* XXVI 301-303, thinks the legend in Le Bel Inconnu (see XXII 4) is more primitive than that in *Yvain,* and explains it.

[7] *Op. cit.,* p. xiii; this view is controverted in *Ltbl.* 1889, 221.

[8] *Op. cit.,* 88, 94 ff.

Avanc of the Lake (= the Black Knight of the Fountain) at Peredur's hands Rhŷs explains [1] as the development of a Welsh myth on the victory of the sun over night and its cold blasts.

The madness of Yvain was probably suggested to Chrétien by the madness of Tristan and his life in the woods. [2] The grateful lion is that of Androcles, a Greco-Roman invention; [3] the ring of invisibility, that of Gyges; the silk weavers were probably figures drawn from life. [4]

The ME. *Ywain and Gawain* is a 'tolerably close but condensed translation' [5] of Chrétien's *Yvain*. No one of the extant French MSS., can have served as the direct source of the English poet; [6] but differences between the French and the English poem are, for the most part, to be attributed to changes made by the translator. [7]

A detailed comparison of the English poem with its French original has been made by Steinbach and by Schleich. Steinbach notices principally the respects in which E [8] surpasses C. [9] In E, as the result of condensation, the progress of the narrative is quicker and more lively. There is also a more frequent, almost dramatically vivid use of direct discourse; in this feature, as in the frequent use of set epithets, the style recalls that of the old folk-epic. In many instances of course, E shows adaptation to the conceptions of the poet as well as to those of his time and people. [10] In numerous single instances and especially in his conception of the characters and of the religious feeling, he shows a 'deeper penetration into the material of his

---

[1] p. 97.

[2] Baist, *Die Quellen des Yvains*, *Zs. f. Rom. Phil.* XXI, Heft III, p. 403.

[3] Holland, p. 162; Baist, *op. cit.*, 404; cf. Rhŷs, pp. 96, 97.

[4] Gröber, 501.   [5] Steinbach, 8.

[6] It is probable that he used a MS. of the β-class. Schleich, 1889, p. 18.

[7] Ibid. p. 19. For possible gaps in the English text, see Schleich's ed. pp. xl—xliii; cf. Kaluza, *E. St.* XII 85.

[8] E = The English poem.   [9] C = Chrétien's poem.

[10] pp. 23—24.

original'. In more formal features, especially in regard to what concerns smoothness and elegance of style, he is noticeably inferior to Chrétien, the courtly poet.

Schleich [1] emphasizes, with especial fullness of detail the frequent superiority of the French poet, not only in mastery over expression, but in imagination, insight, and feeling. In description C is superior; the descriptions of E are less exact and less rich in coloring. Schleich cannot agree with Steinbach that E has deepened the delineation of character or, on the whole, of religious feeling. In the delineation of character, E is far less passionate, far less realistic than C. For example, although the delineation of the heroine is more tender in E, nevertheless the more passionate delineation of C reveals a far greater knowledge of human nature. In the characters drawn by them are mirrored the characters of the two poets: 'Chrétien, the animated, realistically minded Frenchman; the Englishman, the calm, more ideally inclined son of Albion'.

5. Metre. [2] 4032 four-stressed verses, rimed in couplets. Alliteration is employed, but not carried out according to any fixed scheme. [3] Many of the alliterative combinations, especially in the descriptions of battle, are typical formulae of ME.; others are original with the poet.

6. Date. The first half [4] or the beginning [5] of the 14th century. According to Schleich, the MS. seems to belong to the first half of the 14th century, and there are no linguistic objections to assigning the poem to the same period.

7. Dialect. [6] Northern. The language has much in common with that of the celebrated Hermit of Hampole (Richard Rolle).

---

[1] 1889.　　[2] Schleich's ed., pp. xxv—xxxviii.
[3] Cf. *E. St.* XII 89.　　[4] Schleich, i, xxiv.
[5] Kölbing, *Sir Tristrem*, lxxii.
[6] Schleich, pp. iv—xxiv; Kaluza, *E. St.* XII 83—4.

8. Author. Unknown.

9. Bibliography.

Manuscripts: E. IX. Galba, Brit. Mus.

Editions: Ritson, *ÆMR.* I 1—169; notes, III 219—42, 437—38.

Schleich, Oppeln and Leipsic, 1887. Collated with the MS., in *E. St.* XII 139.—On the text: Schleich, *Angl.* XII 139; Holthausen, *Angl.* XV 429—31; Kölbing, *E. St.* XXIV 146—50. *Revs.:* Einenkel, *Ltbl.,* 1886 (6), 262—3; Breul, *Ltzt.,* 1888 (11), 394—5; Kaluza, *E. St.* XII 83—9; Wülker, *Lt. Cbl.,* 1888 (41), 1417.

Long extracts, in Warton's *History of Eng. Poetry,* ed. Hazlitt, L., 1871, IV pp. 93—107.

The OF. *Yvain:* Holland, Hannover and Paris, 1861, 1880; Foerster, Halle, 1887, 1891 (smaller ed.).

General References: Brandl, § 64.

Monographs: Steinbach, *op. cit.* on p. 133; Schleich, *Ywain and Gawain, Über das Verhältniss der me. Romanze zu ihrer altfrz. Quelle,* Berlin, 1889, prgr. rev. by Kaluza, *E. St.* XV 429—31.

XX. Sir Gawain and the Green Knight.

1. Subject. The proving of Sir Gawain; being the outcome of a challenge made at Arthur's court by a mysterious knight.

2. Specimen. Vv. 2374—87:

'Corsed worth cowarddyse & couetyse boþe!
In yow is vylany & vyse, þat vertue disstryeȝ.'
Þenne he kaȝt to þe knot, & þe kest lawseȝ.'
Brayde broþely þe belt to þe burne seluen:
'Lo! þer þe falssyng, foule mot hit falle!
For care of þy knokke cowardyse me taȝt

To a-corde me with covetyse, my kynde to for-sake,
Þat is larges, & lewte, þat longeȝ to knyȝteȝ.
Now am I fawty, & falce, & ferde haf been euer;
Of trecherye & un-trawþe boþe bityde sorȝe & care!
    I bi-knowe yow, knyȝt, here stylle,
    Al fawty is my fare,
    Leteȝ me ouer-take your wylle,
    & efte I schal be ware.'

3. Story. In Arthur's hall at Camelot, the court has just begun the New Year's feast. As the sound of the music ceases after the serving of the first course, a man of gigantic stature rides into the hall. Men marvel much at his color, for he is green all over; his steed is of the same hue. In one hand he bears a sharp axe, in the other a holly bough. Halting in the doorway, and looking toward the high dais, he announces that he has come to seek a boon, a Christmas jest: if one of Arthur's knights dare to strike the Green Knight a blow with the latter's axe, he will abide the blow unarmed, upon condition that, in just a year's time, he may give his opponent a blow in return. All are silent through astonishment and fear. 'What, is this Arthur's hall?' cries the knight tauntingly. Arthur starts up in anger and offers to strike the blow, but Gawain begs for the privilege. After binding himself by oath to the stranger's terms, Gawain takes the axe; the Green Knight bares his neck, and Gawain strikes him a blow that severs the head from the trunk. The Green Knight, never faltering, quickly dismounts, seizes his head, and remounts. As he turns his horse to depart, the head, lifting its eyelids, calls upon Sir Gawain to keep his appointment the next New Year's morn at the Green Chapel.

The year quickly passes. The morning after All Hallows Day, Sir Gawain richly armed sets forth, amid the sorrow of the court, in quest of the Green Chapel. After a perilous journey, he finds himself on Christmas eve in a thick forest. He prays to the Virgin to guide his steps to some shelter where he may hear Mass on Christmas morn. Soon he

11

comes to a fair castle, to which he is readily admitted, and where he is most hospitably entertained by the lord of the castle and his beautiful wife. After three days of feasting, Gawain inquires the way to the Green Chapel, which he must find by New Year's morn. Upon learning from his host that the chapel is but two miles distant, he is persuaded to remain at the castle until the New Year.

The lord of the castle now proposes that on the morrow Gawain shall remain in the castle and rest, while he starts before daybreak on the chase; upon his return each shall present to the other what the day has brought him. To this plan Gawain agrees. For three successive mornings, while Gawain lies half slumbering in bed, he is surprised by a visit from his hostess. Seated beside him, she speaks of many matters and ever shows her love for him, which he persistently turns aside. When she leaves him the first day, she gives him a kiss, which Gawain faithfully gives his host at night. The second evening Gawain has two kisses to bestow upon him; the third evening, three. During his last interview with the lady, after he has refused to receive from her a gold ring, he accepts, as a secret gift, a green lace or girdle, which, she tells him, will preserve its wearer from death and wounds.

On New Year's morn, Gawain is conducted to the Green Chapel, which proves to be a hollow green mound. At Gawain's call the Green Knight appears from over a hill. Gawain bares his neck for the blow, but as the axe falls, he shrinks a little; the Green Knight reproaches him with cowardice. Gawain replies that he will flinch no more. The second time, the Green Knight feigns a fierce blow but does not let it fall; the third time, the blow falls upon Gawain's neck, inflicting, however, but a slight wound. Springing to his feet, Gawain seizes his sword; but the Green Knight explains that all that has occurred—the challenge, the wooing by his wife, (for the lord of the castle and the Green Knight are one), the feigned blows—has been planned only to try Gawain, the most faultless hero in sooth that ever trod the earth; but since he has broken faith a little, he has been punished a little. Gawain, cursing his cowardice and covetousness, gives the girdle to the knight, but finally consents to receive it again; he will wear it, he says, as a safe-guard against self-sufficiency.

Refusing the cordial invitation of the knight to return to his castle, Gawain starts for Camelot. At the court he relates his entire adventure, showing the green lace as the token of his shame. But the king and his court comfort him, and it is agreed that each knight of the Round Table shall wear a baldric of bright green for the sake of Sir Gawain.

4. Origin. *Sir Gawain and the Green Knight* has been called 'the jewel of English literature in the Middle Age'.[1] It is the only long ME. romance devoted to Gawain.[2] The central incident of the poem, namely, the challenge to the blow with the privilege to the challenger of repayment in kind, and the happy termination of the adventure for the courageous hero, are found as incidental features in four French poems:[3] the continuation of Chrétien de Troyes' *Perceval* by Gautier de Doulens, the prose *Perceval*, *La Mule sans Frein*, and *Gauvain et Humbart*. The incident is also found in the German poem, *Diu Krône*, and in the Irish *Fled Bricrend (Bricriu's Feast)*. In *La Mule sans Frein, Gauvain et Humbart,* and *Diu Krône,* as well as in the English poem, the hero is Gawain; in Gautier's poem he is a nephew of Arthur, called Carados; in the prose *Perceval,* Lancelot; and in the Irish tale, Cuchulinn. Of these versions, the Irish tale, according to Miss Weston,[4] contains to all appearance the oldest version now accessible;[5]

---

[1] G. Paris; cf. Ten Brink, I 337, 347—8.

[2] The English, like the French Gawain-romances, are episodic in character, each centering in some one adventure of Gawain's. On the episodic Gawain-romances, see G. Paris, *op. cit. infra.*

[3] Weston, Ch. IX 90—92 (references to W. refer to *The Legend of SG,* unless the translation is named); G. Paris, *op. cit. infra,* 75.

[4] p. 92.

[5] G. Paris considers the presence in the Irish epic of the theme under discussion proof of its Celtic origin.

and of the remaining versions, those ascribing the adventure
to Gawain contain more archaic features than do the others.[1]
Since Gawain is the hero of four versions of the legend,
and since in other respects the legend of Gawain strikingly
resembles [2] that of Cuchulinn, the hero of the oldest version
of the adventure under consideration, Miss Weston concludes [3]
that the original hero, so far as connected with Arthurian
legend, was Gawain and Gawain alone.

In its version of the central incident, *SG* presents some
peculiar features: (1) The curious color of the strange knight;
(2) It is the only narrative that combines the two versions of
the giving of the blows, found in the two Irish manuscripts; [4]
(3) The challenge is differently stated; in all the other
versions the proposition is that the hero cut off the challenger's head, on condition that the latter may afterward
return the attention. (4) Of the Arthurian narratives, *SG* alone
contains the *three* blows of the older Irish manuscript. (5) In
no other version is the central incident coupled with that
of a testing of the hero's honor and chastity. The character
of the wife of the Green Knight is, Miss Weston [5] thinks,
perhaps a reminiscence of the Queen of the Magic Castle
or Isle, daughter or niece of an enchanter, who at an early
stage of Gawain's story was undoubtedly his love. [6] The
magic girdle of invulnerability is found nowhere else in
our legend; but, in other connections, it is a possession both
of Gawain and of Cuchulinn. [7]

No direct source for the English poem can be pointed

---

[1] *e. g.* The three blows of the older Irish MS. are found only in
SG; Weston, 94—5.

[2] Weston, 17, 28—31, 101.   [3] p. 102.

[4] See Weston, 92—4. In the older MS., the scene of the giving
and of the returning of the blow is at the abode of the magician; in
the later MS., it is at the court of the king.

[5] Translation of *SG*, p. ix.

[6] See *Diu Krône*; *The Carle of Carlile* (*infra*): Weston, 96 ff.

[7] Weston, p. 95, n. 1. (This note also points out resemblances
between *SG* and the Celtic *Lay of the Great Fool*.) On Gawain as
originally a solar hero, see Rhŷs, 14, and cf. Malory's *Morte Darthur*,
Bk. XX. Chs. XXI, XXII.

out. Madden, who notices the parallels to *SG* in the poetical
and in the prose *Perceval* and in *La Mule sans Frein,*
says:[1] 'The immediate original of the *Grene Knight* appears
to exist in the *Roman de Perceval*';[2] and again:[3] 'It is
highly probable that the author may have mingled together
several narratives for the purpose of rendering his own
more attractive.' The view of Madden is elaborated by
Miss Thomas:[4] The episode of the loyalty of Gawain to
his host, is borrowed, she thinks, from the adventure of
Gawain with the sister of Guigambresil in Chrétien's part
of the *Perceval*;[5] while the elaboration of *SG* has been
influenced by the *Perceval* as a whole. G. Paris,[6] on the
other hand, considers the resemblance between *SG* and the
episode in the *Perceval* very feeble, and the hypothesis
that the author of *SG* drew from both the poetical and
the prose *Perceval* unnecessarily complicated. The simpler
conclusion is that *SG* represents an independent derivation
from the common source, *i. e.* a French episodic poem, which
had for its principal subject what in the other texts is only
an incident. The charming details of our poem Paris would
still attribute to the English poet.

Our romance presents the original conception of Gawain's
character, that of a model knight.[7] Brandl sees in it a
further development of the romance of chivalric virtue introduced into English literature in *Ywain and Gawain.* This
species of romance has in *SG* 'become more original, more
thoughtful, and more national than in *Ywain,* though at the
same time somewhat skeptical, a quality which in Chaucer's
Troilus was to break out into irony.'[8]

---

[1] p. 305.

[2] This version is regarded as the source of *SG* by Morris, Ten
Brink, Brandl, and Wülker.

[3] p. 307.   [4] pp. 37—58.

[5] Cf. Brandl, and Weston, 96.

[6] *Op. cit. infra,* pp. 78, 72.

[7] Weston, (*Translation*) pp. x, xi; so Rhŷs, 183.

[8] For 15th century popularizations of *SG*, cf. *infra, The Grene
Knight,* and *The Turk and Gowin.*

5. Metre. 2530 verses combined in staves of varying length, each stave being composed of a succession of alliterative long lines followed [1] by five short riming lines technically known as a bob and a wheel; rime order, *ab ab a*. The romance is divided into 'fyttes' or cantos; this division, 'which earlier poets had nearly always done mechanically, of necessity follows from the organic construction of the story'.[2] The alliteration shows many irregularities.

6. Dialect. The West Midland, probably that of Lancashire.[3] The dialect of the *Pearl*, a poem generally assigned to the author of *SG*, is pronounced by Fick[4] W. Midland with a Northern tendency. Knigge[5] finds that the poem was copied by a scribe who spoke the more Southern dialect of *William of Palerne* and the *Alexander* fragments.

7. Date. 1350—1400. Madden[6] assigns the MS. to the reign of Richard II (1377—1398), and the poem itself, upon grounds of costume, armor, and architecture, to the same period or a little earlier. Luick[7] gives the second half, and Fick, upon linguistic grounds, the end, of the 14th century.

The order of composition for the poems ascribed to our author, is given by Ten Brink[8] as follows: *Sir Gawain, The Pearl, Cleanness, Patience. The Pearl* he looks upon as a transition from *SG* to the poems having 'a decided religious coloring', the most mature product of the poet's art. Miss Thomas[9] gives additional reasons for the priority of *SG* and *Pl* over *Cl* and *Pa*, perhaps the most important being that neither of the two former show any trace of

---

[1] Cf. the stanza of 13 lines; *e. g.* in No. XV.

[2] Ten Brink, I 347.

[3] Morris, *EE. Allit. Poems, EETS.*, No. 1, 1864, 1869, p. xxii; Ten Brink, I 336.

[4] p. 7.   [5] p. 117—18.   [6] p. 301.

[7] *Angl.* XI 572. For opinions not cited here, see Thomas, 27—32.

[8] I 348—350.   [9] pp. 18, 32.

Langland's influence, while the two latter, particularly *Cl*, show in their expression the influence of the first [1] and the second [2] version of *Piers Plowman.* Miss Thomas [3] would, however, place *Pl* before *SG*, both because the close connection between *SG* and *Cl* is better accounted for if the *Pearl* be not interposed between them; and because the latter poem, in its more subjective and more mystic character, in its less vigorous diction, in the greater number of comparisons used, and in its metrical form ('it is rhymed in complicated lyric strophes') seems to stand apart from the other poems, and to represent the earlier stages of the poet's maturity.

8. Author. Except as revealed in his works, [4] the 'Gawain-poet' is unknown to us. To him have also been assigned the religious poems, [5] *The Pearl, Cleanness, Patience,* and, according to later investigations, the legend of *St. Erkenwald.* [6] Morris [7] attributes the *Pl, Cl,* and *Pa* to the Gawain-poet because of similarity in dialect. Trautmann, [8] who considers this reason insufficient, bases the same conclusion upon correspondences in vocabulary, phraseology and verse-structure; in the case of *Cl* and *Pa* he notices also the resemblance in subject matter and in treatment. Miss Thomas [9] strengthens the case for *Pl* by pointing out similarities to the other poems in thought, expression, and style. [10]

9. Bibliography.

Manuscripts: Cotton, Nero A X, Brit. Mus.; desc. by Madden, *op. cit. infra.*

Editions: Madden, *Syr Gawane,* for the Bannatyne Club, L., 1839.

---

[1] Trautmann, 32, 33. [2] Thomas, 27—32.

[3] pp. 14, 22—25. [4] See Ten Brink, 1 336—37.

[5] On these poems, see Ten Brink, I 348—351; Brandl, § 74; Wülker, 107, 108; Körting § 105.

[6] Ed., Horstmann, *Altengl. Legenden,* 1881, p. 265.

[7] *Op. cit.* [8] pp. 26—31. [9] pp. 8—12.

[10] On the question of the identity of the poet with the Scottish Huchown, see p. 187.

R. Morris, *EETS.* No. 4, 1864, 1869; emendations of text, Fick, *op. cit. infra,* 5—7.

Retold in modern prose, with a brief introduction and notes by J. L. Weston, L., 1898, (published by D. Nutt as No. 1 of a series entitled *Arthurian Romances Unrepresented in Malory's Morte d'Arthur.*

Selections: Mätzner, *Spr. P.* I 311 (vv. 232—465).

General References: Ten Brink, I 422; Brandl, § 74; G. Paris, *Hist. Litt.,* XXX 71—78; J. L. Weston, *The Legend of Sir Gawain,* L., 1897.

Monographs: Trautmann, *Über die Verfasser und Entstehungszeit einiger allittericrender Gedichte des Altenglischen,* Leipsic, 1876, and *Angl.* I 117; Rosenthal, *Angl.* I 417 (on the metre); M. L. Thomas, *Sir Gawayn and the Green Knight, A Comparison with the French Perceval, preceded by an Investigation of the Author's other Works,* Zürich, 1883, diss.; Fuhrmann, *Die alliterierenden Sprachformeln in Morris' Early Engl. Allit. Poems und in Sir G. and the Green Knight,* Kiel, 1887, diss.; Knigge, *Über die Sprache des Dichters von Sir Gawayn and the Green Knight, und in den sogenannten Early Engl. Allit. Poems,* Marburg, 1885, diss.; Fick, *Zum me. Gedicht von der Perle, eine Lautuntersuchung,* Kiel, 1885, diss.; Steinbach, (*op. cit.* on p. 133) 48—50, (on *SG* and some other Gawain-poems); Schwann, *Die Konjugation in Sir Gawain und in den sog. EE. Allit. Poems,* Strassburg, 1884, prgr.

XXVI. Golagrus and Gawain.

1. Subject. The courtesy and magnanimity of Gawain.

2. Specimen. Golagrus refuses to yield to Gawain, vv. 1038—1050:

'Wes I neuer yit defouillit nor fylit in fame,
Nor nane of my eldaris, that euer I hard nevin;
Bot ilk berne has bene vnbundin with blame,
Ringand in rialte, and reullit thame self evin.

Sall neuer sege vndir son se me with schame,
Na luke on my lekame with light nor with levin,
Na nane of the nynt degre haue noy of my name,
I swere be suthfast God, that settis all on sevin.
Bot gif that wourschip of were win me away,
I trete for na favour;
Do furth thi devoir;   [1] Doutles, this day.' [1]
Of me gettis thou na more,

3. Story. King Arthur is on the march to Tuscany to take ship for the Holy Land.[2] Provisions failing, Kay at his own request is sent to a city that they approach to purchase food. Entering a splendid hall unmolested, he seizes upon food for himself, and answers roughly when reproved by the lord of the hall, by whom he is finally knocked down. Kay returns to Arthur and tells him that no food can be obtained in that city. Gawain, advising that a more courteous messenger be employed, is himself sent to the castle. The lord of the castle, charmed by Gawain's courteous bearing, promises Arthur as a free gift plenty of provisions and thirty thousand fresh troops.

Arthur, journeying through many far countries, comes to a strange castle, whose lords have never paid allegiance to any man. Arthur declares that when he comes again the lord of the castle [3] shall do him homage. Accordingly, having made his offering in the Holy City, upon his homeward journey he again halts before the castle. Gawain, Lancelot, and Ewain announce to its lord that Arthur desires his friendship. Golagrus replies that as none of his elders have ever done homage to any man, he must withhold his allegiance; that reserved, he cannot do too much for Arthur.

Upon hearing this, Arthur prepares to besiege the city. Next occurs a succession of single combats between knights

---

[1] The last line of the stanza.

[2] In the French story, Arthur and fifteen knights set out to deliver a knight imprisoned in Chateau Orgueilleux.

[3] Chateau Orgueilleux, in the French.

from the respective sides. Finally Golagrus and Gawain find themselves opposed; each knight is nearly overthrown by his opponent, but at length Golagrus is struck down. He refuses to give up his sword to Gawain; he will die, but his honor shall remain unstained. In vain Gawain, with promises of gifts and honors, tries to induce him to yield. At last Gawain inquires if there is not some way by which both the knight and his honor may be preserved. Golagrus replies that there is one way; let Gawain follow him to his castle as if conquered, and he shall be rewarded for the act of friendship. Gawain consents, and permits Golagrus to arise; the knights fight for a little while, then they sheathe their swords, and Gawain follows Golagrus to his castle. All Arthur's army weep because of the capture of the flower of knighthood.

In his hall, in the presence of his retainers, Golagrus says to Gawain: 'In my hour of need I experienced your friendship, now I will be your subject.' They go to Arthur's camp, where Golagrus relates how Gawain conquered, and submits himself to Arthur. When Arthur leaves the castle, where he has feasted for nine days, he releases Golagrus from his allegiance.[1]

4. Origin. The author of *Golagrus and Gawain,* according to Madden,[2] borrowed the entire outline of his romance from the French *Roman de Perceval.* Notwithstanding obvious correspondences, *GG* diverges so much from the French narrative that Trautmann is inclined to consider the latter only the indirect source of the former;

---

[1] In the French story, Gawain spares his opponent in order to preserve the life of the latter's *amie*, and receives from him a promise to submit to Arthur. Gawain then follows his opponent to the castle and gives up his sword to the lady; whereupon the lord frees the prisoner and does homage to Arthur.

[2] *Syr Gawane*, p. 338; so G. Paris, *Hist. Litt.*, XXX 41; Trautmann, 402, who gives for the corresponding French passages, Potvin (Mons, 1866—70), III pp. 239—49, 303—45. For summaries of these passages, see Madden, pp. 338—40.

whatever may have been the author's direct source, it is certain that he took liberties with it. This is clearly seen from the fact that in *GG* the majority of all the names given to the combatents are unknown to Arthurian legend. Most of the strange names were undoubtedly invented by the poet in the interest of the alliteration. In the source of the poem, in the choice of subject, a chivalric test, in the use of the stanza of thirteen lines, and in the verbal agreements with *The Aunters of Arthur*, Brandl sees the work of a poet of the Gawain school; and in the stubborn refusal of Golagrus to renounce his freedom, he sees revealed the Scotchman.

5. Metre. [1] 1362 verses, in 105 alliterative-riming stanzas of 13 lines,[2] having the rime-scheme, *ab ab ab ab cdddc.* The first nine lines of each stanza are 4-stressed alliterative verses of the regular sort with medial cesura; verses 10, 11, 12 are 3-stressed; v. 13, 2-stressed. The 4-stressed verses have, most frequently, four alliterating letters, though not seldom one less and sometimes one more; the 3-stressed verses have frequently three, though often only two, alliterating letters, and sometimes none; the 2-stressed verses often dispense with alliteration. In *GG*, and also in the *Aunters of Arthur,* of the last four verses of a stanza, the first three have the structure of the first half of the alliterative long line; the last verse, that of the second half.[3]

6. Dialect. [4] Scottish, influenced by Southern forms.[5]

7. Date. [1] The second half of the 15th century, or shortly before 1500. To this period point the vocabulary and style, which have much in common with that of Blind

---

[1] Trautmann, 407—9.

[2] Cf. *Rauf Coilyear,* p. 82, *The Aunters of Arthur,* p. 176; see further Trautmann.

[3] Luick, *Angl.* XII 438.   [4] Trautmann, 406—7.

[5] See Noltemeyer.

Harry, Holland, Gawain Douglas, and Dunbar. The poem has also been assigned to the first half of the 15th century.[1]

8. Author. Owing to allusions in two Scottish poems of the 15th century to the 'Awntyre'[2] and to the 'awnteris'[3] of Gawain, *GG* has been ascribed respectively to the Scottish poets Huchown and Clerk of Tranent. Trautmann[4] rejects the authorship of Huchown, and also maintains[5] that *GG*, on account of differences in language and metre, cannot have a common authorship with any of the eight poems that have also been ascribed by different scholars to Huchown. The author, he thinks, was Clerk of Tranent; for the title of 'awnteris of Gawane' given to Clerk's poem by Dunbar, might be applied to *GG*, which narrates two distinct adventures; again, the author of *GG* was undoubtedly a Scotchman; and finally, *GG* is the only poem of Scottish origin that, upon the ground of Dunbar's passage, can be ascribed Clerk.

9. Bibliography.

Manuscripts: None extant.[6]

Editions: An old print, Edinburgh, 1508, now in the Advocates' Library, H. 30. a; facsimile edition of the above, Edin., 1827.

Pinkerton, *Scottish Poems*, L., 1792, vol. III.

Madden, *Syr Gawane*, (*supra*, p. 168) 131—33; notes, pp. 336—44.

Trautmann, *Angl.* II 395 ff.

F. J. Amours, in *Scottish Alliterative Poems in Riming Stanzas*, I, *Scottish TS.*, Edin., 1891—92.

---

[1] Madden, *Syr Gawane*, 338; Brandl, §§ 132, 133.

[2] Wyntoun's *Cronykil of Scotland*, 1795, 2 vols, Bk. V, Ch. 12, vv. 301—6.

[3] Wm. Dunbar's *Lament for the Makaris*, St. 17, in his poems, ed. Laing, Edin., 1834, II 355.

[4] *Angl.* I 109 ff.

[5] *Angl.* I 127—30; II 405—7.

[6] See Madden, 336—7; *Angl.* II 398.

General References: Brandl, § 133; Wülker, 111; M. L. Thomas, (*op. cit.* on p. 168) 87—9.

XXVII. The Aunters of Arthur at the Tarnewathelan.

1. Subject. (1) The appearance to queen Guenever of her mother's spectre. (2) The combat between Sir Gawain and a Scottish knight in order to determine the rightful possessor of the latter's land, which Arthur has conquered.

2. Specimen. Stanza VII:

Thus on fote con thay founde, these frekes vn-fayn,
And fled to the forest fro the fau fellus;
Thay ran to the raches, for redeles of rayn,
For the snyterand snaue, that snaypely hom snellus;
So come a lau oute of a loghe in lede is noȝt to layn,
In lykenes of Lucifere, lauyst in hellus;
Glydand to Dame Gaynour, hyre gates were gayne,
Ȝauland ful ȝamerly, with many loude ȝelles;
Hyt ȝaulit, hit ȝamurt, with wlonkes full wete,
And sayd with sykyng sare,
'I banne the byrde that me bare,
For noue comyn is my care,
I gloppen and Y grete!'

3. Story. While Arthur and his court are hunting in the forest near Carlisle, the queen and her escort Sir Gawain become separated from the rest of the company. At noon it becomes dark as midnight; then a flame arises from a lake 'in the likeness of Lucifer lowest in hell', and a gruesome spectre comes gliding towards the queen, yelling lamentably and saying with sore sighing, 'I curse the woman that bore me'.

'Gaynour[1] the gay' wails and weeps, but Gawain bids her not to fear; he will speak to the spectre, if perchance he can amend its sorrow. Accordingly he conjures the spectre by Christ to tell him why she walks in the woods. She replies that she was once a great queen, and begs him to let her have a sight of 'Gaynour the gay', whom she then bids to look upon her loathsome self, saying: 'King, duke, and emperor shall all be thus. Take heed while you may; have pity on the poor; in death nothing but holy prayer will avail'. The pity of the queen, who speaks of her own dead mother, elicits the information that the spectre is the queen's mother, and that, if thirty trentals of mass are said for her between nine in the morning and noon, her soul will soon be brought to heaven; let the queen be generous with her goods while she has them.

In answer to questions of the queen, the spectre says that pride most excites the anger of Christ, and that measure and meekness, and pity upon the poor have most power to bring souls to bliss. She then speaks of Arthur's past victories in France, foretells his triumph over the Romans, the treason of one of his knights, who shall seize the crown, the death of Gawain, the wounding of Arthur, and the slaying of the knights of the Round Table. After telling them to remember the masses for her soul, she glides away with 'grisly greeting'. Then the sun comes out; the clouds disperse; the king's bugle is heard; the royal route comes up; they all go to Rondall-seat Hall for their supper.

As Arthur sits upon the dais, there enters a 'seteler'[2] and a 'lovesome lady', who leads a knight dressed in white armor and carrying a silver shield. The knight tells the king that he is Sir Galrun of Galway, whose lands Arthur has taken in war and given to Gawain; Sir Galrun now comes to fight for his possessions in a fair field.

---

[1] Also written 'Waynour'.

[2] 'A player upon a citole, a sort of hurdy-gurdy': Halliwell's glossary.

Gawain takes up the challenge and the combat begins. The queen weeps for Gawain the Good; and when Sir Galrun is wounded, his lady laments shrilly for him. Gawain's steed is slain and the knights fight on foot; both are covered with wounds; Gawain escapes a mortal wound but by a hair's breadth. Finally, however, he has his foe in his grasp. Sir Galrun's lady entreats the queen to have pity upon him. The queen kneels before the king, begging him to command peace. Sir Galrun resigns his rights to Gawain as the most valiant knight he has ever met. The king makes Gawain a duke or ruler over Wales, and bids him restore to Sir Galrun his lands, which is done. Galrun is then made a duke and a knight of the Round Table.

The queen orders masses for her mother's soul.

4. Origin. No direct source for the *Aunters* has to my knowledge yet been pointed out.[1] Ten Brink[2] considers the 'short and attractive poem' 'a clear case of the separate growth of known saga material'. 'Cumberland, Westmoreland, the districts between the Tyne and Tweed and all the south of the Scotland of to-day, are rich in names of places that point to a localizing and a more or less independent growth of the Arthurian traditions in that region.' The popular Arthurian framework seems to have been used by the writer to impress his own convictions or views. 'The religious and political tendency', says Brandl, 'is clear'.

The ground-work of the first adventure Madden[3] finds in a religious legend, very popular among Latin Mediaeval writers, of the appearance of a woman in torments, who has been punished for her want of chastity and for her pride and vanity, and whose salvation is procured by a certain number of masses said for her soul. There is an inedited English poem of the 15th century, called *The*

---

[1] Lübke announces the future publication of a critical edition of the romance.

[2] I 336.   [3] p. 328.

Trental of St. Gregory,[1] founded on the same story, in which Pope Gregory plays the part that queen Guenever does in the Scottish romance. Of the second 'adventure' Madden knows no prototype, but calls attention to the fact that in Malory's *Morte Darthur,* 'professedly compiled from the French', 'Syr Galleron of Galway' is introduced as a knight of the Round Table,[2] and that he is also one of the knights that watch for the surprising of Lancelot in the queen's chamber.[3] Of this company, Malory says that 'all they were of Scotland, either of Sir Gawain's kin, either well willers to his brethren'.

5. Metre.[4]   702 verses,[5] in 55 alliterative-riming stanzas of 13 lines,[6] each stanza consisting of nine successive alliterative long lines with two stresses in each half line, and four not necessarily alliterative short lines of two, less frequently of three stresses. In the first and in the ninth line of a stanza, one or more words of the preceding, occasionally of a more distant line, are repeated. Both in respect to this repetition and in respect to the rime order, part first[7] of the poem is very regular, part second, very irregular. Nearly half of the alliterative long lines have four alliterating letters, two in each half line; of the remainder, the majority have three alliterating letters, two of which fall for the most part in the first half line. Alliteration in the last line is lacking in nearly half of the stanzas.[8]

6. Dialect. The North of England, probably Lancasshire[9] or the vicinity of Carlisle[10] (Cumberland), where the

---

[1] British Museum, MS. Cott. Calig. A. II f. 84[b]. Madden prints about 29 lines, p. 329.

[2] Bk. XVIII, Chs. X, XI; Bk. XIX, Ch. XI.

[3] Bk. XX, Ch. II.   [4] Lübke, 13—19.

[5] Madden's numbering; there are some gaps in the MSS.

[6] Cf. *Golagrus and Gawain*, p. 171.

[7] Stanzas I—XXV.   [8] See further, p. 171 *supra*.

[9] Ten Brink; Robson, for the MS., pp. x, xi.

[10] Brandl; Robson, p. xiv, for the native place of the author.

scene is laid. All the places named except one are still recognizable and apparently well known to the writer.'[1] The dialect of MS. *L* is very different from that of the other two.[2]

7. Date. 1350—1400, perhaps about 1380. Ten Brink gives the date as 'perhaps about, or some time before the middle of the 14th century; but in no case long before 1350, and still less before 1300, as has been claimed.'[3] Lübke[4] points out that the poet evidently knew the alliterative *Morte Arthure,* and that his work in turn influenced[5] *Thomas of Erceldoune* (1400 or 1401). His conclusion is that, since the date of the *Morte Arthure* has not been fixed, that of *AA* cannot be exactly determined; but if the former poem was written about 1360,[6] then 1380 is the probable date for the *Aunters.*

8. Author. On account of differences in phraseology and in metre, Trautmann concludes that the *Aunters* cannot be by the author of *Golagrus and Gawain,* as Madden and others have thought; neither can it belong to any of the other N. English poets to whom it has been assigned. Lübke,[7] who also rejects the common authorship of *AA* and *GG,* concludes further that *AA* is composed of two originally independent poems, very loosely united in the twenty-sixth stanza. The author of part II knew and imitated part I, but the two parts were probably put together by still a third writer.[8]

9. Bibliography.
Manuscripts: J. Ireland, in Hale, beginning of the 15th century; desc. in Robson's ed., pp. xxxvii—xlv.
L. Lincoln or Thornton (see p. 133).

---

[1] Robson, p. xiv.   [2] Lübke, p. 1.
[3] See Robson, pp. xix, xxi.   [4] pp. 28—9.
[5] See p. 38 of Brandl's ed. of *T. of E.,* in Zupitza's *Sammlung engl. Denkmäler,* II, Berlin, 1880.
[6] *Infra,* p. 187.   [7] pp. 20—27.
[8] Stanza IV belongs both by content and vocabulary to part I.

Douce, Bodl. Libr., Oxford, reign of Edward IV;[9] desc. by Madden, *infra*, p. lviii.

Editions: D. Pinkerton, in *Scottish Ballads*, 1792; see Madden, 326.

L. Laing in *Ancient Popular Poetry of Scotland*, 1822.

Madden, in *Syr Gawane* (see p. 167), 95—128 (notes, 326—36).

J. Robson, in *Three Early English Metrical Romances*, L., 1842.

General References: Ten Brink, I 336; Brandl, § 75; *Hist. Litt.*, XXX 96, 97.

Monographs: Lübke, *The Aunters of Arthur* etc., Part I (MSS., Metre, and Author), Berlin, 1883, diss.; Trautmann (on the author), *Angl.* I 129—131; Luick (on the metre), *Angl.* XII 452.

XXVIII. The Avowynge of King Arther, Sir Gawain, Sir Kaye, and Sir Bawdewyn of Bretan.

1. Subject. The vows made during a boar-hunt by Arthur and three knights; the fulfilment of these vows, especially of the threefold vow of Sir Baudwin of Britain; his narrative in explanation of his vow.

2. Specimen. The vows of the knights, stanza IX:

> Then vnsquarut Gauan,
> And sayd godely a-gayn,
> 'I a-vowe to Tarnewathelan,
>   To wake hit alle nyȝte.'
> 'And I a-vow,' sayd Kaye,
> 'To ride this forest or daye;
> Quo-so wernes me the waye,
>   Hym to dethe diȝte!'

---

[1] Madden.

Quod Baudewyn, 'To stynte owre strife,
I a-vow, bi my life,
Neuyr to be jelus of my wife,
    Ne of no birde bryȝte;
Nere werne nomon my mete,
Quen I gode may gete,
Ne drede my dethe for no threte,
    Nauthir of king ner knyȝte.'

3. Story. Arthur and three knights are hunting a boar. When they have tracked it to its den, Arthur vows that if the boar be Satan himself, he will kill him without help before the next morning. At Arthur's bidding each of the knights makes a vow: Gawain, to watch all night at the Tarn Wadling; Kay, to ride in the forest until day, prepared to award death to all opponents; Baudwin, never to be jealous of his wife or of any fair woman, to refuse no man food when he has it, and never to be afraid of death.

Each knight now goes his own way. Arthur attacks and kills the boar, then, after thanking Mary for the victory, falls asleep from weariness. Meanwhile, Kay, meeting a knight who has captured a maiden, rides against him and is overthrown. At Kay's request they all ride to Tarn Wadling to ask Gawain to pay Kay's ransom. Gawain rides one course with the knight in behalf of Kay, and another in behalf of the maiden, and in both courses is victorious. He sends the knight and the maiden to the queen from her own knight Gawain; the ransom of the prisoners is to be at her will. The queen gives the knight to Arthur, who makes him a member of the Round Table.

Kay now wishes to put Baudwin's vow to the test. Accordingly, with the king's permission, six armed men surprise Baudwin while riding and order him to turn another way; Baudwin refuses, and overcomes them all. In order to test the knight's hospitality, the king sends his minstrel to Baudwin's castle with the order to stay there forty days and see whether any man is sent away without food. The minstrel finds that every comer is welcome to sit at Baudwin's table without even asking permission. Finally, the king tests Baudwin's indifference to the conduct of his wife by presenting to his eyes seeming proof of the lady's intimacy with one of Arthur's knights. Baudwin's only remark is that all has been by the lady's will. At the king's request Baudwin explains, by an account of his experiences in a besieged castle, how he came to hold the convictions expressed in his vow.

4. Origin. For this poem as a whole no source is known; G. Paris[1] says that nothing proves or disproves a French original; Miss Thomas[2] classes it among the romances showing a more original treatment of the Arthur legend; Brandl sees in the romance the influence of the Gawain-poet, for here again the chivalric test is the theme.

A story like the first tale of Sir Baudwin is found in the twenty-sixth *fabliau* in Montaiglon's *Recueil général*; G. Paris,[3] who points out the resemblance, thinks that the French version may repose upon some actual occurrence in Palestine. To the same set of stories belongs the short Latin 'tragedy' of the sixty soldiers and the two women, contained in the *Poetria* of Johannes de Garlandia.[4]

5. Metre. 72 16-line 'tail-rime' stanzas, having the rime scheme *aab ccb ddb eeb*[5] (class III). Alliteration is part of the metrical plan.

6. Dialect. The North of England.[6] *The Aunters of Arthur,*[7] found in the same MS., is in the same handwriting and dialect.

7. Date. 1350—1400.[8]

8. Author. Unknown.

---

[1] p. 113, *op. cit. infra.*   [2] *Op. cit.* on p. 168.
[3] *Op. cit. infra,* p. 112.
[4] Kittredge, *Mod. Lang. Notes,* VIII (8) 502—503.
[5] Cf. *Sir Perceval,* pp. 125, 132.
[6] Brandl, p. 665.   [7] See p. 176.
[8] Brandl; cf. G. Paris, p. 112, *op. cit. infra.*

9. Bibliography.

Manuscripts: Ireland, in Hale (*supra,* p. 177).

Editions: Robson (*supra,* p. 178).

General References: Brandl, § 75, p. 665; G. Paris, *Hist. Litt.,* XXX 111—113; M. C. Thomas (*op. cit.* on p. 168), 83—84.

XXIX. Morte Arthure.

1. Subject. Arthur's war against Rome; the treason of Modred; the death of Arthur.

2. Specimen. (1) Modred's praise of Gawain, vv. 3876—86:

'He was makles one molde, mane be my trowhe;
This was syr Gawayne the gude, þe gladdeste of othire,
And the graciouseste gome that undire God lyffede,
Mane hardyeste of hande, happyeste in armes,
And the hendeste in hawle undire hevene riche;
Þe lordelieste of ledynge qwhylles he lyffe myghte,
Ffore he was lyone allossede in londes i-newe;
Had thow knawene hym, syr kynge in kythe thare he lengede,
His konynge, his knyghthode, his kyndly werkes,
His doyng, his doughtynesse, his dedis of armes,
Thow wolde hafe dole for his dede þe dayes of thy life!'

(2) The Death of Arthur, vv. 4325—32:

'I foregyffe alle greffe, for Cristez lufe of hevene!
3ife Waynor hafe wele wroghte, wele hir be-tydde!'
He saide *In manus* with mayne one molde whare he ligges,
And thus passes his speryt, and spekes he no more!
The baronage of Bretagne thane, bechopes and othire,
Graythes theme to Glaschenbery with gloppynnande hertes,
To bery thare the bolde kynge, and brynge to the erthe,
With alle wirchipe and welthe þat any wy scholde.

3. Story. When Arthur had subdued all Great Britain and France and had made tributary many states, he rested

and held the Round Table. During the Christmas feast at
Carlisle, ambassadors from the Roman emperor, Lucius
Iberius, summon him to pay homage at Rome. After a
council with his barons, Arthur sends Lucius a defiant
message, promising soon to be with him. Upon receiving
the message, Lucius prepares to march to meet the Britons.
Having appointed his nephew Modred, who would prefer to
go with the army, viceroy and guardian of the sorrowing
queen, Arthur embarks with his army at Sandwich for
France.

During the voyage he dreams of a many-hued dragon
fiercely attacked by a black bear, but finally victorious.
The dream is interpreted to mean that Arthur will overthrow some tyrant or giant. Landing in Normandy, he
hears of a giant, who has just abducted the young Duchess
of Brittany, a cousin of Guenever's. Going alone to the
giant's haunt, Arthur finds the duchess' aged foster-mother
mourning over her child's grave. After a terrific encounter
with the giant, Arthur kills him and carries away as
keepsakes, the giant's club and his kirtle bordered with the
beards of kings.

Arthur learns that Lucius is ravaging France; Gawain,
a messenger with others to the emperor, provokes an attack
by the Romans; reinforced, the Britons defeat the Romans
with great slaughter and plunder their camp. Thus has
Arthur richly rebuked the Romans forever! Lucius invades
Saxony and is there suprised by Arthur, who slays with
'Colbrand' six hundred Roman giants, and finally kills
Lucius.[1] The bodies of the emperor and other Romans
are sent by Arthur to Rome as the arrears of tribute due
from Britain.

Arthur, advancing into Lorraine, lays siege to Metz.
Sir Florent, one of his knights, is sent with a detachment
in search of supplies. Gawain, one of the company, going
forth alone in search of adventure, encounters and severely
wounds Sir Priamus, descended from Hector of Troy. Florent

---

[1] v. 2255; in v. 2074 Lucius has already been slain by Lancelot.

is attacked by the Duke of Lorraine, who is later reinforced by the main body of the enemy; Priamus and his men desert to the British because their wages have not been paid; the enemy is defeated, and Metz is taken the same day.

Arthur now crosses the Alps into Italy, where the Pope offers to crown him king of Rome. Arthur has a dream of a beautiful 'duchess' and her wheel, interpreted as prophesying a reverse of fortune for him. Almost immediately he learns from a pilgrim, a British knight in disguise, that Modred has seized all England, has called in Saracens as allies, and has married Guenever. Vowing vengeance, Arthur leaves knights to govern Italy and embarks for Britain.

At Southampton his fleet encounters and utterly defeats that of Modred. Gawain, rashly attempting a land battle, is slain by Modred, who weeps bitterly over him. The now repentant Modred retreats into Cornwall; Guenever, on hearing of his defeat, enters a convent. Arthur, having landed, slays ten thousand of the enemy with the loss of but sevenscore knights. After burying Gawain with great honor at Winchester, he follows Modred into Cornwall, attacks, and, in spite of a vastly inferior force, defeats and kills him; but receives from his nephew's hand his own death-blow. Wishing that Guenever may fare well, if she has done well, Arthur dies, and is buried at Glastonbury. This is the end of Arthur, who was of the blood of Hector and Priamus of Troy, as 'the Bruytte tellys'.

4. Origin.[1] The author of the *Morte Arthure* refers to his sources as 'romawns' and 'cronycles'. By chronicles we are doubtless to understand the accounts of Arthur's heroic deeds as generally believed by the people; by romances, the narrative of the adventures and love-affairs of the knights of the Round Table. The author's use of more than one source, and these differing in kind, is shown

---

[1] Based almost entirely upon Branscheid, to whom the page numbers refer.

both by various contradictions in his narrative, and by the difference in the character of the episodes.

The basis of the narrative is undoubtedly the *Historia Regum Britanniae* of Geoffrey of Monmouth, which is followed most closely in the first part of the poem (to l. 2385), much more freely from l. 3591. A number of features from Layamon's *Brut* are worked in,[1] some of these being divergences from Geoffrey's narrative, others, additions to it. There are also some correspondences[2] with Wace's *Brut*, all of which are, however, found in G., or in L., or in both. Besides the chronicles just mentioned, the narrative gives evidence of the use of two French romances, one belonging to the cycle of Arthur, the other not;[3] also, in one or two places, of the use of still other sources.[4]

In spite, however, of the fact that the substance of the narrative is borrowed, the originality of the poet is constantly in evidence. He has used his borrowed material freely, often expanding[5] it and weaving into it his own inventions.[5] The following seem to be original touches: Arthur's reception of the message of the Roman ambassadors, who quail before his glance; Modred's unwillingness[6] to be left in Britain as Arthur's viceroy (ll. 679—688); Guenever's

---

[1] See p. 211.   [2] pp. 185, 187, 210.

[3] From an Arthurian romance was taken, probably, the feature of the boastful vows of Arthur and his knights, ll. 320—394, 2044—94, 3164—75 [cf. the *gas* in the *Pélerinage de Charlemagne*; cf. also *King Arthur and the King of Cornwall*, Child, I 283; Madden, *Syr Gawane*, 275]; from a non-Arthurian romance, the kernel of Arthur's conquest of Lorraine, ll. 2385—3205.

[4] pp. 194—196, 210, 219. Sommer, (III 274, n. 1) does not 'think it at all likely that the poet took the trouble to combine his information from so many sources, but rather that he had only one'. He also suggests (pp. 274—5) as a possible source for the account of Arthur's Roman expedition a *Suite de Lancelot*; see *infra*, No. XXXII: 4.

[5] See ll. 395—553; 554—624; 1222—1588 (the fight with the giant, where the poet 'has skilfully woven together three originally independent legends'); 1222—1588; 1588—1949; 2483—3031 (The Gawain episode). See pp. 189—91, 193—5, 216.

[6] Cf. Wülker (see p. 85), p. 15.

sorrow at parting with Arthur (697—704); the death of Lucius at the hand of Arthur (2255); the many-colored dragon (764—70), the fight with the giant (2111—2134), which is 'in part drawn with truly original humor'; many of the details in the dream of Fortune and her wheel[1] (3206—3455). In the last part of the poem, after Arthur's return to Britain, the narrative as compared with that of the chroniclers is noticeably expanded and changed; we have nowhere a clear indication which chronicle was used, and much, especially towards the end, was added by the poet himself.[2]

In his account of the death of Arthur the divergence of the poet from the version of Geoffrey and of Layamon[3] is of especial interest. Influenced, doubtless, by his desire to present Arthur as a national hero, the poet says nothing of the removal of the fatally wounded king to Avalon, the Celtic Paradise or Isle of the Blessed, where he is to be healed of his wounds, but records his death, and his burial at Glastonbury.[4] He thus adopts not the mythical, or legendary, but the historical version of Arthur's death.[5]

The influence of the poet's own country and age upon his work has been pointed out[6] in his love for the sea shown in the vivid description of a sea battle[7] not even suggested by the source; in the features of the border warfare between Scotland and England seen in many of the descriptions of battle; in the fondness for allegory; in the traces of classical influence; and in his endeavor to give his readers history, not romance, as witnesses particularly his full account of the death and burial of Arthur.

As a poet the author of the alliterative *Morte Arthure*

---

[1] On the dream, see pp. 201—3.

[2] *e. g.* l. 4326, quoted on p. 181.

[3] For a translation of Layamon's very poetical account of Arthur's last battle, see Ten Brink, I 191—2.

[4] See *supra,* p. 103.

[5] Cf. the version of the rimed *Morte Arthur,* No. XXXII: 3, 4.

[6] Wülker, *op. cit.,* pp. 13—15.

[7] Vv. 3667 ff.

has received no slight praise.[1] In literary merit his poem has been pronounced by both Trautmann[2] and Wülker[3] superior to the work of Malory.[4]

5. Metre.   4346[5] alliterative long lines.   According to Luick,[6] the metrical model followed by the North English author belonged not only to the West Midland in general, but to the alliterative poems of Lancashire, especially as represented by *Sir Gawain and the Grene Knight.*

6. Dialect.   That of N. England or of S. Scotland. Authorities are divided between these two localities; the two dialects were, however, in the 14th and to the middle of the 15th century, 'scarcely to be distinguished'.[7] Morris[8] speaks of the dialect as Northumbrian with N. Midland peculiarities due to the scribe. Trautmann[9] thinks that the original dialect may have been Scottish, since it illustrates some linguistic peculiarities—*i. e.* the use of the same alliterating letter through several successive lines, and the interchange at pleasure of *w* and *v*—found in other Scottish, but not in English, poems. Luick,[10] who speaks of the territory as Northern and of the author as N. English, maintains that the linguistic characteristics mentioned by Trautmann are not peculiar to the Scottish dialect, but occur also in that of N. England.

The dialect of the *Susanna,* thought, with considerable probability, to be the work of the author of *MA,* is also

---

[1] See Ten Brink, II[2] 51—52.   [2] p. 143.

[3] *Op. cit.,* p. 16.

[4] *MA* was the principal source of Malory's fifth book: See Sommer, III 8, n. 1, 148—175; on Malory's literary merit, pp. 8, 294.

[5] After l. 2590, Perry counts one line too many.

[6] Angl. XI 585—97.

[7] Luick, p. 586, in citing Murray on *The Dialect of the Southern Counties of Scotland;* cited also by Brade, p. 21.

[8] *Early English Alliterative Poems, EETS.,* No. 1, 1864, pp. vi-vii; 2nd ed., 1869.

[9] p. 139.   [10] p. 585.

uncertain; but both Brade[1] and Köster[2] favor the opinion
that it is Scottish colored by more Southern forms.

7. Date. Probably about 1360, if Huchown be considered the author. This is the date assigned by Morris
and Skeat,[3] and accepted by Trautmann.[4] Lübke[5] doubts
the date, because he doubts the authorship of Huchown.
Ten Brink assigns *MA,* as a redaction of Huchown's poem,
to the beginning of the 15th century.

8. Author. The author of *MA* has very generally been
believed to be the Scottish poet Huchown, mentioned and
warmly praised by Wyntoun in his *Cronykil of Scotland.*[6]
According to Wyntoun,

> '*He made þe gret Geste of Arthure*
> *And þe Awntyre of Gawane*
> *Đe Pystyl als of Swete Swsane.*'

The identity of Huchown's *gret Geste* with *MA* was
first maintained by Madden, upon the ground that Wyntoun
reports Huchown as having called Lucius Iberius 'Emperoure'
instead of 'Procurature', which is also the case in *MA.*
The view of Madden is opposed by Morris[7] upon linguistic
grounds; but supported by Panton[8] and by Trautmann[9]
upon the ground of the resemblance between *MA* and the
outline of Huchown's *Geste* given by Wyntoun. Trautmann
argues further that Wyntoun himself in his list[10] of the
countries ruled over by Arthur has followed *MA*; and that
the ME. metrical version of the legend of Susanna, which
is very generally conceded to be Huchown's '*Pystel*', shows
in linguistic and in metrical peculiarities, a surprising agreement with *MA,* and is, therefore, by the same author.[11]

---

[1] pp. 21, 22.   [2] pp. 49, 62.

[3] *Specimens of Early English,* II p. XXXIX.

[4] p. 148.   [5] p. 30.   [6] See p. 172.

[7] *Op. cit.* on p. 186, n. 1.

[8] *Destruction of Troy, EETS.,* 39, 56, 1869/74.

[9] *Angl.* I 134—41.   [10] vv. 253—60.

[11] T.'s argument for the authorship of Huchown is considered
strong by Ward (I 388) and conclusive by Sommer (III 8).

The authorship of Huchown is rejected by Lübke upon the following grounds: (1) Wyntoun says expressly that he has found 'na wryt' on Arthur's death, whereas *MA*, in opposition to the general legend, gives a full account of it. (2) The contents of Huchown's poem, as reported by Wyntoun, agree better with the general legend than with *MA*. (3) Lucius is also called 'emperoure' by Geoffrey of Monmouth and in the *Chronicle of England*; by Layamon he is continually called 'kayser'. (4) *MA* does not deserve the praise given by Wyntoun to Huchown for his truthfulness; he diverges more than a 'lytil' from 'Suthfastness', *i. e.* from the version of the old chronicles, as for instance, in the Gawain episode, in the account of the abduction of the French duchess, and in the close of the poem. (5) The correspondence between the names of the countries given by Wyntoun and by the author of *MA* is not close enough to justify the conclusion that the *gret Geste* and *MA* are the same work.

Ten Brink [1] holds that *MA* is probably a North English reproduction of Huchown's *Geste* in connection with his *Awntyre of Gawane*; in all essential points the reproduction may have been almost literal. Brandl speaks of *MA* as possibly, and the *Susanna* as certainly, Huchown's. Wülker [2] assumes him to be the author of *MA*.

The *Awntyre of Gawane,* ascribed by Wyntoun to Huchown, has been thought by some scholars [3] to be *Sir Gawain and the Grene Knight,* by others, *Golagrus and Gawain.* But neither of these poems, Trautmann [4] maintains, nor any other known romance to which the title of '*Awntyre of Gawane*' might be applied can possibly be the work of the author of *MA* and the *Pystyl*; the *Awntyre* is none other than the Gawain episode (vv. 2371—3083), [5] inserted by the poet into his story of Arthur, but which has really nothing to do with the *gret Gest.*

Huchown himself, it is generally granted, must have been a Scotchman. The name has been explained as

---

[1] II[2] 51.   [2] *Op. cit.*   [3] See Trautmann, 120—121.
[4] pp. 141—42.   [5] Cf. *supra*, p. 184.

'apparently a diminutive of Hugh'.[1] Wyntoun (v. 281)
speaks of the poet as 'Huchowne of þe Awle ryale' (*aula
regalis*), and it has been conjectured that he was the 'gude
Schir Hew of Eglintoun',[2] mentioned among other poets
by William Dunbar in the fourteenth stanza of his *Lament
for the Makaris*;[3] for it seems improbable that Dunbar
would have left unmentioned the author of the *gret Gest*.
Sir Hugh de Eglintoun flourished about the middle of the
14th century, was brother-in-law to Robert II, and occupied
different high offices; he died in 1375 or 1376.[4]

9. Bibliography.

Manuscripts: Thornton, A. 1. 17, Lincoln Cathedral Libr.,
ca. 1440: desc. by Halliwell (see p. 133); by Madden, *Syr
Gawane,* pp. 1—lviii.

Editions: Halliwell, L. 1847.

Perry, *EETS.,* No. 8, 1865; Brock, 1871 (Perry's ed.
with revised text); on the text, see *Angl.* VIII 227—36.

Selections and Ballads: Wülker, *AE. LB.,* II 109,
vv. 4073—4342. *The Legend of King Arthur* (100 verses
in ballad measure summarizing, in the first person, Arthur's
history principally as given by the chroniclers): *PF. MS.*
III 297; *Reliques,* Bk. VII, No. 5; Child (1857), I 50—54.

General References: Ten Brink, II[2] 49—52; Brandl,
§ 75; Wülker, (see p. 85) 12—16.

Monographs: Branscheid, *Über die Quellen des stab-
reimenden Morte Arthure, Angl.* VIII 179—236; Trautmann,
Der Dichter Huchown und seine Werke, Angl. I 109—49;
Luick (on metre), *Angl.* XI 585—97; Lübke, *Aunters of
Arthur* (see p. 178) 30—33.—On the *Pystyl of Swete Susan*:
Brade, Breslau, 1892, diss.; Köster, Strassburg, 1895 (*QF.* 76).

---

[1] Jamieson, *Etymolog. Dict. of the Scott. Lang., Supplement,*
cited by Trautmann, 147.

[2] See Trautmann, 114, 115, 146—149; Köster, 10—12.

[3] See p. 172, n. 3.

[4] Ten Brink, II[2] 50, gives 1320—1381, as, with tolerable certainty,
limiting his lifetime.

XXX. Arthur.

1. Subject. That of the alliterative *Morte Arthure.*[1]

2. Specimen. Vv. 427—44:

> But Arthour was not dysmayd,
> He tryst on god, & was wel payd,
> And prayd þe hye trynyte
> Euer hys help forto be;
> And alle hys Men wyþ oo voyse
> Cryde to god wyþ Oo noyse,
> 'Fader in heuene, þy wylle be doon;
> Defende þy puple fram þeire foon,
> And lat not þe heþone Men
> Destroye þe puple crystien:
> Haue Mercy on þy se[r]uantis bonde,
> And kepe ham fram þe heþone honde:
> Þe Muchelnesse of Men sainfayle
> Ys nat victorie in Batayle;
> But after þe wylle þat in heuene ys,
> So þe victorie falleþ y-wys.'
> Than seyd Arthour, 'hyt ys so:
> Auaunt Baner & be Goo.'

3. Story. The writer prefaces his narrative with a brief account of Arthur's birth, and praises him as the strongest and most courteous of kings.[2]

After conquering Scotland, Ireland, and Gothland, Arthur lives twelve years in peace. He then invades France and conquers 'Frollo'. After his return to Britain, while holding a splendid feast in Caerleon at Easter, he receives the message from the Roman emperor.[3] He sails from Southampton. After landing at Barflete, he fights and kills

---

[1] p. 181.

[2] Seven times during the course of his narrative, when an important part of the action has been closed, the writer says, 'Let us stop here and say a *pater noster*', or, 'Let us say a *pater noster* and a *ave*'.

[3] This portion of the narrative corresponds in essentials with that of the *Morte Arthure.*

a giant from Spain, who has ravished and killed the fair Elayne. He learns that Lucius is approaching with a great army of Christians and Saracens. He will not flee, as advised, but with all his men prays to God for help, then says, 'Forward!' Lucius trusts in his men, and is therein beguiled. The battle begins; men are well shod with brains and blood; Lucius is slain by an unknown hand. Arthur sends his body to Rome, and remains in France during the winter.

He is preparing to cross the mountains to Rome, when news comes of Modred's treachery. Arthur returns home and wages a 'strong batayl' against the traitor. Gawain and many other knights are slain. Modred flees towards London, then to Winchester, and thence to Cornwall. The queen, having no hope of mercy, becomes a nun at Caerleon. Arthur sends Gawain's body to Scotland; then, assembling a great host, he meets Modred in Cornwall. The two hosts fight till blood comes down as a river; Modred and all his are slain. Arthur sorely wounded, is brought to Avalon, a place 'Fayr and Mury' now called 'Glastyngbury', where he makes his ending and is buried. Because he escaped the battle, some British and Cornish men say that he lives yet, and will come again and be king. All this was in the year 542 A. D. God willing, the writer will rehearse in this place all the kings that followed Arthur. He that wishes to know their deeds let him read in the French book.

4. Origin. Of the origin of *Arthur,* Furnivall says: 'The six hundred and forty-two English lines here printed occur in an incomplete Latin Chronicle of the kings of Britain. The old chronicler has dealt with Uther Pendragon and Brownsteele (Excalibur), and is narrating Arthur's deeds; when, as if feeling that Latin prose was no fit vehicle for telling of Arthur, king of men, he breaks out into English verse,

'Herkeneþ, þat loueþ honour,
Of kyng Arthour & his labour.'

The story he tells is an abstract, with omissions, of the earlier version of Geoffrey of Monmouth,[1] before the love of Guinevere for Lancelot was introduced by the French-writing English romancers of the Lionheart's time (so far as I know), into the Arthur tales.'[1]

5. Metre. 642 4-stressed lines rimed in couplets.

6. Dialect. Southern,[2] but with some isolated Northern forms.[3]

7. Date. 1350—1400, according to Brandl. Wülker[4] gives *ca.* 1400.

8. Author. Unknown.

9. Bibliography.

Manuscripts: Liber rubrus Bathoniae, in the possession of the Marquis of Bath; ten or twenty years before 1450.[5]

Editions: Furnivall, *EETS.*, No. 2, 1864 and 1869.

General References: Brandl, § 70.

XXXI. Lancelot of the Laik.

1. Subject. How Lancelot in the service of Love wins renown in the war between Arthur and Galiot.

2. Specimen. Lancelot before battle, vv. 3269—3280, 3287—8:

> The blak knycht than on to hyme-felf he faid:
> 'Remembir the, how yhow haith ben araid,
> Ay fen ye hour that yow was makid knycht,
> With love, aȝane quhois powar and whois mycht
> Yow haith no ftrenth, yow may It not endur,
> Nor ȝhit non vthir erthly creatur;

---

[1] Sommer, III 2, n. 2, (3) gives the sources as the '*Historia*, etc.'.
[2] Ed. of 1864, p. vi; cf. Brandl, § 70.
[3] Körting, § 102.   [4] p. 110.
[5] Furnivall's ed., p. vi.

And bot two thingis ar the to amend,
Thi ladice mercy, or thi lyvys end.
And well yhow wot that on to hir preſens
Til hir eſtat, nor til hir excellens,
Thi febilneß neuermore is able
For to attan, ſche is so honorable.

. . . .

Of euery poynt of cowardy yow ſcham,
And in til armys purcheß the ſum name.'

3. Story. The poet, whose heart the sword of love
carves, falling asleep in a garden, receives through a green
bird a charge from the God of Love either to report his
woe to his lady, or to write his plaint in some metrical
treatise that will please her. Awaking, he dares not dis-
obey Love's command, and finally thinks of the romance of
Lancelot of the Lake, which, as treating of love and arms,
is suited to his purpose.

Because of his ignorance he will not translate all of
the French romance, which is 'passing large', but will tell
of the wars between Arthur and Galiot; how Lancelot won
renown therein, made peace, and was rewarded by Venus
with his lady's love.

King Arthur at Carlisle has bad dreams, which his
clerks at last, under pain of death, interpret to mean that
those he trusts will fail him, unless the watery lion, the
leech, and the flower can help him. A knight brings a
message from king Galiot, threatening invasion unless Arthur
submits to him or pays tribute, terms which Arthur stoutly
refuses. With but a small force he marches against Galiot.
After a brave fight, his men are finally driven back, with
the exception of Gawain, their commander, who fights alone
until nightfall, when the enemy retire; Gawain, covered
with wounds, swoons upon his horse.

Lancelot, held a prisoner by the lady of Melyhalt,
because he has slain one of her knights, laments his 'heavy
charge of love' and the loss of his liberty. Hearing of
Gawain's deeds, he finally obtains from the lady release on

13

parole. Galiot assembles a fresh force. The lady of Melyhalt gives Lancelot a red horse, shield, and spear. Riding
forth to battle, he sees the queen looking over a parapet,
and Love catches him by the heart. He sits upon his
horse as still as any stone, and is aroused only when water
is thrown upon him. Rushing into battle, he so fights
that Gawain praises, and the queen prays. Galiot, fearing
lest he may conquer too easily, proposes a year's truce.
Lancelot wounded returns to the Lady of Melyhalt, who
secretly loves him.

Amytans, a learned clerk, rebukes Arthur for his failures
as king, and at great length describes the ideal king. He
explains the lion, leech, and flower as God the Father,
Christ the Son, and the Virgin. The lady of Melyhalt
decides to accept Lancelot's ransom, and provides him with
black armor for his next battle. Arthur, obeying the counsel
of Amytans, gives largely, and thus gains his people's love.

After the expiration of the truce, Gawain, in the first
encounter with Galiot, is most sorely wounded. Lancelot,
hearing of this, laments greatly. He enters the battle, and,
strengthened by a message from the queen exhorting him
to help the king in his need and to deserve her thanks,
works nothing but wonders, utterly eclipsing the Red Knight.
Finally he is borne to the ground, but is remounted by
Galiot.[1] [Galiot several times remounts the Black Knight,
for whom he has conceived the greatest admiration. Lancelot
accepts Galiot's invitation to pass the night in his tent. In
order to win the friendship of the Black Knight, Galiot
voluntarily submits to Arthur. The queen requests Galiot
to arrange an interview for her with the strange knight,
who then reveals himself as Lancelot. Urged by Galiot, the
queen promises Lancelot her love. The Lady of Melyhalt
wishes to be made a fourth in the circle of friends, and the
queen accordingly wins for her the promise of Galiot's love.]

---

[1] End of the MS. The remainder of the story that the poet
has said he proposes to tell is briefly outlined according to the
French text.

4. Origin. This romance, Skeat states,[1] is a loose paraphrase of not quite fourteen folios of the first of the three volumes of the French prose romance, *Lancelot du Lac*.[2] The English paraphraser has set aside the French prologue and written a new one; then, after an enumeration of the events in the earlier history of Lancelot, of which he says he will not treat, he has translated and amplified that portion of his original treating of the invasion of Arthur's territory by Galiot. Judging from his introduction, it seems to have been the writer's intention to carry his work to the point where Lancelot wins the love of Guenever. In the long lecture (vv. 1320—2130) delivered to Arthur by the 'clerk' or 'master', Amytans, the author has greatly expanded the French text. Skeat states that for many of the precepts of Amytans the author was indebted to Gower,[3] and that some lines of the lecture seem to hint at contemporary events in Scotland.[4]

In the choice of subject, Brandl sees the influence of the court of James IV of Scotland, 'the last knight' of Britain, who in his palace of Holyrood held tournaments in imitation of those of Arthur's court; in the use of the heroic couplet and in the attempt to use the literary language of the Londoner, he sees further indication that the romance was intended for the courtly reader. The romance gives evidence also of the influence of Chaucer and of Lydgate upon the chivalric poetry of the time.[5]

In that part of the Lancelot legend covered by our Scotch paraphrase, the feature of principal legendary interest is the love of Lancelot for the queen. The characters of

---

[1] Ed. pp. ix, x.

[2] Ed. of 1513. Paris dates the romance (first redaction) *ca.* 1220. The four parts of the romance as given by Sommer are: (1) and (2) *The Lancelot* proper, dealing not only with the life and adventures of Lancelot but with the adventures of Gawain, Agravayne, etc.; (3) *The Quest of the Holy Grail*; (4) *The Death of King Arthur*. The whole is sometimes also called *The Book of Arthur*.

[3] p. 109, n.   [4] p. xii.

[5] Wülker, 184; cf. Skeat, p. xix.

Galehaut and the Lady of Mallehault, are, according to Paris,[1] inventions of the later romancers; they are perfectly unknown to the verse romances. In what follows on the origin of this legend only two topics are discussed: (1) The earliest version of the Lancelot legend; (2) The origin of the love of Lancelot and Guenever. The earliest mention of Lancelot is found in the *Erec* of Chrétien de Troyes.[2] In this poem and in *Cligès* Chrétien mentions Lancelot among the most celebrated knights of the Round Table. But what is probably the oldest extant version of Lancelot's story is found in a German poem, *Lanzelet*,[3] written by Ulrich von Zatzikhoven shortly before 1200, and representing a French original[4] of about 1160.[5]

The story of Lancelot's early years, as found in the poem of Ulrich, corresponds in essentials with that of the better known prose *Lancelot*; but after the hero has left the home of the Lady of the Lake and begun his life of adventure in the world, the two narratives are almost entirely different. In the *Lanzelet,* while some of the adventures are peculiar to the hero, most of them are found in other romances of the same epoch and of the same character. For example, certain features find parallels in the legend of Perceval and of the Fair Unknown.[6] Rhŷs[7] holds that the story of Lancelot was originally identical with that of Peredur (the Welsh Perceval) and that 'Lancelot'[8] was only another name of Peredur's. Lancelot's three love affairs have a striking resemblance, and are, Paris

---

[1] *Rom.* XII 486.   [2] *Rom.* X 470.

[3] See *Rom.* X 471—96; analyzed on pp. 472—76.

[4] P. Märtens, *Rom. St.,* V 699, 700; G. Paris, § 61 and *Rom.* X 471, 478. Golther, *Geschichte d. deutschen Litt.,* 1893, I 168, says that in the *Lanzelet* motives from the works of Chrétien de Troyes are several times recognizable, but that Ulrich perhaps also drew from Chrétien's source. Cf. Märtens' *stemma,* p. 700.

[5] G. Paris.

[6] Cf. *supra,* p. 140; *Rom.* XXVI 298—99; *Rom.* X 494, n. 2.

[7] p. 133.

[8] See Rhŷs, 253, n. 1. Zimmer (*Zs. f. franz. Sprache u. Litt.,* XIII 43—58) derives the name from one or both of two Lantberts who

declares, only variations of a widely spread theme. As a whole the *Lanzelet* is one of those romances in which a certain number of adventures are attached to a certain number of names without there being between the names and the adventures any constant relation; hence the lack of individuality in the heroes.[1] Lancelot next appears as the hero of Chrétien de Troyes' *Conte de la Charrette*.[2] This romance centers in Lancelot's rescue of the queen from king Meleaguant, who has carried her away to his kingdom of Goire, 'whence no stranger ever returns'. It is in Chrétien's poem that Lancelot first appears as the queen's lover; in *Lanzelet*, he is merely her deliverer.[3] G. Paris holds that in the first stage of his story Lancelot was not the lover of the queen,[4] that it is perfectly useless to try to find in Celtic tradition the origin of their loves,[5] and that these were unknown even to the most ancient French romances of the British cycle.

But may not Lancelot, in his rôle of lover of the queen, have been merely a substitute for some earlier character? Two twelfth century stories are of interest here: According to the story told in the *Vita Gildae*,[6] Guenever is carried by Melwas, king of *Aestiva Regio*,[7] to his stronghold of *Glastonia*.[8] Arthur, having searched for her for a year, prepares to besiege Melwas, but through the intervention of the abbot and Gildas the queen is given up. This is evidently an earlier version of the legend known to the

---

played a conspicuous part in Brittany in the 9th century. See also *Rom.* X 488—89, 492, n. 1; Golther (*op. cit.*) 168.

[1] *Rom.* X 472, 476, 496.

[2] See *Rom.* XII 459—534 (analyzed on pp. 464—81). This tale, in a version based in all probability upon the poem of Chrétien (Paris, *op. cit.*, whose argument, Sommer, III 276, n., considers conclusive) occurs also in the prose *Lancelot*.

[3] As are other knights in other romances; see *Rom.* XII, 507, n. 4.

[4] See *Rom.* X 477—8, 486—96; XII 506—7, 516.

[5] So Rhŷs, 50.

[6] On the date, see p. 207.

[7] Sommerset.

[8] Glastonbury.

writer of Ulrich's source,[1] to Chrétien, and to later romance writers. The legend is generally believed to be an echo of a Celtic 'other-world' myth,[2] which had assumed a historical form[3] and had been localized in Somerset; but features of the romance versions, notably of Chrétien's poem,[4] point to the original mythical significance. The fact that the rescuer of the queen in the romance versions is not her husband but one of his knights is due, according to Paris,[5] to a general tendency of the Breton tales in the Anglo-Norman period to put Arthur in the second place, and to accomplish all the exploits by means of his knights.[6]

According to the well known version of Geoffrey of Monmouth, the queen's lover is the usurper Modred, the king's nephew, whom 'queen Guanhumara, in violation of her first marriage, had wickedly married'.[7] Here the inference is that the yielding of Guenever was voluntary;[8] this is insisted upon by Layamon, writing at the beginning of the 13th century.

In the earliest French verse romances, according to Paris,[9] Geoffrey of Monmouth's version of the infidelity of the queen is not found; on the contrary she is represented as 'the model of spouses and of queens';[10] 'she tenderly loves her husband and inspires in the knights that surround him only sentiments of respectful devotion'. These senti-

---

[1] In the *Lanzelet*, Guenever is imprisoned by king Falerin in a castle surrounded by an impenetrable girdle of monsters, serpents, etc., and is plunged into a magic sleep.

[2] G. Paris, § 61, *Rom.* XII 508—16; (cf. Zimmer, *Zs. f. franz. Sprache u. Litt.* XIII 43 ff.); Rhŷs, 50—57, 25—37.

[3] According to Paris (*Rom.* XII 512, 514), before the story became known to the Anglo-Normans.

[4] Rhŷs, 54—56. Cf. Malory's version, Bk. XIX.

[5] *Op. cit.*, 513.

[6] Cf. the position of Charlemagne among his peers in the later poems of the Charlemagne cycle.

[7] *Historia Regum Britanniae*, Bk. X, Ch. xiii.

[8] Cf. also Bk. XI, Ch. i.

[9] *Rom.* X 488; see also the manual, p. 89.

[10] Cf. *Hist. Litt.* XXX 220.

ments, a little more strongly marked than usual in the case of Ulrich's Lanzelet, 'may have suggested to a later writer,[1] who wished to give to Arthur's wife a lover worthy of her, and to show in the *liason* between them a type of *l'amour courtois*, the idea of choosing Lancelot of the Lake for the rôle'.[2]

Rhŷs[3] regards the idea of the love between Lancelot and Guenever as originating in a blunder on the part of Chrétien or of his authority; namely, in the mistaking the 'Empress' of whom Peredur (cf. *supra*, p. 196) was in search for Arthur's queen.

5. Metre. 3486 four-stressed verses, rimed in couplets. Skeat[4] notices the similarity of the rhythm to that of Chaucer.

6. Dialect.[5] The Lowland Scotch dialect has undergone a 'remarkable transformation' through the introduction of many Southern forms. This is to be attributed, for the most part, to the influence of 'southernism', especially to the influence of Chaucer, upon the author. The handwriting of the extant MS. is certainly Scottish.

7. Date.[6] The last quarter of the 15th century. The MS., as is shown by the handwriting, belongs to the very end of the 15th century. The poem may have been written towards the end of the reign of James III or in the reign of James IV.

8. Author. Unknown.

9. Bibliography.
Manuscripts: Kk. 1. 5, Cambridge Univ. Library.
Editions: Stevenson, for the Maitland Club, L., 1839; Skeat, *EETS.*, 1865, No. 6; 2nd ed., 1870.

---

[1] Chrétien, in all probability; G. Paris, § 57, 61; *Rom.* XII 507, 516.
[2] Paris (*Hist. Litt.* 200; cf. 204—7) cites the knight Ider as one who, before Lancelot, was said to have loved Guenever.
[3] p. 135.   [4] Ed., p. xix.   [5] Skeat, pp. xv—xxii.
[6] Skeat, p. xii.

Selections: Wülker, *Æ. LB.,* II 115, (vv. 1166—1272). [1]

General References: Brandl, § 138. Analyses of the French prose Lancelot: P. Paris, III; Dunlop, I 179 ff. On Lancelot: G. Paris, in *Rom.* X 465—96, XII 459—534.

XXXII. Le Morte Arthur.

1. Subject. The love of Elaine for Lancelot; the condemnation of the queen as a poisoner and her rescue from the stake by her champion, Lancelot; the disclosure to Arthur of the guilt of Lancelot and the queen; Mordred's treason and the death of Arthur.

2. Specimen. Vv. 3494—3517:

> To the kynge A-gayne wente he thare
> And sayd, 'leve syr, I saw An hand;
> Oute of the water it cam Alle bare,
> And thryse brandysshyd that Ryche brande.'
> 'helpe me sone that I ware there.'
> he lede hys lord vnto that stronde;
> A rychè shyppe wyth maste And ore,
> Fulle of ladyes there they fonde,
> The ladyes that were feyre and Free,
> Curteysly the kynge gan they fonge,
> And one, that bryghtest was of blee,
> Wepyd sore, and handys wrange,
> 'Broder,' she sayd, 'wo ys me,
> Fro lechyng hastow be to longe;
> I wote that gretely greuyth me,
> For thy paynès Ar fulle stronge.'
> The knyght kest A rewfulle rowne,

---

[1] See *PF. MS.* I 84 (*Reliques,* Bk. 11, No. 9) for a mere fragment of a ballad, *Sir Lancelot Du Lake,* based on Malory's *Morte Darthur,* Bk. VI, Chs. vii, viii, ix,

There he stode, sore and vnsownde,
And say, 'lord, whedyr Ar ye bowne,
Allas, whedyr wylle ye fro me fownde?'
The kynge spake wyth A sory sowne,
"I wylle wende A lytelle stownde
In to the vale of Avelovne,
A whyle to hele me of my wounde."

3. Story. Four years after the Quest of the Holy
Grail is ended, Arthur proclaims a tournament at Winchester
in order to revive the honor of his court. To this tournament Sir Lancelot decides to go in disguise. On his way
to Winchester he lodges in the castle of the Earl of Ascolot.
Almost at sight, the earl's daughter, 'red as blossom on
briar', sets her heart upon him and confesses her love.
Lancelot replies that his heart is bestowed elsewhere; he
consents however to wear her sleeve upon his helmet at the
tournament. Lancelot and one of the earl's sons take the
weaker side in the tournament, that of the challenger,
Galehaut, and Lancelot overthrows the best knights on the
king's side, Bors, Ewain and Lionel. He is himself sorely
wounded and rides away to the house of his companion's
aunt; when better, he is removed to Ascolot. Arthur's
knights search for and discover the abode of Lancelot.
Later, Gawain comes to Ascolot, but finds that Lancelot has
departed. The Maid of Ascolot[1] tells him that Lancelot
has taken her for his 'lover' and shows him Lancelot's
shield. On his return to court, Gawain tells the queen of
Lancelot's new love. When Lancelot arrives and seeks an
interview with the queen, she breaks into lamentation because
he will wed the Earl of Ascolot's daughter. Lancelot says
that he knows nothing of these tidings, but thinking that
the queen wishes him away, he speeds to the forest.

Some time after his departure, there is seen one day
descending the river a boat which bears a dead lady, the
'fairest of maids'. Gawain recognizes her as the Maid of

---

[1] She is not otherwise named.

Ascolot, whom he once asked to be a lover of his own; he finds upon her a letter telling that she dies of unrequited love for Lancelot. She is buried as befits her rank. The queen grieves deeply for Lancelot.

A Scottish knight dies from eating a poisoned apple, passed to him at the table by the queen. Accused by the knight's brother of the crime, Guenever is condemned to be burned, unless within forty days she can find a champion. The queen upon her knees pleads with the bravest knights to espouse her cause, but in vain; the king joins his entreaties to hers, and finally Sir Bors undertakes the championship. Bors, Lionel, and Ector, while praying in a forest chapel for Bors' success, meet Lancelot, who promises to fight for the queen. He comes and wins, whereupon a squire confesses to the poisoning. Lancelot is restored to the favor of the queen.

Agravain, against the will of Gawain, discloses the guilt of Lancelot and Guenever to Arthur, and a plot is then laid to entrap the lovers. During Arthur's absence on a hunt, fourteen knights surprise Lancelot in the queen's chamber. In response to their challenge he admits them one by one to the room, encounters, and kills them all with the exception of Mordred, who flies. More than one hundred knights and squires accompany Lancelot from court. Later they rescue the queen, whom Arthur has condemned to be burned. In this rescue Gawain's two brothers are killed, and Gawain becomes Lancelot's bitterest enemy. Lancelot takes the queen to his castle of 'Joyus Gard', where Arthur in vain besieges him. By order of the pope, the queen is finally restored to her husband. Lancelot retires to his kingdom on the Continent, whither Arthur, with a great host, pursues him. Lancelot desires peace, but Gawain, though twice severely wounded in single combat with Lancelot, is implacable.

News comes of the treachery of Mordred and of his attempt to kill the queen. Arthur hastens home and wins two great battles, but Gawain is slain in the battle at the landing. Warned by Gawain's spirit and other visions not to fight, Arthur proposes a truce; but later, suspecting treachery, begins a battle that rages furiously until evening. Only Arthur, Lucan, and Bedivere are left on the one side, and Mordred on the other. Arthur kills Mordred, who, as he falls, smites Arthur heavily upon the helm. Lucan and Bedivere support the king to a chapel, where the night is passed in prayer. The king commands Bedivere to cast the sword Excalibur into the sea. Bedivere twice hides the sword; but reproached by Arthur for his disobedience, the third time he obeys the king's command. A hand from the water seizes and brandishes the sword, then 'glints away like a gleam'. Bedivere helps Arthur to the shore, where lies a ship full of ladies. The lady 'brightest of beauty' weeps and wrings her hands over the king. Arthur tells Bedivere that he is going to the vale of Avalon for a while to be cured of his wound. The ship leaves the land and Bedivere sees it no more. All night he roams the wood weeping; at daybreak he comes to a forest chapel, where he finds Arthur's tomb, and learns from a hermit that the king was buried there at midnight by ladies.

Lancelot comes with an army to aid Arthur. Hearing of his death, he seeks the queen, who has become a nun; she refuses him a kiss, and bids him go home and marry. Instead, he lives seven years a penitent, prayerful monk at the hermitage where Arthur lies. When dying he sees Heaven open to him. His brother Ector buries him in Joyus Gard. Ector finds the queen dead, and buries her beside the king. The place is now called Glastonbury. The monks sing

> 'Jhesu, that suffrèd woundès sore
> Graunt vs Alle the blysse of hevyn.'

4. Origin. Sommer, in his investigation of the sources[1] of Malory's *Morte Darthur,* reaches the following conclusion in regard to the sources of *Le Morte Arthur.*[2]—It is based

---

[1] Vol. III, to which the page numbers in the notes following refer.
[2] To be designated as M. H.

on two French sources, which in some points contradict each other: The Vulgate-*Lancelot*[1] is the source of the first part (ll. 1—1181) up to the gap; for the remainder (ll. 1318— 3969), the source was that used by Malory for his last two books,[2] namely a *Suite de Lancelot,* only a fragment[3] of which is extant but which must have been a modified version of the long Vulgate-*Lancelot,* characterized by greater precision and dealing more exclusively with the hero.

At the point where the poet probably began to follow the *Suite de Lancelot, i. e.* after l. 1181, a folio or leaf of the manuscript is missing;[4] and after the gap the narrative begins abruptly in the middle of the episode of 'Guenever and Mador de la Porte', already narrated, with the exception of the closing scene, in ll. 832—951.[5] The first part of the episode thus rewritten is conjectured to have been on the missing leaf, and is represented in substance by ll. 832—911; the episode as rewritten is completed without interruption.[6] The arrangement finally adopted by the poet for ll. 1—1671 is accordingly represented by the following order: (1) Introduction and the episode of 'Lancelot and Elaine', ll. 1—831, 952—1181; (2) Episode of 'Guenever and Mador de la Porte', ll. 832—911, 1318—1671.[7]

---

[1] Cf. *infra,* p. 8.

[2] Sommer concludes that for these books Malory also used M. H. Wechssler (*Graal-Lancelot-Cyclus,* Halle, 1895) p. 36 and Mead, pp. 305—10, conclude that M. used only the French source. The ballad on *King Arthur's Death* (see infra, p. 208) has, Sommer holds (p. 269, n. 1), the same source.

[3] Eighteen folios, corresponding substantially to Malory's books xi and xii. It was only after Sommer had reached his conclusions that he discovered the fragment of the *Suite de Lancelot* in a manuscript of the *Tristan* (British Museum, Ms. Add. 5474): pp. 272—78.

[4] After folio 102.

[5] On the cause of this confusion, see Sommer, p. 11, n. 1, last paragraph; cf. p. 249.

[6] Cf. the position of ll. 952—1181.

[7] Sommer (p. 11, n. 1) omits ll. 912—927 as being to a certain extent repeated by ll. 1318—1331, and ll. 928—951, as being an apparent contradiction to ll. 1467—1503.

The version of Arthur's death in our romance is also essentially the version of Malory.[1] In the latter version an additional fact of special interest is that one of the ladies in the boat was Arthur's sister, Morgan le Fay.[2] The prose *Lancelot* says nothing of Arthur going to Avalon; he is taken away in a boat by Morgan and other ladies, and later his tomb is found in the 'black chapel', which is not said to be in Glastonbury.[3]

The version of Arthur's death represented by the prose *Lancelot*, M. H., and Malory, unites two earlier versions, the mythical and the historical; the historical version has clearly triumphed. Zimmer[4] points out the following facts concerning the two versions: The historical version was that of the ancient Welsh hero-legend; the *Annales Cambriae*, belonging to the 10th century, for the year 537 records the death of *Arthur* and *Medraut* in the battle of Camlan. Avalon and its connected conceptions were unknown in Welsh literature before Geoffrey of Monmouth (1135). The mythical version came from Brittany.[5] It was evidently known to William of

---

[1] Cf. *supra*, p. 185. For valuable notes and references on the principal features covered by the story of M. H., see Mead. On the love of Lancelot and Guenever, see *supra*, pp. 197—99.

[2] Rhŷs, 348, holds that Morgan and the Lady of the Lake are the same person viewed under different aspects: 'At one time as kind and benevolent and at another as hostile and truculent'. Cf. her rôle in *Sir Gawain and the Green Knight*, *supra*, p. 210.

[3] I follow the analysis of Summer, pp. 268—271.

[4] *Zs. f. franz. Sprache u. Litt.*, XII 238—256 (*Bretonische Elemente in der Arthursage des Gottfried von Monmouth*).

[5] Avalon was the Breton name for an isle of the Western ocean, in the region of the setting sun; it was the land of the dead, including the abode of the Blessed. (*Rom.* XII 510—12. Cf. *supra*, pp. 146—50.) The 'isle of glass' described in Chrétien's *Erec*, vv. 1933, sq., and of which *Maheloas* was lord is also to be identified with Avalon. (Cf. the story of Melwas, p. 197, *supra*; see Zimmer, *op. cit.*, 251—2.) Mortals who had not died sometimes visited the 'happy isle' and returned thence. (Cf. pp. 148—9; Child I 318.) Rhŷs (*Celtic Heathendom*, 1888) cites numerous Irish and Welsh stories of visits to Hades, of which a few place the Celtic Elysium on an island (pp. 342, 343, 550, 641).

Malmesbury in 1125,[1] and the narrative of Hermann of Laon, who wrote in 1146 of events occurring in 1113, shows that by the latter date the belief in the return of Arthur had gained a hold in Cornwall and that the legend was already known, but discredited, in Normandy.[2] The statement of Geoffrey that Arthur was fatally wounded shows the influence of the mythical version by the historical. This 'union' of the two versions may have been the work of Geoffrey,[3] or he may have found them already united in Cornwall, Devonshire, or Somerset, where after 1067 Bretons, *i. e.* Armoricans, received gifts of land from William I. In Geoffrey's account of Arthur's last battle, Rhŷs,[4] in accordance with his general theory of the origin of the Arthurian legend, sees a 'quasi-historical' version of a Celtic solar myth on the conflict between light and darkness, disturbed, however, by the influence of a historical fact.

Another feature of the tradition concerning Arthur's death, which undoubtedly influenced the later historical version, is first recorded by William of Malmesbury in 1139 in his *Antiquitates ecclesiae Glastoniensis*,[5] when he says that the ancient British name for Glastonbury was *Yniswitrin* [isle of glass], of which the English name was a rendering.[6] Then, without further explanation, he adds that the place was also called the isle of Avalon, signifying in British the 'isle of apples',[7] or named from a certain

---

[1] *Gesta regum Angliae*, I § 8.

[2] Zimmer, *op. cit.*, XIII 106—112.

[3] Earlier in his narrative (Bk. VII, 3) Geoffrey causes Merlin to prophesy that Arthur's end would be uncertain.

[4] pp. 13—18; cf. Mac Callum, 15—16.

[5] San-Marte, 423 (*op. cit.* on p. 115). On the genuineness of the passage, see *Germania* XII 276; Paul u. Braune, *Beiträge*, III 326; Baist, *Zs. f. rom. Phil.* XIX 326—45.

[6] A false etymology, of course. The Old English form was Glaestingabyrig, Glaestingaburh. (See *Rom.* X 491; Zimmer, *op. cit.*, 245.) Glastonbury, surrounded as it is by marshes, has always been compared to an island; see William of Malmesbury, *Gesta Pontificum*, p. 196; cf. Rhŷs, 330, n. 2.

[7] In the *Vita Merlini* of Geoffrey, the island to which Arthur is carried for healing by Morgen is also termed '*insula pomorum*'.

Avalloc,[1] 'who is said to have dwelt there with his daughters on account of the secrecy of the place.' In this passage William says nothing of Arthur. The *Vita Gildae,* which can scarcely be much later than Geoffrey's *Historia* and Malmesbury's *Antiquitates,*[2] makes Glastonbury the stronghold of Melwas, who was, as we have seen,[3] originally the king of the dead. This identification of Avalon with Glastonbury is thought by some scholars to represent the localization of an ancient Celtic 'other-world' myth.[4] Zimmer, on the other hand, regards it as merely a 'erudite fable' suggested by the union of the historical and the mythical version of Arthur's death, and in turn suggesting the claim made by the abbot of Glastonbury in the last quarter of the 12th century that Arthur's grave had been discovered there.[5]

The belief underlying the return of Arthur has not been confined to the Celts.

5. Metre.[6] 3834[7] verses in stanzas of eight lines rimed alternately. The stanza is a doubling of the four line ballad-stanza;[8] irregularities in the scheme of both stanza and rime are not infrequent. As an ornament to his verse the poet makes a 'very rich use' of alliteration.

6. Dialect. N. W. Midland, according to Seyferth;[9] Morris, whose opinion is quoted by the editor,[10] pronounced

---

[1] According to Rhŷs, 336, a Celtic dark divinity. Zimmer, *op. cit.,* 249, suggests an Armorican derivation for Avalon, meaning 'isle of air'.

[2] Zimmer, *op. cit.,* 251—2. [3] pp. 197—98.

[4] *Rom.* XII 512—14; Nutt, *Studies,* 223. The romance of *Durmart* several times speaks of *Glaestingebieres* as the residence of Arthur: *Hist. Litt.,* 153. On the localization of the marvellous in the Middle Age, see Bedier (*op. cit.* on p. 153) 856.

[5] Giraldus Cambrensis, *Speculum ecclesiae,* II 9. See Baist, (*op. cit.* on p. 207, n. 1) 336—39.

[6] Seyferth, pp. 59—74.

[7] Furnivall allows 136 lines for the folio missing after fol. 102 (l. 1181); Sommer (p. 11, n. 3), but 82 lines.

[8] Cf. the *Sowdone of Babylone,* p. 57.

[9] p. 57. [10] p. xv.

the dialect E. Midland. The manuscript is the work of two scribes, the home of the first (vv. 1—1091) having been the E. Midland; that of the second (vv. 1092 ff.), the borderland between the E. Midland and the South.[1]

7. Date. The end of the 14th century; at the latest, about 1400.[2] Furnivall dates the MS. from about 1460, the language of the poem being somewhat earlier.

8. Author. Unknown. On linguistic grounds, Seyferth[3] rejects Sommer's conjecture that the poem is by the author of the romance, *The lyfe of Ipomydon*,[4] found in the same manuscript.

9. Bibliography.

Manuscripts: Harleian 2252, British Museum.

Editions: Furnivall, L. and Cambr., 1864.[5]

General References: Brandl, § 125; Herbert Coleridge in the Introduction to Furnivall's ed.; Ellis (analysis), 143—187; Newell, *King Arthur and the Table Round,* II 199—239 (an abridged rendering in prose), Boston and N. Y., 1897; Mead, *Selections from Malory's Morte Darthur,* Boston and London, 1897 (notes).

Monographs: Seyferth, *Sprache und Metrik des mittelengl. strophischen Gedichtes 'Le Morte Arthur' und sein Verhältniss zu 'The Lyfe of Ipomydon',* in *Berliner Beiträge zur germ. u. rom. Philologie,* VIII; Bruce, J. D., *On the Relation between Harl. MS. 2252 and Malory's Morte Darthur,*[6] 1900.[7]

---

[1] Seyferth, 56—59.

[2] Seyferth, 58.   [3] pp. 74—8.

[4] Ed. Weber, II 279; Kölbing, Leipsic, 1890.

[5] The fragment of a ballad or short poem on *King Arthur's Death* is printed in *PF. MS.* I 501—507; (*Reliques,* Bk. 7, No. 4; Child, 1857, I 40).

[6] This came to my notice too late for examination.

[7] The two romances named below have a slight external connection with Arthurian legend.—Sir D e g r e v a n t: Ed. Halliwell, *Thornton Romances* (see p. 133). 1904 vv. in the 16-line tail-rime stanza. Northern

XXXIII. Romance Poems on Gawain.[1]

1. The Green Knight.

1. Subject. See No. XXV.

2. Story. The following are the principal points in which the story of this 'romance poem' differs from that of its original, *Sir Gawain and the Green Knight*.

The wife of Sir Bredbeddle, a man of the 'west Countrye', loves Sir Gawain, though she has never seen him, because he is bold in battle. This lady's mother, a witch named Agteb, induces her son-in-law to go to court to prove Sir Gawain.[2] After reaching the court, Sir Bredbeddle proposes that one of the knights shall, if possible, strike off his head, upon condition that after a twelvemonth he may give the knight a return-stroke at the Green Chapel. Each man present is ready to do the deed, but Gawain says to the king: 'Remember I am your sister's son. It would be a great villainy if you did not put this deed on me.' The blow is not struck until after the feast. After

---

dialect, 1350—1400 (Brandl, § 79). Except that the hero is said (vv. 1—32) to be a knight of the Round Table and a nephew of the king (who is not named), the romance has no connection, so far as I am aware, with the Arthurian cycle. Lübke (*op. cit.* on p. 178) p. 27, finds that the author has undoubtedly made considerable use of the *Aunters of Arthur.*—Sir Cleges: Ed. Weber, *Metrical Romances*, L., 1811, I 329; Treichel, in *E. St.* XXII 345—89. 570 vv. in the 12-line tail-rime stanza. N. Midland dialect, beginning of the 15th century. Sir Cleges is a rich, generous, and pious knight of the Round Table of Uther, the father of Arthur. Like Launfal, Sir Cleges becomes impoverished through the feasts that he gives. The leading motive, in its oldest and simplest form, is found in an Oriental tale.

[1] In French romance Gawain, the model of chivalric perfection, has, properly speaking, no biography; he is the hero of numerous episodic romances: *Hist. Litt.*, 33. On Gawain in Arthurian legend, see *op. cit.*, pp. 29—45.

[2] As three lines are missing here, we do not know her precise request.

telling of the departure of the Green Knight, the author remarks that all this was done by enchantment. The Green Knight upon his return home will not tell his folk what doughty deeds he has done; he knows certainly that his wife loves Sir Gawain.

At the castle where Gawain is entertained, the identity of his host with the Green Knight is disclosed to the reader. After the pledge between the knights and the departure of the host for the hunt, the witch leads her daughter to Gawain's bedside, and tells him to take her, as she loves him. The lady kisses him thrice and tells him of her love, but Gawain refuses to be untrue to his host. He however accepts from her a white lace as a protection in combat. At the Green Chapel, the knight strikes at Gawain but once, slightly wounding him; Gawain then draws his sword, saying that the knight is entitled to but one blow. The knight, after discovering himself to Gawain, says that he will consider himself paid for the white lace, if Gawain will take him to Arthur's court, which Gawain does.

This story shows why a Knight of the Bath wears the lace until he has won his 'shoen', or a lady of high estate shall take the lace from his neck for his doughty deeds. King Arthur decreed this at Sir Gawain's request.

3. Origin. The original of the *Grene Knight* is undoubtedly *Sir Gawain and the Green Knight,* though some intermediate form of the story may have been the direct source of the present version.[1] The witch Agteb was probably suggested by Morgan le Fay, who appears in the original as an ugly old woman, the instigator of the challenge with the purpose of putting Queen Guenever into deadly fear.

In the 15th century, 'the school of the Gawain-poet', says Brandl, 'thrown into shadow by that of Chaucer, is running out in variations, increasingly vulgar, of its favorite motive of the chivalric test.'

---

[1] Madden, 352.

4. Metre. 528 vv. in the tail-rime stanza of six lines
aab ccb).

5. Dialect. That of the more Southern Midland.[1]

6. Date. 15th century.

7. Author. Unknown.

8. Bibliography.

Manuscripts: Percy MS., latter half of the 17th century;
Madden, p. lxiii, says that a minute account of the MS.
with a list of the first fifty-nine articles in it is found in
Dr. Dibdin's *Bibliographical Decameron,* III 338—344.

Editions: PF. MS. II 56; Madden, 224—42 (notes, 352).—
Brandl, § 113.

2. The Turk and Gowin.

1. Subject. Gawain accepts a challenge from a Turk
to give and receive a buffet, and has strange adventures
in the Isle of Man.

2. Story.[2] One like a Turk appears at Arthur's court
and asks who is hardy enough to give and take a buffet.
Gawain evidently accepts the challenge. The Turk threatens
to make Gawain as afraid as any man in 'middleearth' ere
he sees the court again. Gawain says that he will never
flee from any adventure, and goes with him. They come
to a hill, where the earth opens and closes again; Gawain
is a-dread. When they have reached an underground castle,
the Turk, strange to say, implores Gawain to give him
another buffet.[3]

[4]We next find them sailing over the sea as friends;
they arrive at a castle inhabited by the King of Man

---

[1] Brandl; cf. *supra,* p. 151 on *Landavall.*

[2] The MS. is very imperfect.

[3] According to Hales and Furnivall, I 88. Madden says, 'the
counter-buffet is demanded by the Turk'. The MS. here is very imperfect.

[4] From this point the summary is Madden's.

(a heathen soldan) and a rout of giants. A trial of skill
takes place at tennis in which Gawain is assisted by the
Turk, who passes for the knight's 'boy'. Other trials of
strength follow, which end in the discomfiture of the giants.
The soldan and one of his rout lay some plan to kill
Gawain, but are prevented by the Turk, who, putting on
a coat of invisibility, throws the giant into a boiling cauldron
of lead and the soldan into the fire. After this, the Turk
desires Gawain to strike off his head. Gawain at first refuses;
but on his compliance in place of the Turk rises up a
stalwart knight, Sir Grower by name, who sings a *Te Deum*
by way of thankfulness and to prove his orthodoxy. By
this feat the ladies and knights confined in the castle are
delivered from thraldom. The kingdom of Man is bestowed
by Arthur upon Sir Grower.

3. Origin. [1] The commencement is probably borrowed
from the *Green Knight* [2] and imperfectly amalgamated with
the main story. This embodies certain superstitions of the
isle of Man, where it was 'firmly believed for many a
century that the island was tenanted by a population of
giants'; traditions of magnificent underground apartments
also exist there.

4. Metre. 335 verses, in the tail-rime stanza of six
lines (*aab ccb*) with frequent alliteration.

5. Dialect. N. Midland or the North; the author may
have come from the Isle of Man. [3]

6. Date. 15th century (Brandl); 16th century (Paris) [4].

7. Author. Unknown. From the versification, Madden
judges that the poem evidently proceeds from the same
hand as *The Grene Knight*. 'Nor will it, perhaps, be wrong
to assign to one hand the greater part, if not the whole,
of the romance-stories in the manuscript.' [5]

---

[1] *PF. MS.* I 88.

[2] Or from a different version of that poem: Madden, 355.

[3] Brandl, p. 708.   [4] *Hist. Litt.*, 78.   [5] p. 355.

8. Bibliography.

Manuscripts: Percy Folio; see *supra,* p. 212.

Editions: PF. MS. I 88—102; Madden, 243—55 (notes, 355).—Brandl, § 127.

3. The Jeaste of Syr Gawayne.

1. Subject. A love-adventure of Gawain's.

2. Story. [Gawain, having left the siege of Branlant, finds in a magnificent pavilion a beautiful maiden,][1] whose full favor he wins.[2] The lady's father enters the pavilion, and upon seeing Gawain with his daughter insists, in spite of Gawain's offer of amends, upon fighting with him. Gawain overthrows and wounds the father, who promises to fight no more against him that day. Two brothers, in turn, share their father's fortune; last comes the oldest brother, Brandles, 'Of knyghthode he had no peere.' With him Gawain fights until dark; both are wounded, but neither asks for mercy. Finally Brandles proposes that they shall swear upon their swords, whenever they meet again to fight to the death. To this Gawain assents, and after requesting kind treatment for the lady, departs on foot for the court. Brandles reviles and beats his sister, who leaves the pavilion and goes wandering to and fro; they never see her again. Sir Brandles and Gawain never meet again, whereof they are full glad.

3. Origin. The source of the *Jeaste of Gawain* is an episode in the first continuation of the *Perceval* of Chrétien de Troyes.[3] Except for the loss of the opening lines, the English poem seems complete in itself, but it covers the first part only of the story found in the French, and then, in a few additional sentences, gives an entirely different

---

[1] According to the French; the opening lines of the English poem are wanting.

[2] According to one account in the French (*Perceval,* v. 11987, sq.), the lady offers herself to Gawain, having long loved him for his fame.

[3] Vv. 16885—17481: *Hist. Litt.,* 192, n. 2.

ending. According to the French,[1] the first part of the narrative closes with the departure of Gawain from the pavilion. At a subsequent part of the romance, Arthur and his court arrive at a stately castle, which proves to be that of Brandelys. Here Gawain relates his former adventure, his narrative differing widely, at least as regards his wooing of the lady,[2] from the earlier account.[3] When Gawain has finished his story, Brandelys enters, and the two knights fight by candle-light. The lady appears upon the scene with her child, whom she interposes between the combatents; Brandelys brutally kicks the child away, to the great indignation of Arthur. Brandelys is struck down, and finally persuaded to yield. He is made a knight of the Round Table, and grants forgiveness to the penitent Gawain, who begs it on his knees.

This story concerning Gawain serves in the French as an introduction to the adventures of his son. 'The greatly abridged manner in which the author speaks of these adventures,' says Paris,[4] 'shows that he referred to a source where they were recounted in detail.' In the second continuation of the *Perceval*, the son of Gawain appears for an instant under the surname of the *Bel Desconeü*. From the first continuation, it is seen that his youth much resembled that of Perceval and of Tyolet. 'The primitive hero of the adventure of the *fier baiser* had a similar youth, and this is without doubt the cause of this adventure being attributed to the son of Gawain.'[5]

4. Metre. 541 verses in stanzas of six lines; rime-scheme, *aab ccb*.

5. Dialect. The South or more Southern Midland (Brandl).

6. Date. 15th century (Brandl). The Douce MS. 'contains transcripts of several Romances apparently taken from editions earlier than Copland's' (cf. *supra*, p. 31).

---

[1] As summarized by Madden.
[2] See Madden's summaries.   [3] See ref., n. 3 on p. 213.
[4] *Op. cit.*, 192—93.   [5] *Op. cit.*

7. Author. Unknown.

8. Bibliography.

Manuscripts:[1] Douce, Bodl. Library; 1564; desc. by Madden, p. lxiii.—Harleian 5927, art. 32, preserves the last leaf of another edition in black letter, printed by Thos. Petyt.

Editions: Madden, 207 (notes, 348).—Brandl, § 113.

4. Syre Gawene and the Carle of Carelyle.

1. Subject. Gawain's adventure with an evil host.

2. Story. Gawain, Kay, and Bishop Bawdewyn take shelter for the night in the castle of the Carl of Carlile, a host of evil reputation. When the knights are admitted to the carl's presence, a boar, a lion, and a bear rise from before the fire and would have killed the strangers, but for the carl's command. Gawain greets his host, kneeling before him. After being treated to wine from a golden cup holding nine gallons, each knight in turn goes out to see how his steed fares. The Bishop, and then Kay, finds a foal of the carl's standing by his palfrey, eating with him. Each turns the foal away, Kay turning her out into the rain, and each is struck to the ground by a blow from the watching carl. Gawain brings the foal back into the stable, puts her beside his own steed, and covers her with his mantle. The carl thanks him courteously many times. When supper is ready, the carl bids Gawain cast a spear full in his face, adding that it will not hurt him. Gawain obeys; the carl bends his head, and the spear breaks against the stone wall. Gawain is seated opposite the carl's wife, whose beauty renders him unable to eat or drink. After supper, the carl's daughter, with shining golden hair and garments gleaming with jewels, comes in and plays upon the harp, singing of love and of Arthur's arms. Then they are led to their chambers. The carl takes Gawain to his own room, tells his wife to enter the splendid bed, and then bids Gawain

---

[1] Madden, p. 348.

to take her in his arms and kiss her. When Gawain has obeyed, the carl dismisses him, but takes him to his daughter's room.

The next morning, the carl tells Gawain that twenty winters ago he made a vow that every man who lodged with him should be slain unless he would do his will; he then shows Gawain the bones of his victims lying in their blood. He will now amend his ways and found a chantry, where ten priests shall sing masses for the souls of the murdered men until Doomsday.

Gawain and his companions, taking with them the carl's daughter, return to Arthur's court. Arthur accepts an invitation to dine the next day with the carl, and thinks that he never had a better dinner. Arthur makes the carl lord of the country of Carlile, and a knight of the Round Table. Gawain is wedded to the carl's daughter. The poem closes formally with 'Amen'.

3. Origin. The original of this romance poem is said by Madden to be 'the beautiful French fabliau' *Le Chevalier à l'épée*. The English poem corresponds, but only in general outline, with the first of the two originally unrelated parts of the French poem. In this first part, according to G. Paris, the primitive tale, undoubtedly of Welsh origin, is much altered and united [1] with the episode of 'the perilous bed', which figures several times in narratives relating to Gawain, but which has nothing in common with the tale in question. The English poem Paris regards as much nearer the primitive form of the tale, and as representing 'without doubt a lost Anglo-Norman source'. A ballad of the 16th century, evidently a working over of the older English poem, contains a different denouement, which Paris thinks must be primitive, but which on account of its fantastic character, the copyist of the older poem may have suppressed. The additional incident is as follows: When Gawain, after a night spent as in the older version, bids the carl adieu, he is conducted

---

[1] In the *first* part of the fabliau.

into a room hung with swords and ordered to smite off his host's head. Gawain obeys only when the carl threatens him with a similar fate. When Gawain has struck the blow, the carl, who was forty cubits high, rises up the height of Sir Gawain. The carl says that forty winters ago he was 'so shapen by necromancy' until a knight of the Round Table should smite off his head. A similar adventure forms the close of *The Turk and Gowin*,[1] whose beginning recalls *Sir Gawain and the Green Knight*.

4. Metre. 660 vv. in the 12-line tail-rime stanza, with the rime-scheme, *aab ccb ddb eeb.*

5. Dialect. Classified by Brandl with the literature belonging to the N. Midland or to the North.

6. Date. Brandl assigns it to the 15th, G. Paris,[2] to the 14th century.

7. Author. Unknown.

8. Bibliography.

Manuscripts: 10 Porkington Library; desc. by Madden, (*op. cit.* on p. 168) pp. lviii—lxiii.

Editions: Madden, 188—206, (notes, 344—51). *The Carle off Carlile* (16th century, 500 vv. in ballad measure, though some stanzas have six lines): Madden, 256—74 (notes, 356); *PF. MS.,* III 275.—Brandl, § 125; G. Paris, *Hist. Litt.,* XXX 67.

5. The Weddynge of Syr Gawen and Dame Ragnell.

1. Subject. How Gawain, in order to save Arthur's life, weds a hideous woman, and how his deference to her will effects her disenchantment.

2. Story.[3] Arthur while hunting in Ingleswood, is met by a groom, Gromer Somer Joure, who, enraged because Arthur has taken his lands, threatens the life of the defence-

---

[1] See p. 212.   [2] p. 68, *op. cit. infra.*

[3] The summaries of Child and of Paris have been followed.

less king, unless within a twelvemonth and a day Arthur
shall tell him what women love best. Arthur confides his
situation to Gawain, and the two ride in different directions
far and near, asking the question of all and collecting the
answers in a book. In the last month of the time Arthur,
who is by no means confident of the success of his efforts,
meets in Ingleswood a lady, hideous beyond description,
riding on a richly caparisoned palfrey. She tells him that
she knows his secret, and knows that of all the answers
he has collected not one will avail. She will save him,
but on one condition only: that Gawain may become her
husband. The king refers the matter to Gawain, who
exclaims: 'Is that all! I will wed her once and again, else
were I no friend.' On the day when the king must give
his answer, the hideous lady, Dame Ragnell, tells him that
above all things women desire to have the sovereignty.
This answer alone saves the king. Gromer upon hearing
it says that she who gave it was his sister, and wishes
that he may see her 'burn on a fire'. Dame Ragnell insists
upon a splendid wedding. Her appetite at the wedding
dinner is all but as horrible as her person.[1] . . . 'Give me
at least', says she, 'a kiss for courtesy'. The unhappy
Gawain, turning towards her, beholds the fairest creature
upon whom his eyes ever rested. But the lady tells him
that he must choose whether she shall be fair by night
and foul by day, or fair by day and foul by night. Gawain,
in this strait, leaves all to her. 'Gramercy!' says she.
'Thou shalt have me fair both day and night.' Then she
tells Gawain that her stepmother had transformed her into
an ugly old woman, not to recover her own shape until the
best knight in England had wedded her and given her the
sovereignty in all points. The next morning, Arthur and
others, full of anguish, come to see whether Gawain has
not been slain by the monster with whom they left him.
What is not their surprise and joy to see him come forth

---

[1] A leaf of the MS. is wanting here, but the connection is easily
inferred. The scene is in the nuptial chamber.

radiant from the nuptial chamber, leading his young and beautiful wife, who promises always to obey him in every thing!

3. Origin. The story of this romance, probably of the 15th century, had already been told, with different settings, by Gower,[1] and by Chaucer in his *Wife of Bath's Tale*. A ballad in seven fragments, *The Marriage of Sir Gawain*, later than the romance-poem, tells essentially the same story. In the ballad Arthur offers Gawain to the lady, if she will help him; her answer to the question is 'a woman would have her will'; she tells Gawain that the knight who asked the hard question of the king is her brother, who was under a spell to challenge men either to fight with him at odds[2] or to answer his question. Paris would not derive the ballad from the poem. Gower and Chaucer both have the variation, 'beyond doubt original in the story, that the man whose life is saved by rightly answering the question has himself to marry the monstrous woman'.[3] Chaucer's tale is not now thought to be derived from Gower's. Vv. 6507—14 of Chaucer's, ed. Tyrwhitt, are close to vv. 409—420 of *The Wedding*.[4] Paris[5] regards the three as independent derivations, whose relations are not very clear, from some ancient source, which it is not rash to suppose was a Breton lay.

Paris finds in the story the union of two elements originally distinct. The first is that of the beautiful maiden enchanted by an evil power, who recovers her beauty when, in spite of her hideous form, she is loved and married;[6] this is an element in the romance of *Guinglain*,[7] and may be regarded as the feminine counterpart of *Beauty and the Beast*: the second element is the pretended divulgence of woman's secret.

---

[1] *Confessio Amantis*, ed. Pauli, Bk. I 89—104.

[2] Cf. the case of the Carl of Carlile, *infra*, p. 217.

[3] Child, 291.   [4] Child, 292.   [5] p. 102.

[6] Child, 292, calls attention to the change made by Chaucer in this element of the story.

[7] Cf. *supra*, p. 136.

Tales resembling *The Wedding of Gawain* are found in English, Gaelic, and Scandinavian literature;[1] they must have been widely spread during the Middle Ages. An Irish parallel found in manuscripts of the 12th and 14th centuries contains the feature of the 'sovereignty'.[2] 'Good is thy journey', says the transformed hag to the hero, 'for *I* am thy Sovranty, and *thou* shalt obtain the sovranty of Erin'. This feature proves, Mr. Nutt thinks,[3] the dependence of the English ballad upon the Irish tale.[4] In English literature, the Border ballad of *King Henry*[5] has much in common with the story under consideration and is regarded by Child as probably much earlier. Analogues have also been pointed out in Oriental and in African stories.[6] The having one shape by day and another by night is a common feature in popular tales.[7] Generally the person is some kind of an animal by day and a man at night; in one case, he is a ring, and in another, a pumpkin, by day.

4. Metre. With a leaf that is wanting there would be about 925 lines, in stanzas of six lines, with the rime-scheme, *aab ccb*.

5. Dialect. The South, or the more Southern Midland (Brandl).

6. Date. The 15th century probably.[8]

7. Author. Unknown.

---

[1] See Child, 289; Clouston, 483; Skeat, 448.

[2] Told in *Acad.*, 1892, p. 399.

[3] *Op. cit.*, 425.

[4] On the 'loathly lady' in Mediaeval romance, see Thomas (*op. cit.* on p. 168) 62—64; *Litbl.*, 1885, 212; *Acad.*, 1889, p. 255, and 1892, p. 425.

[5] Ed. Child, I 298; Scott, *Minstrelsy of The Scottish Border*, 1802, II 132.

[6] See Clouston and Skeat.

[7] Child, I 290, n., who cites Curtin: *Myths and Folk Lore of Ireland*, 1890, pp. 51, 68, 69, 71, 136.

[8] Child.

8. Bibliography.

Manuscripts: Rawlinson C 86, Bodl. Library; close of the reign of Henry VII (Child I 289); desc. by Madden, *infra,* p. lxiv.

Editions: Madden, 297.—*The Marriage of Sir Gawaine,* ballad: Madden, 288; *PF. MS.* I 105; *Reliques* (1794), III 350; Ritson, *AEMR.,* I, p. cx; Child, I 288.

General References: Brandl, § 113; Clouston, *Originals and Analogues,* p. 483 (published by the Chaucer Society, 1887); Skeat, *Sources of The Canterbury Tales,* 447—50, in his *Complete Works of Chaucer,* Oxford, 1894.[1]

---

[1] *King Arthur and the King of Cornwall,* since it is written in ballad measure and is printed by Child, is not treated here, although Madden prints it with his other 'romance-poems'. Ed. Madden, 275; Hales and Furnivall, *PF. MS.,* 61; Child, I 283.

APPENDIX A.

CONCERNING THE ORIGIN OF THE ARTHURIAN LEGENDS.

THAT the Arthurian legends have a Celtic nucleus is not now disputed. Arthur, it is safe to say, represents a war-leader of the British Celts in their 'heroic age', the period of their struggle against the German invaders. Professor Zimmer, in his study of Nennius,[1] through whom (*ca.* 796) our earliest account of Arthur comes, reaches the following conclusions: Arthur fought in the wars between the Britons and the Saxons that terminated in the victory of *Mons Badonis* between 495—501. In the renewed wars of the latter half of the sixth century Arthur's memory was cherished by the hard-pressed Britons of the North and South, and was carried to Armorica by Britons migrating thither during this century.[2]

The legends of which Arthur was the hero assimilated older Celtic myths and legends, and through the succeeding centuries were constantly modified and altered. Special stress is laid by Rhŷs upon the mythical contributions to the legend. Arthur he regards as originally a Celtic Culture-hero, and other leading characters and features in the

---

[1] *Nennius Vindicatus*, Berlin, 1893, pp. 283—290.

[2] See *GGA.*, 1890, p. 818 sq. For additional evidence of the early fame of Arthur, cf. *supra*, pp. 205—206; *Rajna*, in *Rom.* XVII 161—85 355 – 65 (showing that Arthur and Gawain were known in Italy at least as early as the close of the 11th century); Pütz, *Zur Geschichte der Entwicklung der Artussage*, Bonn, 1892, diss.

Arthurian legend as originating in Celtic solar myths which were later given a historical form; the myth of Arthur, the Culture-hero, was 'disturbed by a historical fact'.[1]

But how did the Arthurian legends become known to the trouvères? Was the nucleus of the *matière de Bretagne* furnished by Wales or by Brittany? The two theories claiming to answer this question, may be briefly stated as follows. (1) The Theory of Paris.[2] Professor Gaston Paris holds that the Welsh imparted the Arthurian legends in lays and tales, to the English, to some extent, and much more fully to the Anglo-Normans. The favorite themes of the British lays were made the subjects of short Anglo-Norman poems, also called *lais*. In time, the term came to be extended to short poems on romantic themes not necessarily Celtic. The *matière de Bretagne* crossed the Channel in versions of the Anglo-Norman lays, written or oral, the latter doubtless often in prose form. It was also, to some extent, doubtless brought into France directly by the Welsh bards and story-tellers. The contribution of Brittany was not made until later, and under the influence of the success of the tales from the Britain beyond the sea.—The Anglo-Norman Arthurian poems that issued from the British lays and tales are nearly all lost; we know them only through redactions[3] English, German, and above all French. The author of the most celebrated of these redactions, Chrétien de Troyes, knew the Anglo-Norman versions only in a very much altered and disfigured state, with many gaps. Geoffrey of Monmouth's *Historia* has been utilized by only a few of the least ancient of the French prose romances; those in verse know nothing of Arthur's marvelous conquests or of the final catastrophe.[4]

The theory of Paris that the French verse-romances

---

[1] *Arthurian Legend.*

[2] *Opp. cit.* on p. 85; also *Rom.* X 465, XII 459.

[3] Cf. *La Litt. Franç.*, § 55, on the lays of Marie de France.

[4] In general agreement with the theory of Paris are: F. Lot, *Rom.*, 1895—96, '99; J. Loth, *Rev. Celt.*, XIII 480; d'Arbois de Jubainville, *La Litt. Celt.*, I 42, 43.

drew from Welsh sources through the Anglo-Normans was assailed by Foerster[1] as both improbable and unsupported by evidence from Anglo-Norman literature.[2] The few allusions to Arthur in the *lais* are, Foerster holds, mere interpolations; and the three romances in the *Mabinognion* corresponding to the three romances by Chrétien on Erec, Yvain, and Perceval, must be regarded as redactions of Chrétien's romances, not of his sources, as Paris holds.[3] Moreover, the French verse-romances do not give us a true hero legend: they represent Arthur as the world-conqueror, who has all his heroic deeds behind him, and who does practically nothing; his rôle is exactly like that of Charlemagne in the later *chansons de geste*. The knights that surround him engage in nothing but adventures, a pure emanation of the French chivalry.[4]

(2) The Theory of Zimmer:[5] Foerster's objections to the theory of Paris are supported further by Professor Zimmer, who holds it more reasonable to suppose that the basis of the romantic Arthurian legend, *i. e.* the legend as found in the French verse-romances, came from Brittany. In support of his theory, Zimmer urges: (a) The long intercourse of the Bretons with their Romanized neighbors, from the seventh century, especially their very close intercourse with the Normans from the tenth to the middle of the twelfth century; (b) the use of the word *breton* by writers of the twelfth century, and of *Britannia* by Geoffrey of Monmouth (the *Historia*, VII 20) to denote, evidently, the Celts of Armorica, while for 'Welsh', 'Wales', the words *gallois*, *Cambria*, *Gualia* were used; (c) the presence in

---

[1] *Christians von Troyes sämtliche Werke*: Bd. II: *Der Löwenritter (Yvain)*, Halle, 1887; Bd. III: *Erec und Enide*, Halle, 1890; *Ltbl.* 1890, p. 265 ff.—Bd. IV: *Der Karrenritter (Lancelot) und das Wilhelmsleben*, Halle, 1899 (this, I regret to say, I have not seen).

[2] *Yv.* p. xxix; *E.* pp. xxiv, xxv, xxxii—xxxiv.

[3] *Yv.* p. xxiv; *E.* p. xxxiv.

[4] *Yv.* p. xxviii.

[5] (a) *GGA.*, 1890, No. 20, 785 ff.; (b) *ZsffSp.*, XII 230 ff. (*op. cit.* on p. 205), and (c) XIII 1—117 (*Beiträge zur Namenforschung in den altfranz. Arthurepen*).

Geoffrey's narrative of proper names based upon French-Breton forms; (d) the presence in the French verse-romances of proper name connected with Brittany linguistically, historically, or in both ways; (e) Avalon and its connected conceptions are entirely unknown to the Welsh hero-legend, but, as testimony from the twelfth century shows, are of Breton origin;[1] (f) the Round Table, first mentioned by the Norman Wace, was also unknown to the Welsh in the eleventh century; (g) the absence of any true hero-legend, in the usual sense of the term, in the French romances, a fact due to the peculiar development of the Arthurian legend in its new home in 'Little Britain'. There the hero-legend was not localized as in Wales, since the recollection of the old home was at first too strong. But as the memory of Arthur's heroic deeds paled, the historical kernel of the legend almost entirely disappeared, while Arthur became more and more, and to a much greater extent than in Wales, the center of the general legendary element; figures like Ywain and Perceval are grouped around Arthur, which, in the Welsh hero-legends, stand as the representatives of a later time.[2] The foreign literary influence, of France and especially of Normandy, also contributed not a little to give the Breton Arthurian legend a different stamp from that of Wales.

Since the Eastern portion of the Breton territory was almost entirely Romanized, it becomes us to be very cautious before accepting any particular element in the French Arthurian legend as genuinely Celtic. The Round Table, for instance, may be considered as a working over of the Arthurian legend under the influence of the Charlemagne legend; and the figure of Kay, who in the Welsh legend is one of the most prominent heroes around Arthur, may have been altered in the Breton legend under the influence of the figure of Ganelon.[3] The Arthurian legend of Brittany, owing to the contact of the Bretons as followers of the

---

[1] Cf. *supra*, p. 205.   [2] *Op. cit.* as (b) p. 232.
[3] *GGA.*, (*op. cit.*) p. 830.

Anglo-Norman princes with the Kymri in Cumbria, Wales, and Cornwall, received new elements,[1] and influenced in turn the hero legend of Wales and Cornwall.[2] The narrative of Geoffrey of Monmouth is, upon the whole, in the spirit of the Welsh hero-legend, but it also contains Breton features.[3]

The Arthurian romances in prose are regarded by Paris as based upon those in verse.[4] But, since the prose romances narrate events concerning Arthur, especially concerning his wars with the Saxons, not found in the verse-romances, and since they also narrate these events more fully and exactly in some particulars than does Geoffrey of Monmouth, the are regarded by other scholars as based, in their original form, upon the narratives of Breton-French *conteurs* and *fableurs*; the present versions are much interpolated from the verse-romances.[5]

---

[1] *Op. cit.* as (c), pp. 86—103.

[2] *Op. cit.* as (b), pp. 299—253, as (c) 18—22.

[3] Cf. *supra*, p. 206. Zimmer's theory is accepted by Foerster, Golther (*Geschichte der deutschen Lit.*) 142—152, Sommer, III 5. Rhŷs, while in the main convinced by Z.'s evidence, maintains that the legend of the Grail is of Brythonic origin (Introduction to *Morte Darthur*). Z.'s theory is controverted by Lot (*opp. cit.* on p. 223).

[4] See *Rom.* XII 485—86, 497—98.

[5] See Foerster's *Erec*, pp. xxxvii—xli; Golther, *op. cit.*, pp. 149—50.

APPENDIX B.

———

1. Sir Gowther. *Story:* Sir Gowther is the son of a fiend (also the father of Merlin) and the Duchess of 'Estryke', the lady having prayed to God for a child, come how it may. From infancy, Sir Gowther was 'full wild'. Learning of his parentage when grown to manhood, he seeks absolution from the pope, and faithfully carries out the humiliating penance imposed upon him. He fights in disguise in the army of the Emperor of Germany, thrice defeats the enemy, then marries the daughter of the emperor, whose successor he becomes.

Origin (Breul's ed.): This romance is a version of the very popular mediaeval legend of Robert the Devil, known in France at least as early as the middle of the twelfth century. No historical identification of Robert is possible. The romantic version of the story is based upon a religious redaction of two widely spread folk-tales; the tale of wishing for a child and that of *Grindkopf* or the male Cinderella. The golden-haired hero, endowed with supernatural strength, who for a time dwells in obscurity, Breul is inclined to trace to a mythical origin. *Sir Gowther* claims as source a Breton lay; it is not based upon any of the extant French versions. English versions of the 16th century, independent of *Sir Gowther,* are: (a) in prose, *Robert the Deuyll,* printed by Wynken de Worde (1510?); (b) a metrical version of (a); (c) a prose romance by Thomas Lodge, 1591.

15*

Metre, etc.: 757 vv., in the twelve line tail-rime stanza, composed in the N. E. Midland at the beginning of the 15th century (Breul's ed., p. 29), or in N. England, 1350—1400 (Kaluza, *op. cit. infra*).—*MSS.:* 19, 3, 1, Advocates Library, Edin.; 17 B XLIII, Brit. Mus.—*Editions:* Utterson, I 157. Breul, Oppeln, 1886; *reviews,*—Brandl, *Anz. f. d. Alt.* XIV 205—210; Kaluza, *E. St.,* XII 78—83; *Rom.* XV 160; *Angl.* VII (2) 6; *Ltbl.,* 1884 (1) 16; *Ltzt.,* 1886, 1458.—Brandl § 80.

2. Chevelere Assigne. This poem appears to its latest editor to be an epitome of the first 1083 lines of a French verse-romance or *chanson* belonging to the end of the 12th or the beginning of the 13th century (ed. Hippeau, 1874—77). Krüger (p. 173, *op. cit., infra*) regards the English poem (*E*) as more nearly related to a Latin version of the 14th century, both having had, probably, a common source *y*, while *y* and the French poem (*F*) probably had a common French source. Two English prose versions, only one (*E. P.*) of which is extant (ed. Thoms, 1858), belong to the 16th century.—*E* closes at the point where the swans, with one exception, regain their human form; *F* recites the adventures of Helyas (the brother who did not lose his human form) in company with his swan-brother, closes the personal history of Helyas with his departure from his wife because of her disobedience to his command not to inquire concerning his kith and kin, and then connects the story of his descendants with the history of his grandson, Godfrey of Bouillon; *E. P.* (which follows the French folio printed in 1504) tells of the return of Helyas to his own country, of the swan-brother's recovery of his human form, of the retirement of Helyas from the world, and of his reunion with his wife and daughter upon his death-bed.

In the French poem, which represents the least primitive of the 12th century versions, two tales originally independent have been welded. The presence of the swans in the tale concerning the children (see G. Paris, *Rom.* XIX 314—340) probably suggested its union with the legend of the mysterious Knight of the Swan as an explanation of his origin. The former tale is connected, though remotely, with other tales, originally of mythical significance (see *Germ.* I 488), in which children are condemned to a bestial form (cf. Grimm, nos. 9, 11, 25, 49). The legend of the Knight of the Swan has been investigated by Blöte. At first, attributing to it a mythical origin (*ZsfdA.* XXXVIII 272), he later concludes that it was a natural development of some facts in the life of a Roger de Toëni (*ca.* 1040), whose emblem was a swan. The marriage of Roger's granddaughter with Baldwin, the brother of Godfrey of Bouillon, led, probably, to the connection of the emblem and the legend with the house of Bouillon (*ZsfrPh.* XXI 176; see also Blöte in *ZsfdA.* XLII). G. Paris dissents from Blöte's view; he regards the story of the Knight of the Swan, as an ancient Lorraine legend, *sans doute primitivement totémique*, attached arbitrarily in the 12th century to the kings of Jerusalem (*Rom.* XXVI 581).

Metre, etc. (see Gibb's ed.): 370 allitterative long lines, though with many irregularities. *Dialect*, probably an E. Midland transcript of a text of the N. or N. W. (cf. p. xiii). *Date*, the latter part of the 14th century.—*MS.:* Cotton, Caligula A. 2, Brit. Mus.—*Editions:* Utterson, for the Roxburghe Club, 1820. Gibbs, *EETS. ES.* no. 6; on text, *E. St.* 17, p. 174; *Angl.* 21, p. 441.—*References:* Krüger, in *Arch.* LXXVII 169; Brandl, § 73.

INDEX

TO THE ROMANCES TREATED.

ADDITIONS AND CORRECTIONS.

Metre. Stanzas in tail-rime, *Class I, II, etc.*, see Wilda.

p. 11, *King Horn*, on text, *Angl.* 20, p. 459.

p. 23, *Editions*, l. 5, for *E. St.* 19 read 18.

p. 23, *Havelok*, see *Argentile and Curan* in Percy's *Reliques*.

p. 28, l. 1, read *adventurers*.

p. 29, *Guy of Warick*: on its ascetic features, see p. xviii.

p. 31, l. 15, read *Copland*.

p. 40, *Bevis of Hampton*: for the dialect of the later versions, see p. xiii.

p. 44, l. 12, read *original MS.*

p. 63, *Rouland and Vernagu*, on text, *Angl.* 21, p. 366.

p. 66, l. 15, read 14th.

p. 71, *Otuel*, on text, *Angl.* 21, p. 369.

p. 85, *General References*: G. Paris; Golther, *Geschichte der deutschen Literatur*, I 1893, pp. 142—181; Körting, p. 108, n.; Newell (*op. cit.*, on p. 209).

p. 91, l. 7, p. 108, l. 5, read divergences.

p. 95, Röttiger's monograph, rev. in *Rom.*, 1898, pp. 608—19.

p. 101, l. 7, *The Round Table before Arthur,* by C. L. Brown, is to appear in *Harvard Studies.*

p. 108, n. 1, cf. Rhŷs, p. 166, n. 1, 167—8.

p. 112, l. 6, read *Pendragon.*

p. 112, ¶ 3, l. 4, read *declaring.*

p. 113, ¶ 1, l. 4, omit *Arthur.*

p. 116, l. 23, read *Geoffrey.*

p. 117, l. 10, read *Geoffrey.*

p. 119, ¶ 2, l. 4, read *correspondences.*

p. 121, l. 2, for 14th read 13th.

p. 123, add to *Editions*: MS. P. *PF. MS.,* I 422—96; MS. H., Turnbull; Engl. prose *Merlin,* Mead *EETS.,* 1899.

p. 124, on origin, cf. Sommer, III, 17, n.

p. 138, l. 17, for *troie* read *traie.*

p. 148, *Sir Launfal,* Origin: see Schofield, *The Lays of Graelent and Lanval and the Story of Wayland,* Baltimore, 1900.

p. 160, **9.** J. L. Weston: *"Ywain and Gawain" and "Le chevalier au lion"*; see *JB.* XX p. 212.—on text of *Y. and G., Angl.* 14, p. 319.

p. 167, T. G. Foster, *The Revised Text of SG.*; see *JB.* XIX p. 311.

p. 204, n. 1, read cf. *supra,* p. 195, n. 2.